Sailing in the Wake of the Ancestors

Reviving Polynesian Voyaging

Bishop Museum Press
1525 Bernice Street
Honolulu, Hawai'i 96817

Printed in Australia
First trade edition, November 2003

Front cover image: *Hawai'iloa* during sea trials © Monte Costa
Back cover image: *Hawai'iloa* during sea trials © Moana Doi

Cover design: Angela Wu-Ki

Hard Cover ISBN 1-58178-025-7
Soft Cover ISBN 1-58178-024-9

Library of Congress Cataloging-in-Publication Data

Finney, Ben R.
Sailing in the wake of the ancestors : reviving Polynesian voyaging /
By Ben Finney.
p. cm. -- (Legacy of excellence)
"Sponsored by Bishop Museum's Native Hawaiian Culture
and Arts Program"--Verso t.p.
Includes bibliographical references.
ISBN 1-58178-024-9 -- ISBN 1-58178-025-7
1. Hawaiians—Boats. 2. Canoes and canoeing—Hawaii.
3. Navigation—Polynesia. 4. Hawaiians—Travel—French
Polynesia—Marquesas Islands.
I. Bernice Pauahi Bishop Museum. Native Hawaiian Culture
and Arts Program. II. Title. III. Series.

DU624.65.F56 2003
910'.9164'9--dc22   2003015286

Sailing in the Wake of the Ancestors
Reviving Polynesian Voyaging

by

Ben Finney

BISHOP MUSEUM PRESS
Honolulu

DEDICATION

To the memory of Myron "Pinky" Thompson, who rescued the Polynesian Voyaging Society when it was foundering and put it back on course; Wright "Bo" Bowman Jr., who built *Hawai'iloa*; Richard Rhodes, who first drew her lines; Pierre Sham Koua, who presided over the ceremonies at Taputapuātea; Lucien "Ro'o" Kimetete, mayor of Nukuhiva who welcomed the fleet to Te Henua 'Enana; Hilda Busby, loving hostess to the *Hōkūle'a* family at Aotearoa; Abraham Pi'i'anai'a, veteran seaman and patron to a new generation of Hawaiian sailors.

Bishop Museum Native Hawaiian Culture and Arts Program

Ua lehulehu a manomano ka 'ikena a ka Hawai'i.
Great and numerous is the knowledge of the Hawaiians.
Ōlelo No'eau 2814

This publication is sponsored by Bishop Museum's Native Hawaiian Culture and Arts Program in celebration of the Legacy of Excellence of Native Hawaiian culture. The Legacy of Excellence volumes are devoted to generating an appreciation of Native Hawaiian traditions, art, and language through education, awareness, and recognition of excellence in Native Hawaiian achievement.

The Native Hawaiian Culture and Arts Program (NHCAP) was created by the U.S. Congress through the American Indian, Alaska Native, and Native Hawaiian Culture and Arts Development Act (Higher Education Amendments of 1986, P.L. 99–498). It was implemented in 1987 upon the execution of the first cooperative agreement between the National Park Service and Bishop Museum. NHCAP is dedicated to making a meaningful and continuing contribution to the well-being of Native Hawaiian people through the perpetuation and growth of Native Hawaiian language, culture, arts, and values.

William Y. Brown
President, Director, and CEO
Bishop Museum

Vice Chairman, Board of Trustees
Native Hawaiian Culture and Arts Program

Contents

A Thirty-Year Timeline of Canoe Voyaging

1965–66	Building and testing *Nālehia*
1973	Founding the Polynesian Voyaging Society
1975	Launching *Hōkūle'a*
1976	First voyage of *Hōkūle'a* to Tahiti
1978	Failed attempt to return to Tahiti
1978	Myron "Pinky" Thompson elected PVS president
1980	Successful second voyage to Tahiti
1980	Emergence of Nainoa Thompson as navigator and leader
1985–87	Voyage of Rediscovery to Aotearoa and five other archipelagos
1989–90	Fruitless search for *koa* logs for a new voyaging canoe
1990	Donation of Alaskan spruce logs
1992	Educational voyage to the Cook Islands
1993	Launching of *Hawai'iloa*
1995	Canoes from four Polynesian nations meet at Ra'iātea near Tahiti
1995	Six canoes sail together from Te Henua 'Enana to Hawai'i

Hawai'iloa *undergoing sea trials off Moloka'i.*

Prologue

In 1995 six voyaging canoes from around Polynesia set sail from the Marquesas Islands, a rugged volcanic archipelago in the South Pacific called Te Henua 'Enana by its inhabitants.

These handcrafted reconstructions of ancient craft were heading north-northwest to commemorate the original discovery and settlement of the Hawaiian archipelago by seafarers thought to have come from Te Henua 'Enana. But the entire effort of creating and gathering these canoes together also celebrated the revival of voyaging that had begun two decades earlier in Hawai'i and had spread across Polynesia. This book tells the story of voyaging's rebirth, focusing particularly on the commemorative journey to Hawai'i and the visionaries, canoe builders, navigators, sailors, and others who made it happen.

In late 1994, several months before the three Hawai'i canoes were to rendezvous with those from Aotearoa (New Zealand), the Cook Islands, and Tahiti, I was approached by representatives of Bishop Museum's Native Hawaiian Culture and Arts Program. They asked me to sail on the voyage and write a book about it, focusing especially on the role that *Hawai'iloa*—a new canoe built expressly for the voyage—would play in the adventure. I had just published *Voyage of Rediscovery*, a work summing up what we had learned over the previous twenty years from sailing around Polynesia with *Hōkūle'a*,* the first of the modern voyaging canoes. Even though I was then developing a new research project on humanity's future voyages into the cosmos and had just started teaching part time at the newly founded International Space University, the prospect of going to sea again and chronicling this oceanic voyage was irresistible.

Yet I wondered if I were the right person for the job. It seemed to me that the story of building and sailing *Hawai'iloa* should be told as part of a larger tale of how Hawaiians and other Polynesians were reviving their ancient ways of seafaring. Although I had helped start that revival, it was the Hawaiians who had really made it work. I thought that a Hawaiian would be better able to describe and explain the process. Those who had invited me, however, insisted that because of my long experience with building, sailing, and writing about voyaging canoes I should accept the assignment. Moreover the Hawaiian elders whose counsel I sought also recommended that I take the job. So I arranged to take a leave from the University of Hawai'i to join the canoes as they assembled at an ancient temple near Tahiti.

My involvement with canoe voyaging began in the spring of 1958, when, fresh out

---

* A macron (*kahakō* in Hawaiian) above a vowel indicates that it is long. A /'/ (*'okina*) before a vowel represents a glottal stop, an unvoiced consonant in Hawaiian and other Polynesian languages.

of the navy, I enrolled as an M.A. student in anthropology at the University of Hawai'i. I had come to study how the ancient Polynesians had explored and settled the Pacific. Just before classes began, I called upon my advisor, noted folklorist Katharine Luomala. After a routine chat about the department's program and requirements, we talked about my interest in Polynesian seafaring. Professor Luomala then handed me a slim book entitled *Ancient Voyagers in the Pacific* that had recently been published by Andrew Sharp, a New Zealand bureaucrat turned amateur historian.[1] She had just reviewed it and warned me I might not like it.

As I read the book that evening, I realized what she meant. Sharp rubbished the then-common belief that the ancient Polynesians had been great seafarers who had intentionally explored the Pacific and purposefully settled the many islands they found there. Why? Because he judged that their canoes and ways of navigating were much too crude for such an immense task. Instead, he asserted that they had been castaways who had strayed or been blown off course while making short trips, or had been driven to take to their canoes by war or famine, and then were pushed by wind and current to uninhabited islands. To Sharp, a long series of such accidental drift and exile voyages— not planned voyages of exploration and settlement—had randomly scattered the Polynesians over the Pacific.

The almost gleeful way Sharp demoted Polynesians from pioneering seafarers to hapless castaways made me angry, particularly since I could see how he had selected only evidence that supported his thesis and ignored any that gave Polynesians credit for being able seafarers. A number of knowledgeable scholars shared my view, including Professor Luomala and Bishop Museum's Kenneth Emory, who taught part time at the University of Hawai'i and became my tutor in Polynesian archaeology. Nonetheless, Sharp's reasoning appealed to those who apparently could not imagine how Stone Age people without ships, compasses, charts, and other navigational aids could have intentionally discovered and settled so many mid-ocean islands.

As I followed the ensuing debate, I realized that the issue could not be resolved with the information at hand. It hinged on how well the old canoes sailed and how accurate were traditional methods of navigation. Yet the two main sources on Polynesian voyaging then available—migration legends and explorers' reports—did not provide precise enough information to settle the issue. We needed the actual double-hulled canoes, but they (and their navigators) had long ago disappeared from Polynesian waters. The only way to get the needed information was to reconstruct the old canoes and ways of navigating and then test these over the legendary sea routes of Polynesia.

As a graduate student, I was hardly in a position to undertake such an ambitious program, and so kept my ideas to myself while finishing my M.A. and then earning a

Ph.D. (with a dissertation on contemporary Tahitians). After a year spent teaching at the University of California at Santa Barbara, I finally took the plunge, though in a measured way. Rather than immediately building a large, deep-sea canoe, I decided first to construct and test a smaller one in order to learn how double canoes sailed.

In the fall of 1965 I began work on a 40-foot long replica of a Hawaiian *wa'a kaulua*, literally a "double-placed canoe," and launched her the following spring. Once we had the sleek canoe sailing in Hawaiian waters, the renowned Hawaiian scholar Mary Kawena Pukui named her *Nālehia*, "The Skilled Ones," from the way her twin hulls rode so gracefully over the swells. After sea trials with *Nālehia* confirmed that double canoes were well-adapted to sailing in the open ocean, the next step was to build a full-size voyaging canoe and test it over a legendary voyaging route. Hawaiian tales about chiefs and high priests sailing between Hawai'i and Tahiti suggested just the route to challenge Andrew Sharp. He had announced that Polynesians could not have intentionally sailed to islands more than 300 miles away. Sailing back and forth across the more than 2,000 miles of blue water separating Hawai'i and Tahiti would constitute a crucial test of Sharp's claims.[2]

After a research detour to New Guinea to study the first generation of native businessmen in the Highlands, I returned to Hawai'i in 1970 to teach anthropology and build the voyaging canoe of my dreams. A pair of like-minded canoe enthusiasts joined me: Hawaiian artist Herb Kawainui Kāne, who after spending most of his adult life in the Midwest, had just returned to Hawai'i to reconnect with his Hawaiian roots; and canoe paddler Tommy Holmes, a *haole* (Caucasian) graduate student who had been born and raised in Hawai'i. In 1973 we founded the Polynesian Voyaging Society to raise money, build the canoe, and make the voyage. Two years later we launched a 62-foot voyaging canoe christened *Hōkūle'a*, the Hawaiian name of Arcturus, the bright star that currently passes directly over the Islands. After a hard year spent learning how to handle the big canoe, we set sail for Tahiti in May of 1976.

Elia "Kāwika" Kapahulehua, an expert catamaran sailor originally from the isolated Hawaiian island of Ni'ihau, was our captain. There were no surviving Polynesian navigators to guide us, so I recruited Pius "Mau" Piailug, a master navigator from a remote atoll in Micronesia where they still navigate by methods similar to those once used in Polynesia. And to pilot us safely past the dangerous atolls of the Tuamotu Archipelago just to the north-northeast of Tahiti I brought on board Rodo Williams, an experienced Tahitian sea captain and an old friend who had just sailed up from Tahiti.

As Tahiti lies 2,250 miles southeast of our starting point and the trade winds blow from east to west across the route, the main problem was to make enough easting into the trades and not let them push us west of Tahiti. Thanks to Kāwika's seamanship and

Mau's uncanny skill at navigation, after a month at sea we made landfall as planned on an atoll at the western end of the Tuamotu chain. With Rodo piloting we carefully sailed from there to Tahiti, where some 15,000 people crowded the shore to greet us.[3]

The voyage undermined Sharp and his theories and went a long way toward reestablishing the reputation of ancient Polynesian canoes and ways of navigating. Yet when *Hōkūle'a* tied up in Tahiti, the Polynesian Voyaging Society was deeply troubled.

We had planned our endeavor as an effort in cultural revival as well as an experiment in voyaging. We gave public talks and hands-on workshops around the islands, recruited Hawaiian crewmembers for the voyage, and invited a number of Hawaiian educators to join the governing board of the Polynesian Voyaging Society. Our hope was that a successful voyage would restore pride in ancestral technologies and accomplishments, and that afterwards the newly trained Hawaiian sailors would turn *Hōkūle'a* into a "floating classroom" for schoolchildren to learn about canoe sailing and Hawai'i's voyaging heritage. That vision proved to be naive. As soon as we launched the canoe and began sailing her around the archipelago in preparation for the long voyage to Tahiti, some highly vocal protestors started campaigning to take her over in the name of Hawaiian nationalism.

That Herb Kāne had designed *Hōkūle'a* and supervised her construction, Kāwika Kapahulehua was the captain, and Hawaiians made up the majority of the crew was not enough. They objected to having any non-Hawaiians on *Hōkūle'a*, as well as to the research purpose of the canoe and even to sailing her to Tahiti. Having me, a *haole* professor, leading what they thought should be an exclusively Hawaiian endeavor was particularly galling. If the protestors had been sailors and were dedicated to voyaging to Tahiti as planned, some of them might have been welcomed as crewmembers. But they were not experienced blue water sailors and wanted to keep the canoe in Hawai'i and only make short trips between the islands.

So great was their appeal among some Hawaiians, including more than a few crewmembers, that for a while it looked like the project might dissolve in controversy. The Society's board of directors was split, and Herb, caught in the middle and in financial trouble for having neglected his profession to work on the canoe, resigned. Nonetheless, with the timely intervention of several farsighted Hawaiians we did manage to set sail—but not before having to endure a final dockside protest replete with fiery denunciations, placards, and television news cameras.

Despite hopes that we had left the troubles on shore, they erupted again at sea. Two weeks into the voyage a half-dozen novice crewmembers (out of a total crew of fifteen) went on strike. After denouncing "the leaders" for overworking and underfeeding them, they quit standing watch and spent the rest of the voyage eating, sleeping, smoking foul-smelling hand-rolled cigarettes, and generally making life difficult for those of us who were actually sailing the canoe. We kicked them off the crew upon landing, but Mau Piailug and Tommy Holmes nonetheless quit in disgust. Although the young Hawaiian men and women flown down from Honolulu to replace the striking crewmembers did a fine job on the return leg, the damage had already been done. Deeply chagrined that I had not been able to head off the troubles, I resigned the presidency of the Polynesian Voyaging Society after reaching Hawai'i. It was time for me to go back to teaching and also to start work on *Hokule'a: The Way to Tahiti*—a book for which the Society had earlier received a generous advance that had enabled us to start work on the canoe.[4]

Although the new leaders of the Society had some success in using *Hōkūle'a* for education, the troubles left over from the voyage continued to have a baleful influence. In order to clear the air, they decided to sail the canoe back to Tahiti in 1978 on their own. Unfortunately, the new crew lacked the experience of such masters from the first voyage as Kāwika Kapahulehua, Mau Piailug, and Rodo Williams, and had not even bothered to ask their advice. At midnight, six hours after departing from Honolulu, *Hōkūle'a* capsized while sailing hard into gale force winds and mounting seas. The following day champion surfer Eddie Aikau was lost in a valiant attempt to paddle his surfboard to shore to summon help. At dusk the canoe's overturned hulls were finally spotted from a passing airliner just as the winds and accompanying currents were pushing the wreckage southwest away from the islands. That night the Coast Guard rescued the rapidly weakening survivors, and the next day a cutter towed the canoe back to Honolulu.

The tragedy frightened many people away from the project, and those who remained had only a battered canoe, the humiliation of having failed, and the grief of having lost a beloved comrade. Some urged them to admit that voyaging was too dangerous, donate the canoe to a museum, and dissolve the Polynesian Voyaging Society. Fortunately, a nucleus of determined sailors refused to quit, including Nainoa Thompson, a slim, pensive Hawaiian youth who aspired to be a traditional navigator. They insisted that *Hōkūle'a* must be rebuilt and, after proper preparations and training, sailed to Tahiti to complete the aborted second attempt. Urging them to do it right and really make the Hawaiian people proud was Nainoa's father, Myron Thompson, a true Hawaiian patriot and an experienced social worker. As the newly elected president of the Polynesian Voyaging Society, he firmly turned the ailing organization around.

Captain Kapahulehua and others from the first voyage were asked for their advice, and apologies were extended to Mau Piailug, who graciously agreed to come back to Hawai'i and teach Nainoa how to navigate the canoe to Tahiti. After months of intensive training the master navigator pronounced the young Hawaiian ready for the task. In March of 1980 *Hōkūle'a*, which had been rebuilt to meet Coast Guard safety standards, set sail with a unified, well-trained crew. They reached Tahiti and returned to Hawai'i without any real difficulties along the way. This well-executed voyage did much to rehabilitate the battered reputation of contemporary Hawaiians as sailors, particularly since Nainoa had guided the canoe both ways without using any instruments, charts, or other navigational aids. He emerged as just the cultural hero Hawaiians needed—a courageous and dedicated youth who was striving to learn and apply traditional skills in order to help his fellow Hawaiians regain their bearings in today's world.[5]

At this point the justly proud sailors could have relaxed and gone back to school, work, and family, satisfied that they had done their part in rescuing Hawaiian honor. Yet they knew that there was much more to be done. *Hōkūle'a* had only been to Tahiti, and other island groups within the Polynesian Triangle beckoned. So they organized a "Voyage of Rediscovery" that took *Hōkūle'a* from Hawai'i to Aotearoa (New Zealand) and returned, stopping at the Tuamotus, Tahiti, the Cook Islands, Tonga, and Sāmoa along the way. This 12,000-mile odyssey, which took from 1985 to 1987 to complete, opened Hawaiian horizons to the rest of Polynesia and inspired their cousins from the South Pacific to think about building and sailing their own voyaging canoes.

In addition, the voyage helped to settle another dispute about Polynesian settlement. The 1976 voyage demonstrated that sheer distance had not been a barrier to Polynesian voyagers. The 1980 voyage replicated that experiment and illuminated basic principles of canoe navigation. However, sailing back and forth twice between Hawai'i and Tahiti had not directly addressed the issue of how the ancestors of the Polynesians were able to migrate from Southeast Asia into the Pacific, sailing eastward against the direction from which the trade winds blow.

Thor Heyerdahl, famed explorer and author of *Kon-Tiki: Across the Pacific by Raft*, had claimed that canoe voyagers coming from Southeast Asia could not have tacked eastward into the Pacific against what he called "permanent trade winds." He concluded that Polynesia must have been settled by people coming from the Americas, sailing before the trades and drifting with the accompanying currents.[6] The flaw in Heyerdahl's theory is that the trades are not permanent. They seasonally weaken and are displaced by spells of westerlies—winds blowing from the west. Heyerdahl also did not know that Polynesians and other Pacific sailors were well-aware of these wind shifts and used them to sail to the east.

Nainoa and the crew were able to test this strategy on the return leg from Aotearoa. First they sailed *Hōkūle'a* north to Sāmoa in order to position her for the crossing to Tahiti, which lies 1,250 miles to the east-southeast of Sāmoa—directly upwind with respect to the normal trade wind flow in that part of the Pacific. After waiting for the onset of the Austral winter, they set sail from Sāmoa at the first sign of westerly winds from storms developing south of the tropics. Sailing with successive spells of these "winter westerlies," they worked *Hōkūle'a* to the Cooks and after a pause proceeded to Tahiti. By demonstrating how canoes could sail eastward across the tropical Pacific, this crossing demolished Heyerdahl's thesis that Polynesia could only have been settled from the Americas.[7]

After returning home, the Hawaiians began thinking about taking the voyaging revival a step further by building a new voyaging canoe, which, unlike *Hōkūle'a*, would be created solely out of traditional materials. Judging from early drawings and descriptions, the hulls of most deep-sea voyaging canoes were not carved from single dugout logs. Instead they were built from planks and shaped sections of logs cut from several trees, which were then carefully fitted, caulked, and lashed together to form deep, wide, and complexly curved structures capable of carrying heavy loads. As we reckoned that it would have taken us years to master this method of construction, we built *Hōkūle'a*'s twin hulls using milled lumber framing covered by molded plywood strips and sealed with a layer of fiberglass and resin. And although we had wanted to lash the hulls and other components together with coconut-fiber sennit, we could not obtain enough of this now scarce cordage and instead used commercial rope. We also tried making a pair of woven pandanus sails, but as only one was finished by the time we had to leave, we sailed with cloth ones instead.

Although *Hōkūle'a* had proven to be a magnificent vehicle for recovering lost knowledge, and had become a beloved cultural icon in the process, by the late 1980s it was time to go back to basics. The Polynesian Voyaging Society decided to build a new voyaging canoe with hulls made from *koa*, Hawai'i's premier timber for making canoes, lashed together with *'aha*, cordage plaited from the fibers of coconut husks, and rigged with sails woven out of *lauhala*, the leaves of the pandanus palm.

In 1989 Nainoa Thompson went to the Native Hawaiian Culture and Arts Program to request funding for an all native-materials canoe. This program had been created a few years earlier by Congress at the initiative of Daniel Inouye, Hawai'i's senior senator, and through the passage of the American Indian, Alaska Native, and Native Hawaiian Culture and Arts Development Act. The Department of the Interior funded the program through the U.S. Park Service with a grant to Bishop Museum. The mission of the program, called NHCAP for short, was to foster Hawaiian art and culture by awarding grants and contracts to individuals and groups for specific projects. Nainoa proposed that from 1990 through 1994 NHCAP fund the construction and sailing of a native-materials canoe. The individual awards and contracts would first go for recovering ancient techniques of canoe building, sail weaving, and cordage making, as well as reviving the prayers, rituals, and chants integral to these. Then they would be dedicated to the actual construction of the canoe, and then the commemorative voyage from Te Henua 'Enana to Hawai'i.

To support his substantial request, the navigator argued that important benefits would flow from recovering lost knowledge and employing it to recreate a truly native voyaging canoe:[8]

> Two hundred years ago, we lost basically all that we knew about our traditions and it's going to be through research and through projects like this that we can regain it. But we're not just regaining an artifact. We are regaining the pride in the culture of the people—a proud, courageous people.

Herb Kāne, who was then serving on NHCAP's board of trustees, immediately registered his support, explaining that the canoe would provide a focus for the efforts of people in different areas of culture and the arts. Later he more fully explained the rationale in a letter to me:

> My support as a board member for Nainoa's desire to build a voyaging canoe using traditional materials was based on the possibility that this could become a catalyst project, providing a central objective toward which each of the NHCAP-supported practitioners in the traditional arts could make a contribution. Virtually all the Hawaiian arts could be brought to bear in some way on this project, going far beyond the building of the canoe to include everything an ancient canoe would carry. These would include tools, utensils, fishing equipment, waterproofed tapa, medicines, provisions, seeds, cuttings, young breadfruit plants—everything required for transplanting the culture to an uninhabited islands, as well as fine gifts if a landing were made on a friendly island and weapons if a landing had to be forced on a hostile island. There would also be special requirements relating to lore and ceremony which would include the performing arts and language arts.

After several weeks of discussions and negotiations, the NHCAP trustees accepted Nainoa's proposal. The Hawaiians would have a new canoe that would further the voyaging revival by recreating the arts and crafts that went into building, launching, and sailing their ancestral vessel.

Chapter One

Hawaiʻiloa

ON A HEAVILY FORESTED island off the coast of southeast Alaska, Paul Marks, a slim, handsome Tlingit dressed in jeans, a leather vest, and a richly decorated Northwest Coast blanket draped over his left shoulder, stands before a towering spruce tree. He closes his eyes, raises his open arms, and intones a prayer in his native tongue. He then paraphrases it in English for the benefit of the Hawaiʻi delegates and those who do not understand Tlingit:

> We thank you trees, in Tlingit *askwani*.
> And the tree that we are going to use today.
> That we look at you as a symbol of strength and power.
> And that you would hold up in the storms and weathers to come.
> And that it would be a blessing to the Hawaiian nation.
> And that it would also serve as a link between the three nations,
> Haida, Tlingit, and the Hawaiians.
> And that our love would grow with one another.
> And that it would be an ongoing relationship.[1]

He continues praying in Tlingit for a few moments and then turns to his Hawaiian counterpart dressed in a long flowing cloak. Keliʻi Tauʻā, a gentle yet intense man who teaches Hawaiian, music, and cultural studies at a Maui high school, steps forward to act as the Hawaiians' *kahuna pule*, or prayer expert. At the base of the tree, he places an offering of Hawaiian foods along with a length of red cloth. Stepping back, Keliʻi addresses the four major Hawaiian gods—Kāne, Kanaloa, Kū, and Lono—and then calls to the multitude of gods by chanting:

E kini o ke akua	O forty thousand gods
E ka lehu o ke akua	O four hundred thousand gods
E ka lalani o ke akua	O rows of gods
E ke kukui akua	O collection of gods
E ka mano o ke akua	O four thousand gods
E kaikua'ana o ke akua	O older brothers of the gods
E ke akua mūkī	O gods that suck air through their lips
E ke akua hāwanawana	O gods that whisper
E ke akua kia'i o ka pō	O gods that watch by night
E ke akua 'ala'alawa o ke aumoe	O gods that glance this way and that late at night
E iho, e ala, e 'oni, e 'eu	O come down, awake, move, stir yourselves
Eia ka mea 'ai 'oukou la, he hale	Here is your food, a house

Once Keli'i has the attention of the gods, he calls for Nainoa Thompson to step forward along with Wright Bowman Jr., who will carve the new canoe. As they stand before the tree with bowed heads, Keli'i asks them to join with him to beg the forgiveness of the gods for taking the tree's life and to beseech their blessings in giving the tree a new life as part of a voyaging canoe.

As Keli'i's voice fades, the loggers step forward to begin their task. Led by a rugged, white-haired man called out of retirement just for this job, they quickly attack the trunk with a long chain saw. Starting on the side away from the crowd, the loggers make two chain-saw cuts, angled so that they meet at a point about two feet into the log. On the side facing the crowd, they make two deeper cuts that start out a foot apart and come together about four feet into the trunk. Once they pry out the sections left by the cuts, all 220 feet of the tree stand balanced on a fraction of its massive trunk. The loggers immediately pound thick wooden wedges into the largest gap to lever the tree over so that it will fall away from the crowd. The spruce creaks as the remaining fibers begin to give way, then cracks loudly. The chief logger gives out a yell as the tree falls with an eerie groan and crashes onto the forest floor.

By a ring count, the loggers reckoned that it was 418 years old. This was the second of a pair of spruce trees felled in June of 1990 on Shelikof, a small island that now forms part of forestlands administered by the U.S. National Park Service. The trees were gifts from the Sealaska Corporation—and its Tlingit, Haida, and Tshimshian shareholders—to the Hawaiian people so that they could build their new canoe from whole logs.

IN AN UNSIGNED essay written sometime during the 1830s or early 1840s, a Hawaiian studying to be a teacher in the new missionary schools praised Hawai'i's premier wood for making canoes:

*O ke koa naʻe ka laʻau maikaʻi loa, a ʻoia ka mōʻī o nā laʻau waʻa o
ka wā kahiko.*

The *koa* indeed was the very best and the king of all canoe making timber in
the olden days.[2]

Koa *(Acacia koa)*, a species endemic to Hawaiʻi, grows tall and straight in the
uplands, particularly those of Hawaiʻi Island. Today's canoe paddlers still talk with
great admiration about *koa*, declaring it superior to other timber—and especially to
fiberglass—for building outrigger racing canoes. Not only are canoes made from richly
grained *koa* strikingly attractive, but paddlers swear that the way their hulls flex
smoothly in the ocean swells makes them feel alive. It was therefore natural that the
first priority of the new project was to find a pair of sound *koa* trees tall and thick
enough to build the new canoe.

From September 1989 through mid-March of 1990, Nainoa and a group of volunteers spent several days each week fruitlessly searching for likely trees in the uplands of
Hawaiʻi Island. They also made a few forays into the forests of neighboring Maui. Some
tall, straight trees were located, but each turned out to be insect-ridden or otherwise
diseased. One of the most heartbreaking sights was a fallen *koa* giant. It measured 70
feet from roots to the first branches but was so rotten that an axe could easily be poked
clear through it.

The quest came far too late. The great *koa* forests through which early Western
explorers had walked in wonder were almost all gone, victims of wrenching environmental changes over the last two centuries. While the Polynesians had brought small
pigs with them, Western voyagers later introduced much larger and more destructive
pigs, as well as cattle and goats. These four-legged marauders provided the first shock
as they moved into the forests and began eating and trampling the tender *koa* suckers
and seedlings. Next, great swaths of *koa* were cut down as this beautiful hardwood
found a ready market among local builders and furniture makers and became especially prized overseas. Much of the cleared land became cattle pasture, preventing the
natural recovery of the forests. The remaining *koa* were further stressed by a succession
of introduced pests and diseases.[3]

With great sadness Nainoa called off the search but not the project. There were
alternative ways of building a native-materials canoe. Though expensive, some milled
koa lumber was being used to make racing canoes by gluing the planks edge-to-edge.
But the idea of fabricating the hulls of the new canoe in this way was rejected, apparently because they would not have the structural integrity or the symbolic impact of
ones carved from dugout logs. Fabricating hulls in the manner of the old voyaging

canoes from elsewhere in Polynesia—by fitting and lashing together shaped sections and planks from several logs—does not seem to have been considered. Instead, the Hawaiians looked toward Alaska.

HERB KĀNE took the initiative in making the connection. Some years earlier he had met Judson Brown, a widely respected Tlingit elder. Brown invited him to Alaska to do a painting for Sealaska, a native corporation that controls extensive stands of timber and is heavily involved in logging. When Herb heard that the search for *koa* logs was not going well, he talked with Judson and Nainoa about using Alaskan logs instead. With their encouragement, he contacted Sealaska CEO Byron Mallott, to inquire whether NHCAP could purchase a pair of logs from the corporation. "Hell no, we'll give them to you!" was the Tlingit executive's unhesitating response.

Since the days of the Fur Trade in the late 1700s, Hawaiians have worked and settled in Southeast Alaska, and Byron thought that giving Hawaiians a pair of big logs would extend that connection for everyone's mutual benefit. At the time he and other executives of Sealaska were wrestling with the dilemma of how the corporation could help its native shareholders above and beyond paying them wages and dividends and providing money for scholarships and other worthy causes. When Herb made the request, Byron sensed that helping the Hawaiians might also inspire the shareholders to think about how they too could use their resources for inspirational cultural endeavors.

Yet Byron realized that he had spoken before he knew for sure that Sealaska had trees big enough to meet Nainoa's specifications: eight feet wide at the base and growing straight without branches for at least 70 feet. After several weeks of searching, Sealaska land manager Ernie Hillman located two big spruce trees on Shelikof Island that met the specifications.

First, however, Nainoa had to fly to Alaska and inspect the trees. Ernie Hillman met Nainoa at Ketchikan, the closest town to Shelikof with an airport, and the two took a floatplane to the island. Flying over islands thick with trees, then landing off Shelikof and driving deep into a dense forest filled with bird calls, as eagles soared silently overhead, awed the Hawaiian, who was fresh from the devastated forests of his own land. After parking and walking a short distance, Ernie proudly showed Nainoa the two giant spruces. Nainoa recalls how excited Ernie was about the prospect of using them to build a great canoe and that he had expectantly asked him: "Is this what you need?" But Nainoa remained silent for an embarrassingly long time before finally mumbling to the perplexed Sealaska official that he would have to check with the canoe builder back in Hawai'i.

To understand the navigator's hesitancy, we have to go back several weeks to the day when he gave up searching for *koa* trees. Nainoa and Teikihe'epo "Tava" Taupu, an experienced *Hōkūle'a* sailor originally from Te Henua 'Enana, were conducting one last search in the Kilauea Forest Preserve located on the slopes of Mauna Loa. The two usually walked together, for the rough lava terrain hidden under the dense vegetation and debris of the forest floor contains deep holes into which a lone hiker could fall and never be found. However, to maximize their coverage for this last effort, the two took a chance and separated. Nainoa and Tava hardly spoke when they returned and deject-edly trudged back to the truck. There was nothing to say. Once again they had failed to find any suitable trees. Nainoa recalls that as they walked in silence he felt a great weight on his back, an aching pressure as though he were taking onto his body the pain of the loss of the great *koa* forests that had formerly provided his ancestors with logs for building their canoes.

Nainoa carried that feeling of loss to Alaska, which was why he could not bring himself to answer Ernie's question directly. The conflicted navigator saw that the trees met the technical specifications. But he worried that in accepting them as replacements for *koa* trees that no longer existed, he would be turning his back on Hawai'i's once-flourishing forests and asking Alaskans to sacrifice two of their finest trees to make up for Hawai'i's mistakes. But at the time, Nainoa could not explain that to Ernie.

Once back in Hawai'i, Nainoa was counseled by his father and several other elders to accept the trees and get on with the project. Upon becoming a trustee of the Kamehameha Schools/Bishop Estate in the early 1970s, the senior Thompson had discovered that the estate (the revenues of which are used to educate Hawaiian children) had been logging their upland forest holdings and leasing the land for cattle pastures. He managed to have the estate set aside some of their holdings as a preserve for *koa* and other native trees. His advice to Nainoa was to accept the spruce trees but also develop a plan to replant *koa* so that future generations would have healthy forests from which they could obtain sound trees for making canoes. Nainoa agreed, and before returning to Alaska to witness the felling of the spruce trees, a symbolic replant-ing was held on estate lands on Hawai'i Island. Members of the *Hōkūle'a* family and an Alaskan delegation led by Judson Brown and Byron Mallott set out hundreds of seedlings on logged-over *koa* lands.

ACTUALLY, HAWAIIANS FORMERLY used drift logs from the Northwest Coast to make some of their canoes. The most complete reference to this practice comes from the journal of British explorer George Vancouver during his visit to Hawai'i in the early 1790s. While sailing from O'ahu to Kaua'i, Vancouver's HMS *Discovery* was becalmed in mid-channel. Hawaiians aboard three double canoes and a large outrigger heading from Kaua'i to Maui spied the British ship off in the distance. Taking advantage of the calm, they paddled over to take a look. As they eyed *Discovery*, Vancouver studied the outrigger canoe, noting that it carried sixteen people, measured sixty-one and a half feet long, and was "without exception the finest canoe we had seen amongst the islands." The canoe's long hull caught the explorer's eye for he saw that it had been hewn from "an exceedingly fine pine-tree," a tree that he knew did not grow in the islands.[4]

Vancouver, who had learned some Hawaiian while serving as a midshipman on the Cook expedition of 1778–1779, asked the crew where the wood came from. They told him that the canoe was made from a huge log that had drifted onto the coast of Kaua'i, where it had been set aside in hopes of "a companion arriving in the same manner" so that a double canoe could be built. After waiting for some time, the Hawaiians finally made the drift log into the outrigger canoe that Vancouver was admiring. Once the explorer reached Kaua'i, he saw a double canoe "of a middling size, made from two small pine-trees, that had been driven on shore nearly at the same spot." He also examined several foreign logs that had drifted ashore at different times, but were too "decayed and worm-eaten to be usefully appropriated." All this led Vancouver to conclude that it was not uncommon for "fir timber" (a category in which he apparently included spruce, fir, and pine) to drift from the Northwest Coast onto the shores of the Hawaiian Islands, particularly Kaua'i.[7]

SEVERAL MONTHS LATER, the two spruce logs, reduced to 70-foot long sections weighing about 30 tons each, were off-loaded at Honolulu Harbor. Sealaska had shipped them to Seattle, and a barge operated by Aloha Cargo Transport took them to Honolulu, all without cost to the project. The local firm of McCabe, Hamilton and Renny trucked the logs to Bishop Museum, also without charge, and an off-duty police officer volunteered his services to escort the trucks. The logs therefore arrived at the museum as gifts ready to be shaped into canoe hulls.

Byron Mallott had set the tone for keeping the entire transaction out of the money economy. Not only did he refuse to discuss selling the trees, but he also forbade his employees to calculate what it had cost the corporation to locate and exchange them for Sealaska trees, cut them down, and ship the log sections to Hawai'i. This generosity did more than save the canoe project a lot of money. As both the Native Hawaiians and Alaskans well understood, whereas monetary payments close a transaction, a gift establishes a continuing relationship.

Part of that relationship involved formally presenting the logs to the Hawaiians. A delegation of Native Alaskans flew to Hawai'i in order to personally hand the logs over. At the ceremony held on the museum grounds, Dr. Walter Soboleff, a prominent Tlingit educator, gave the future vessel a Tlingit name: *Khutxh. ayun nah Ha Kayatun*, which he explained meant "Steering by the Stars."[5] Byron Mallott also spoke, briefly characterizing how he saw the impact of the project:

Both the reality and the symbolism of the project breathes hope and inspiration into all peoples seeking to maintain their traditions, heritage and culture in a society that does not place a high priority on such things. In your canoe, you carry all of us who share your vision and aspiration for a people to live and prosper with their future firmly built on the knowledge of their heritage and traditions.[6]

Nainoa already knew how he wanted to acknowledge these gifts from Alaska and further cement this transpacific linkage of native peoples. He promised that upon their return from Te Henua 'Enana, the crew would sail the new canoe up Alaska's Inland Passage, stopping at native communities along the way to show them the vessel that was built with their logs.

WRIGHT BOWMAN JR. had been chosen as the *kahuna kālai wa'a*, the master canoe carver who would build the new canoe. "Bo," as he was usually called, had learned how to work on canoes from his father, a Kamehameha Schools teacher who had created the crossbeams and other components of *Hōkūle'a*. For a large man nearly six feet tall and well over 200 pounds, Bo seemed particularly gentle and soft-spoken. However, his calm demeanor belied an inner turmoil over the challenge before him. The hulls of the new canoe would be much larger than those of the slim racing canoes he was used to building. Moreover, Bo had never made a canoe from spruce logs.

Since Hawai'i is much hotter and drier than the cool, damp forests of southeast Alaska, Bo's immediate task was to manage the drying of the logs. At first the logs were left in the open on the museum grounds. However, the intense sun and heat drove the moisture out of them so quickly that threatening cracks developed. Sprinklers to cool and wet the logs helped, but eventually a long A-frame structure had to be erected to shelter the logs and those who worked on them.

By late March of 1990, nine months after the spruce trees had been felled, the logs were cured enough to begin work. Everyone knew that Bo was not going to try and carve the hulls with stone adzes and other traditional tools. But some were taken aback by the array of modern tools he deployed: long chain saws, templates and jigs assembled out of plywood, planks and steel pipes, hydraulic jacks, power planers and sanders, and a wide variety of modern hand tools. As Bo and the helpers he recruited could only work on weekends, this mechanized approach to canoe building was necessary if the vessel was to be completed on schedule. It was also the way Bo operated. This was the 1990s not the 1790s, and canoe building in Hawai'i had changed radically over the last two centuries.

Dick Rhodes, a scientific illustrator from the University of Hawai'i's School of

Oceanography, with a second career devoted to drawing canoes, had developed the original design for the canoe. After studying the few available old drawings and photographs of canoes from Te Henua 'Enana, Dick created a design with hulls as deep and broad as it was possible to carve from the spruce logs. Instead of curved crossbeams, crab-claw sails, and high prow pieces characteristic of Hawaiian double canoes, he drew straight crossbeams, a single sail with a straight boom, and long, low prow pieces, all features typical of Te Henua 'Enana craft. Subsequently, other designers modified the hull design, slimming the bows, specifying two masts instead of one, and adding Hawaiian-style prow pieces.

Following the latest design, Bo and his crew began the long process of turning round logs into dugout canoe hulls by making a horizontal chain saw cut down the length of each log to produce a flat, slightly concave working surface. Here they drew the outline of each hull as seen from above. Starting with a short-bladed chain saw, the crew began making continuous vertical cuts into the logs, following the hull outlines. Chain saws with successively longer blades deepened these incisions until the flanks of each log had been laid bare.[7]

Next, using winches, jacks, and many hands, the partially shaped logs were laid first on one side and then the other in order to rough out the curving shape of the flanks with shallow chain-saw cuts. Then they planed down the facets left by the chain-saw cuts so that the smooth longitudinal and vertical curves of canoe hulls emerged. Levering each hull over so that it stood upside down enabled Bo to make both sides as symmetrical as possible.

The hulls were then rotated until they rested upright in their cradling jigs. Weeks earlier a big section of wood 30 feet long had been split out of the interior of each hull in order to start the curing process. Now the builders used chain saws to cut progressively deeper into the hulls. After employing wedges and long pry bars to split out successively deeper levels of wood, the builders finished the hollowing-out process with axes, adzes, chisels, power planers and sanders.

When questioned about how he liked working with spruce, Bo said that it was much softer and straighter-grained than *koa*, and was therefore much easier to shape—except for one problem. As the working surfaces dried, long cracks developed. These could be partially controlled by painting the freshly exposed surfaces with hot wax or linseed oil, but in the end a number of major splits had to be filled to keep the hulls watertight.

FOR SOME TIME NHCAP'S board of directors had been searching for a name for the canoe that would evoke the coming of the first people to Hawai'i. After considering many suggestions, they finally settled on *Hawai'iloa*, the name of a chiefly voyager credited in legend with being the first to discover and settle the islands. But the choice was contested. Some students of Hawaiian traditions considered the legend a nineteenth century creation rather than an ancient tale handed down orally from the time of first settlement.

The legend of Hawai'iloa came to public attention in the late 1860s and 1870s through the efforts of three men: the distinguished native historian Samuel Mānaiakalani Kamakau; a younger scholar known as Kepelino (the Hawaiianized form of his baptismal name Zepherin) rather than by his Hawaiian name of Kahoali'ikūmai'eiwakamoku Keauokalani; and Swedish-born Abraham Fornander, who had come to the islands aboard a whaling ship, married into a chiefly family, and rose to become a circuit judge and assistant governor of Maui. At this late stage in his life, Fornander was devoted to gathering and analyzing Hawaiian traditions, and was searching for one about the discovery and settlement of Hawai'i. He naturally turned to Kamakau, who was then publishing article after article in Hawaiian language newspapers, and to Kepelino, who was working on a book of Hawaiian traditions that unfortunately would not be published until 1932. They obligingly provided him with parallel accounts about the first man to discover and settle the islands, a chief called Hawai'iloa by Kamakau and Hawai'inui by Kepelino. Fornander then condensed and edited the materials in English and entitled the account "The Legend of Hawaii Loa."[8]

This legend, which was not published in full until 1919,[9] features a series of tales that start with the creation of the world and its living forms, including the first man, Kumuhonua, who was made from the soil. Subsequent stories relate the adventures of his descendants, including Hawai'iloa, who is introduced as the discoverer and settler of the islands of Hawai'i and Maui:

> Hawaii Loa, or Ke Kowa i Hawaii. He was one of the four children of Aniani Ka Lani. The other three were Ki, who settled in Tahiti, Kana Loa and Laakapu. In his time the ocean was called Kai Holo-o-ka-Ia. It was so-called by Hawaii Loa, and at that time there existed only the two islands of Hawaii and of Maui, discovered by him, the first of which was called after himself, and the second was named after his eldest son. The other islands of this group are said to have been hove up from the sea by volcanoes during and subsequent to the time of Hawaii Loa. These two large islands were then uninhabited. Hawaii Loa and his followers were the first inhabitants.[10]

The text explained that Hawai'iloa and his brothers had been born on the coast of 'Āina Kai Melemele a Kāne, "The Land of the Yellow Sea of Kāne." Hawai'iloa was a great fisherman who liked to roam over the ocean for months on end. During one of his expeditions, Makaliʻi, his navigator-astronomer, urged him to head east toward the rising stars:

> So they steered straight onward and arrived at the easternmost island (*ka moku hikina loa*). They went ashore and found the country fertile and pleasant, filled with ʻawa, coconut trees, etc., and Hawaii Loa, the chief, called that land after his own name. Here they dwelt a long time and when their vessel was filled with food and with fish, they returned to their native country with the firm intention to come back to Hawaii-nei which they preferred to their own country.

After returning with his family, Hawaiʻiloa sailed south to Kahiki to visit his brother. From there he traveled back to Hawaiʻi, taking with him his brother's firstborn son who then married Hawaiʻiloa's favorite daughter, Oʻahu. Thus, the new settlement's chiefly lineage descended from Oʻahu and her son Kūnuiākea, while the commoner lineage descended from navigator-astronomer Makaliʻi.

In addition to compiling this text, Fornander also featured the legend in the first volume of his *An Account of the Polynesian Race*, published in London in 1878. He triumphantly revealed that the legend also contained clues for tracing the Polynesians across two oceans to their original homeland in the Middle East.[11]

Fornander divided the name Hawaiʻiloa into two parts: Hawa, which he identified as the Indonesian Island of Java; and *iʻi*, which he claimed meant "raging, furious with heat" and referred to active volcanism on Java. He then proposed that Hawaiʻi meant "burning Hawa," and that Hawaiʻiloa meant "Great Burning Hawa." (Fornander translated Hawaiʻiloa's alternate name, Ke Kowa i Hawaiʻi, to mean "The Straits of Great Burning Hawa," which he identified as the waters separating Java and the Asian mainland.)

Not content to stop there, Fornander rummaged through the early genealogical layers of the legend for clues to the ultimate Polynesian homeland. He found that the stories about the early descendants of Kumuhonua, the first man, pointed westwards to the Middle East. He hypothesized that Kumuhonua's immediate descendants had lived on the northern shore of the Persian Gulf and, after surviving a great flood, crossed to the Arabian Peninsula. From there, under Hawaiʻiloa's leadership, they sailed across the Indian Ocean to Indonesia, and eventually to Hawaiʻi. Faced with the problem of explaining how Hawaiʻiloa could have left the Middle East and sailed across the Indian Ocean and far into the Pacific during one lifetime, Fornander blithely suggested that a succession of voyagers called Hawaiʻiloa had carried out this migration.

As far-fetched as this might seem today, we must remember that Fornander was not a trained scholar, and was writing well before the necessary research tools had been developed and applied to tracing Polynesian origins. He was one of a number of Westerners living in 19th century Polynesia who had become fluent in the language of their adoptive islands and sought to reconstruct Polynesian migrations from oral traditions, place names, and language. Commonly these amateur scholars seized upon legends, names, and words that seemed to resemble those from continental cultures. Using these dubious identifications, they traced Polynesians back to India and the Middle East, where they supposedly branched off from Hebrews, Cushites, Aryans, or other ancient peoples. Their grand migration scenarios have long since been discarded. New research in linguistics, archaeology, and genetics points to Island Southeast Asia as the jumping-off point for the people moving out into the Pacific who were ancestral to the Polynesians. Some linguists trace them farther back to Taiwan and the adjacent coast of southern China.[12]

Kamakau and Kepelino appear to have set the stage for Fornander's speculations by incorporating biblical elements in their writings. This is evident in the Genesis-like creation of the world, animals, and the first man, the great flood sent to punish the wicked people who turned away from their god, and the building by Nu'u and his family of a "Canoe-like-a-chief's house" to survive the inundation. Such melding of biblical and native narratives was common in nineteenth-century Polynesia. As native intellectuals became literate through reading the Bible, they attempted to give a wider meaning to their oral traditions by connecting them with biblical tales.[13]

In 1937 Māori scholar Te Rangi Hiroa (AKA Sir Peter H. Buck) addressed the origins of the Hawai'iloa legend in his lyrical book about Polynesian migrations, *Vikings of the Sunrise*.[14] Although he based it primarily on oral traditions, he was wary of the Hawai'iloa legend. From his experience in Polynesia, he considered that the belief that Hawai'i Island had been found by an explorer called Hawai'iloa—who then named the island after himself—did not "stand inspection." Among other things, it did not account for the fact that the name Hawai'i and such cognate forms as Hawaiki, 'Avaiki, Havai'i, and Savai'i are found across Polynesia, where they refer either to a distant homeland that is also the place to which the spirits of the dead return, or to an island settled from that homeland.[15] Te Rangi Hiroa therefore suggested that Hawaiian historians had named a mythical voyager Hawai'iloa in order to establish their claim that he was the first to discover and settle the previously named Hawai'i Island.

Dorothy Barrère, who worked for decades at Bishop Museum as Mary Kawena Pukui's assistant, was more resolute in her critique. In her 1969 monograph, she charged that when Kamakau and Kepelino wrote about Hawai'iloa/Hawai'inui discovering Hawai'i they had "departed from Biblically-inspired tales and entered into the realm of pure invention."[16] These were challenging words to those who wanted to name the new canoe after the legendary explorer. Many knowledgeable Hawaiians deeply believe that Hawai'iloa is part of their history. Patience Bacon, Mary Kawena Pukui's daughter and an authority in ancient hula, recalled her mother saying that when she interviewed the *kūpuna* (elders) during the 1920s and 1930s, they spoke of Hawai'iloa as part of "their reality." Similarly, Randie Fong, head of the Kamehameha Schools music program and a passionate scholar of native Hawaiian dance and song, felt that there was no reason to question the age and authenticity of the Hawai'iloa story.[17]

Although not involved in the controversy, I was pleased to hear that *Hawai'iloa* was finally confirmed as the new canoe's name. Literally, *Hawai'iloa* means "long or distant Hawai'i."[18] Whatever its origins, I thought that it made a fine name for a voyaging canoe, one that calls forth visions of far-off lands, as those of us who sailed *Hōkūle'a* to Aotearoa in 1985 had realized upon landing. On shore we heard *Hawaiki Roa*, the Māori way of saying *Hawai'iloa*, repeatedly and resonantly chanted in a mantra about the magnificence, extant, and faraway location of Hawaiki, the legendary Māori homeland:

> *Hawaiki Nui, Hawaiki Roa, Hawaiki Pāmamao*
> Great Hawaiki, Long Hawaiki, Distant Hawaiki

ONCE BO AND HIS TEAM finished turning the logs into slim and gracefully curved hulls, they were trucked from the museum to Pier 36, which lay vacant in Honolulu Harbor. This was an ideal location for finishing the canoe, as there was nobody around to be disturbed by sawing, hammering, or other noisy activities. In addition, the site included a shed big enough for working on *Hawai'iloa* and *Hōkūle'a* at once and an attached building with several rooms for office work, meetings, and storage.

At the pier, many volunteers joined in the work of making canoe components and mating them with the hull bases. They worked under Bo's overall supervision, and with the guidance of such masters as skilled woodworker Jerry Ongais and longtime canoe maker, *Hōkūle'a* sailor, and Polynesian Voyaging Society board member Wally Froiseth. The team carved long *koa* planks and sections of *koa* logs to fashion the side strakes and the prow and stern pieces. They also shaped logs of dense, tough *'ōhi'a lehua (Metrosideros macropus)* to make the crossbeams connecting the hulls, as well as the masts and booms, and worked the softwood trunks and branches of spreading *hau* trees *(Hibiscus tiliaceus)* to make the deck posts and railings. Making these components from Hawaiian woods helped to overcome some of the disappointment about not being able to carve the hulls out of *koa*.

Next to the big work shed was a large kitchen that became a combination cafeteria, meeting room, lecture hall, and recreation center. There volunteers could take a break, have a snack or a meal, and trade stories with experienced canoe makers and sailors, as well as others who dropped by. In addition, formal meetings and lessons about canoe sailing, navigation, and the Hawaiian language were held there. Captain Kapahulehua, whose first language is Hawaiian, and Esther "Kiki" Mo'okini, a Hawaiian linguist and author, gave a series of lessons on the Hawaiian names for parts of a canoe and sailing and navigational terms.

WHEN WORK ON *HAWAI'ILOA'S* HULLS had begun, research also started on how to make lashings, rigging lines, and sails from native materials.

'Aha, a generic term for a meeting or assembly, also refers to the all-important cordage with which the many components of canoes, houses, and other structures were lashed together. Canoe *'aha* was usually made from coconut fibers. After tearing these from the husk, then soaking and cleaning them, *'aha* makers would roll the fibers together on their thighs to make a rough twine. Strands were then braided to make cordage known in English as sennit. Hawaiians commonly used three-strand *'aha* for binding the side strakes *(mo'o)* and bow and stern covers *(manu)* to a dugout hull, and for joining the hulls together with crossbeams *('iako)*.[19] Like sailors elsewhere in the tropical Pacific, Hawaiians also twisted and plaited together many strands of sennit to make rigging lines—the ropes used to stay the masts, hoist the sails, and control their angle to the wind.

The virtues of *'aha* were well-appreciated by foreign seamen. For example, the French navigator Louis Freycinet wrote how he was:

> amazed at the skill and intelligence demonstrated in joining various parts of these floating machines so solidly that they are almost indestructible under the pressure of sea water, even though it is only achieved by means of braided fiber lashings.[20]

Since the coconut is really a great seed that evolved to float across lagoons and to more distant shores, cordage made from the fibers of its husk are highly resistant to salt water. However, this cordage has a relatively low tensile strength, in part because the fibers from which it is made are so short, limited to length of the coconut. When coir ropes made from coconut fiber entered international trade, sailors recognized that they were not as strong as those made from other natural fibers such as manila, sisal, and hemp. Polynesian sailors compensated for this limitation by making many turns around the components they lashed together with *'aha*, and by making the rigging lines extra thick.

As sennit had not been made in Hawai'i for generations, Nainoa asked Mau Piailug to bring several long hanks from his home atoll in order to test them. He was dismayed to find out how weak it was. An instrumented test of a one-inch coir rope was especially disconcerting for it broke well before reaching the maximum load on *Hōkūle'a*'s stays. This meant that miles and miles of sennit line would be needed to join the hulls, crossbeams, and other components, and to make into heavy coir for the rigging. Nainoa began to doubt the feasibility of employing Hawaiian sennit, particularly since its manufacture was a lost art that would have to be revived. And he was unsure that enough canoe-grade sennit could be imported from atolls where it is still being made.

That left another indigenous alternative to consider: cordage made from long fibers stripped from the inner bark of a native shrub, *olonā (Touchardia latifolia)*. Hawaiians used this cordage for making fishing lines, nets, and extra-tough lashings and ropes. In the early days, Western sea captains realized that *olonā* cordage was the strongest available anywhere in the world and bought all they could to replace their worn-out rigging. Even when the manufacture of *olonā* cordage eventually died out, the fibers continued to be exported until nylon and other synthetic fibers made their appearance. Swiss mountaineers are said to have favored these thin, soft, but very tough fibers for making climbing rope. However, when researchers looked into the possibility of using *olonā* for the canoe, their findings were discouraging. They could not find any large concentrations of the shrub growing in the wild and estimated that it could take several years to develop the plantations, processing facilities, and skills needed to produce enough *olonā* for the canoe.

Preliminary trials with mat sails were also undertaken. By the 1830s, gaff-rigged European sails made from sailcloth had largely replaced the Hawaiians' distinctive crab-claw sails that had been fabricated by stitching together narrow strips of matting. When we started building *Hōkūle'a* in 1974, there was no one left in Hawai'i with any experience in weaving and rigging traditional sails. Accordingly, we ordered a number of rolls of finely woven sail matting from Micronesia. However, by the time we had to leave for Tahiti, we had just one finished mat sail. We sailed to Tahiti with cloth sails, although we carried the mat sail as a spare and tried it out in Tahitian waters to good effect.

Mau brought several rolls of narrow sail matting from his home island for *Hawai'iloa*. He and his helpers cut these into strips and stitched them together to make rough sails for testing on *Hōkūle'a*. Although the strips tended to separate in brisk trades, the trials were encouraging enough to have NHCAP commission two expert Hawaiian weavers create matting for a pair of finished sails.

ON A RAINY SATURDAY morning in June of 1993, *Hawai'iloa* sat on the dock at Pier 36, ready for launching. Waiting for the logs to season, working on the hulls only on weekends at the museum, and then carving all the other components and joining them together at Pier 36 had stretched out the construction process. Nonetheless, three years after the spruce trees had been felled, the canoe was ready. Bo, his crew, and the many others who worked on the canoe, had done a remarkable job. Their creation was truly handsome—a 57-foot long double canoe with spruce hulls stained a traditional matte black, finished with shiny *manu ihu* (prow pieces), *manu hope* (stern pieces), and *mo'o* (side strakes) carved from golden brown *koa*.

After a lengthy ceremony carried out in drenching rain (considered a blessing in itself), *Hawai'iloa* was ready to be introduced to the sea. No one seemed to mind that the heavy canoe had to be placed in the water by a giant crane. For the first time in living memory, a big dugout sailing canoe was being launched in Hawai'i.

Once *Hawai'iloa* was gently lowered in the water, thirty of the men and women who had built the canoe climbed on board and, while paddling, chanted *"Ia Wa'a Nui:"*

Ia wa'a nui	That large canoe
Ia wa'a kioloa	That long canoe
Ia wa'a peleleu	That broad canoe
A lele māmala	Let the chips fly
A manu o uka	The bird of the upland
A manu o kai	The bird of the lowland
'I'iwi pōlena	The *'i'iwi pōlena* bird
A kau ka hōkū	The stars appear
A kau i ka mālama	The daylight arrives
A pae i kula	Land ashore
'Āmama ua noa!	*'Āmama*, the *kapu* is free!

This chant, which had been found in an old box in the museum archives, had also been used for the launching of *Hōkūle'a*. Its words capture the feeling of a canoe born of the forest yet meant for the sea, and their recitation at launchings serves to release a vessel from its *kapu*, or sacred state, making it *noa*, that is, secular and free to sail over the ocean.

When the chanting died down, the canoe was formally transferred from Bo to the owner, the Native Hawaiian Culture and Arts Program. Keli'i Tau'ā, the *kahuna pule* who had gone to Alaska for the tree felling, asked NHCAP chairman Clayton Hee, if he found the canoe to be *maika'i*, good and acceptable. Clayton immediately answered *'ae* (yes), and the ceremony ended with the sounding of the *pū* (conches).

SEA TRIALS CONDUCTED over the next several weeks revealed that *Hawai'iloa* was far too heavy and very hard to steer. The excess weight and consequent sluggishness of the canoe had been expected and could be remedied. Nainoa had purposefully left the flanks and keel of each hull extra thick and planned to cut out the excess wood after sea trials. However, the steering problem was a surprise. *Hawai'iloa* sailed bow down, giving her a very heavy weather helm, meaning that she automatically turned hard into the wind and had to be held off by pushing long steering sweeps deep into the sea.

The bows were too narrow and shallow, more like those of an outrigger racing canoe than a sailing canoe. Without enough buoyancy forward to fully support the massive forward crossbeams and the heavy foremast and boom (all made from dense *'ōhi'a*), the bows were pushed low into the water, destroying the canoe's balance. In a video interview, Bo said that he must have taken too much wood off the bows because he was so used to making racing canoes. But he was too hard on himself. Not only did the design he was given call for slim forward sections, but the logs tapered too quickly to make deep and full bows.

The spruce trees were big enough around at the base, but like *koa* they narrowed rapidly as they gained height. The canoe was thus too slim forward and lacked the displacement needed to carry a heavy load of people, plus their food, water, and other supplies. The native Alaskans were able to make large outrigger-less paddling canoes from such logs by widening them. They filled the dugout hulls with water, which they then heated with hot rocks. As the fibers soaked up the hot water, they relaxed, spreading the gunnels. The resultant broad and stable hulls were therefore fit for carrying large loads in inland waterways and the open sea.

But this technique was not used in Polynesia. *Hawai'iloa* had been built in the manner of the dugout canoes seen by foreign explorers in Hawai'i two centuries ago. Except for a few giant ones, such as a 70-footer with hulls three feet deep and wide, the longest canoes were mostly in the 40 to 60 foot range. Cook's artists depicted several of these craft, and a French naval officer took the lines off the 48-foot long *wa'a kaulua* of Kauikeaouli, Kamehameha III. This drawing, which I followed in building *Nālehia*, shows that the hulls were made from a pair of dugout logs to which side strakes were added to raise the freeboard, and prow and stern pieces added to close the ends. Other drawings and descriptions confirm this construction method.[21]

Double canoes constructed in this way were sleek, strong, and well-suited for coastal and inter-island travel along the Hawaiian chain. Their round-bottom, relatively shallow hulls were adapted for the characteristic big swells and breaking surf. But they were not long-range voyaging canoes with ample freeboard and capacity for carrying many people and their supplies over long distances. By the late eighteenth century, Hawaiians apparently were no longer voyaging beyond their archipelago or building canoes for that purpose. Instead they made combination paddling and sailing craft ideally adapted for coastal and inter-archipelago sailing. Their relatively low freeboard

Double canoes (wa'a kaulua) *taking high chief Kalaniopu'u to greet Captain Cook's ships at Kealakekua Bay, 1779.*

made them easy to paddle, as did their narrow central platform. Instead of the wide-deck characteristic of voyaging canoes, they lashed a long, narrow plank called a *pola* atop the arching crossbeams connecting the hulls. The space between each hull and the central *pola* enabled paddlers to alternately stroke inboard and outboard the hull for maximum efficiency and endurance. Yet the lack of a broad central platform, and above all the relatively low freeboard and limited displacement restricted the loads the standard *wa'a kaulua* could safely carry. Kamehameha I found this out in 1796 when his fleet of heavily laden war canoes foundered in heavy weather when attempting to invade Kaua'i from O'ahu. His solution was to create a new kind of canoe, a *wa'a peleleu* (extended canoe) with enlarged hulls for greater capacity. [22]

Trying to turn a pair of highly tapered spruce logs into a voyaging canoe by following the standard *wa'a kaulua* model had put Bo and his helpers into an impossible bind. But what was done was done. There was no time to go back and redesign a new *Hawai'iloa* along the lines of such well known types of deep-sea voyaging canoes as the Tahitian *tipaerua* and *pahi*—which as drawings from Cook's expeditions show, had composite hulls built from planks and shaped sections of logs. The builders had to work with what they had.

After the sea trials, *Hawai'iloa* was hauled out and disassembled so that the excess wood could be cut out from the insides of the hulls and from other components. In

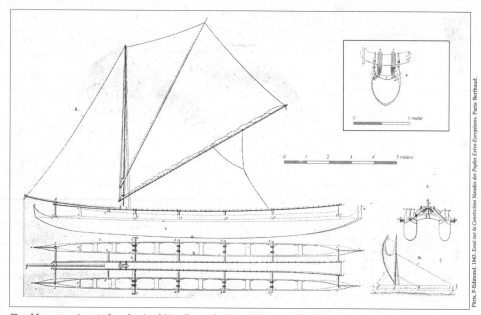

Double canoe (wa'a kaulua) *of Kauikeaouli (Kamehameha III) drawn ca. 1838 by François Edmond Pâris. The sail, which was not shown in Pâris' original drawing, is adapted from his drawing of an outrigger canoe. It represents the Western-style sail that by the 1830s had replaced the Hawaiian "crab-claw" sail, an example of which Pâris sketched in the lower right-hand corner.*

addition one of the forward crossbeams was removed to further lighten the bows. When relaunched seven months later, in July of 1994, the canoe—now lighter by some 6,500 pounds—floated considerably higher in the water and was much livelier under sail. Nonetheless, there still was not enough overall buoyancy, which meant that the size of the crew and amount of food and water carried on the voyage would have to be carefully controlled.

Since there was no practical way to go back and add extra wood to the bow sections, a more radical solution had to be found to correct the weather helm. *Hawai'iloa's* sail rig was reversed, following the practice of the 1920s and 1930s when surfers at Waikīkī adapted their outrigger paddling canoes for sailing. The twin masts and sails that had been mounted toward the forward end of *Hawai'iloa* were instead placed aft. This made what had been the buoyant sterns of the two hulls into the new bows, with the slim former bows becoming the new sterns. Having extra buoyancy forward brought the bows up, making the steering so much easier that everyone soon forgot that they were really sailing the canoe backwards.

Although some components of *Hawai'iloa* had been lashed together with sennit for the initial sea trials, the canoe went back into the water, bound and rigged solely with synthetic cordage and rope. After doubts were raised about the strength of sennit line and coir rope, and the feasibility of making or buying enough to fully rig *Hawai'iloa*, the dream of using only native lashings and rigging died. Similarly, when a pair of traditional sails made from wide strips of finely woven *lauhala* matting kept splitting during sea trials, the goal of equipping the canoe with *lauhala* sails was also regretfully abandoned.

ALTHOUGH *HAWAI'ILOA* only partially met the ideal of a native materials canoe, much had been learned by trying. Failing to find even one large and sound *koa* tree exposed how much the native forests had been devastated over the last two centuries. Accepting spruce logs as substitutes broadened Hawaiian horizons to include Native Alaskans who had gone through a similar colonial experience and were also searching for ways to regain their balance in today's world. Coping with the limitations of single-log hulls and then not being able to make enough native cordage as well as serviceable *lauhala* sails was especially painful. But these experiences did drive home the point that voyaging canoes were highly complex creations that were much harder to recreate than had been foreseen. Nonetheless, despite all the problems, delays, and disappointments, *Hawai'iloa* was finally ready to sail, and everyone involved was immensely proud of their handsome creation.

Their pride was as much about the process of cultural revival as it was for the actual canoe. Randie Fong clearly expressed this point at a celebration held at Pōka'ī Bay on O'ahu's Wai'anae coast, one of the most heavily Hawaiian regions in the islands. The populace welcomed *Hawai'iloa*, along with *Hōkūle'a* and several smaller sailing canoes. Speaking in his capacity as a member of NHCAP's board of trustees, Randie explained to the crowd assembled on the beach that:

> You see, this really isn't just about canoes and voyaging. This is about a race of people realizing the greatness within them—the understanding that as a community we are capable of great things. If we are grounded in our culture and dare to take risks, our Polynesian lifestyle and cultural practices will be the key to our success as a race in the 21st century. That's what this is all about!

The remarkable recitation of the legend of Mō'ikeha that day demonstrated how, despite all the problems, the project was nonetheless fulfilling the stated goal of serving as a focal center for cultural revival. When I had been casting about for the appropriate route to test a reconstructed voyaging canoe, the seaway between Hawai'i and Tahiti

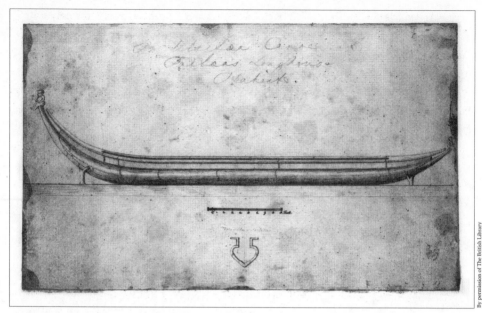

Hull of a pahi *double canoe under construction at Ra'iātea.*

stood out because of Hawaiian traditions about voyaging back and forth between these centers. Prominent among these was the story of the high chief Mō'ikeha and his family, which involved three round trips between Hawai'i and Tahiti—one by Mō'ikeha himself, and one each by his Hawaiian son Kila and his Tahitian son La'a-mai-Kahiki (La'a-from-Kahiki).[23] The presentation at Pōka'ī Bay, given entirely in Hawaiian, caught me unawares. As the first orator Manu Boyd began, I realized he was chanting about Mō'ikeha and his return from Tahiti to Hawai'i. Subsequent orators continued chanting about the successive segments of Mō'ikeha's journey, first around Hawai'i Island, then Maui, Moloka'i, O'ahu, and finally Kaua'i.

There the chiefly voyager spied two beautiful "princesses" *(nā kamāli'iwahine)* out surfing the waves. He promptly fell in love with the two, married them, and became Kaua'i's ruling chief. Kalani Akana, the teacher of Hawaiian chant and dance who organized this stunning performance, closed the presentation with these poetic lines about Mō'ikeha's decision to settle on Kaua'i:

'O Mō'ikeha ka Lani nāna e noho.	Mō'ikeha is the chief who will reside.
Noho ku'u lani iā Hawai'i.	My chief will reside on Hawai'i.
Ola! Ola! Ola kalanaola!	Life! Life! O buoyant life!
Ola ke ali'i! Ola ke kahuna!	The chief and the priest shall live!
Ola ke kilo! Ola ke kauwā!	The seer and the servant shall live!

Noho ku'u lani a lūlana	Settle down my chief and be at rest
A kani mo'opuna i Kaua'i	And increase the generations on Kaua'i
'O Mō'ikeha ka ali'i.	Mō'ikeha is the chief.

Aside from the brilliance of the performance, what really struck me was hearing an oral presentation of the legend that had been so central to the voyaging revival. Back in the late 1950s, we had learned Mō'ikeha's story by reading about it, not by hearing it chanted, as by then such traditions were seldom if ever publicly orated. Inspired by the building of *Hawai'iloa*, and seeking to honor the canoe's coming to Wai'anae, Kalani Akana had gone back to old Hawaiian texts. By vigorously reciting a tale that for too long had languished on paper, he and his associates were fulfilling the promise given by Nainoa Thompson and affirmed by Herb Kāne that building the new canoe would serve as a catalyst for cultural revival.

Chapter Two

For the Coming Generations

THE SIXTH FESTIVAL OF PACIFIC ARTS was scheduled to be held in Rarotonga, the capital of the Cook Islands, in October of 1992. Prime Minister Geoffrey Henry and his advisors had decided that the festival's theme would be "Seafaring Pacific Islanders," but they needed advice from the nation's *tumu korero* (traditionally learned specialists) on how to proceed. At a conference attended by *tumu korero* from around the Cooks, Jon Tikivanotau Jonassen, then the Permanent Secretary of the Ministry of Cultural Development, asked the delegates: "Should the Cook Islands build a voyaging canoe for the festival?" In their discussions, the *tumu korero* admitted that although voyaging canoes were still celebrated in legend, song, and dance, none had been constructed for many generations, and the art of building and sailing them had really been forgotten. One even declared that such a vessel could not be built today.[1]

Jon, who now teaches political science at the Hawai'i branch of Brigham Young University, realized that the *tumu korero* needed some encouragement. Accordingly he called a recess until that afternoon when he knew that a visiting Māori[2] leader from Aotearoa would make some challenging remarks. After lunch the visitor told the assembly that three groups from Aotearoa were planning to build canoes and sail them to Rarotonga for the festival, and then pointedly reminded the *tumu korero* about a shared cultural principle:

> If our three canoes arrive and there are no canoes in Rarotonga to meet our canoes, then we would uphold our common traditions. We will go ashore, and claim the land.

Given such a prospect, the Cook Islanders had no choice. They had to build not one but several canoes in order to greet those sailing to the festival with proper dignity. The Rarotongan delegates said that several of the island's tribes would build large double canoes, and the delegates from the outlying islands of the Southern Cooks— Aitutaki, 'Ātiu, Mangaia, Ma'uke, and Miti'āro—declared that each of their communities would build their own sailing canoe for the festival. Regrettably, the *tumu korero* from the sprinkling of remote atolls that make up the Northern Cooks declined to participate, saying that their islands were too distant and too poor in timber resources. Their decision was unfortunate as the last traditional sailors left in the Cooks live on these atolls, where they still sail small outrigger canoes across interior lagoons and take them fishing offshore.

While plans for the new canoes were being developed, Prime Minister Henry contacted the Polynesian Voyaging Society with an unusual request. He wanted the Hawaiians to sail *Hōkūle'a* to the Cooks to help celebrate the festival's seafaring theme, and to train navigators from the outer Southern Cooks so that they could guide their canoes to Rarotonga for the festival.

The timing was not ideal. The voyage from Te Henua 'Enana to Hawai'i was scheduled for 1994, yet *Hawai'iloa* was not yet finished and the training of a new batch of sailors had just begun. But the Hawaiians could not refuse. *Hōkūle'a*'s voyages, particularly the long one to and from Aotearoa during which the canoe twice passed through the Cooks, had excited people across the South Pacific. Furthermore, the Hawaiians were already dedicated to passing on their newly won skills lest they be lost again and between long voyages had been sailing *Hōkūle'a* as a floating classroom for Hawai'i schoolchildren and youths. They therefore accepted the Prime Minister's invitation, even though it meant putting off *Hawai'iloa*'s voyage until 1995. Aside from the satisfaction of helping out the Cook Islanders, Nainoa and others were attracted to the Cook Islands trip by the prospect of trying out new satellite connections for linking classrooms in Hawai'i with the living laboratory of *Hōkūle'a* at sea.

The Hawaiians named the voyage *No Nā Mamo*, a phrase that hinges on the metaphorical meaning of *mamo*. Although *mamo* refers primarily to a now extinct bird whose yellow tail feathers were prized for making cloaks, it figuratively means "posterity" or "descendants."[3] Hence the phrase really reflected the venture's educational nature. Poet, scholar, and canoe sailor Carlos Andrade captured this meaning by rendering *No Nā Mamo* as "For the Coming Generations" in a song he wrote about the voyage.

THE PEOPLE OF AITUTAKI, a miniature high island surrounded by an atoll ring that lies 140 nautical miles* north of Rarotonga, had a special request for the *Hōkūle'a* sailors, many of whom they had come to know when the canoe stopped there in 1986 on the

---

* One nautical mile equals 1.15 land miles and 1.85 kilometers. Nautical miles are used throughout this book, though hereafter are referred to simply as miles.

way back from Aotearoa. Since Aitutaki had no trees big enough to build even a medium-size double canoe, they asked their Hawaiian friends to find them a pair of albizia falcataria, a fast-growing introduced tree that has become popular for making fishing canoes.

The Hawaiians were only too happy to oblige with two albizias from Hawai'i Island. These were felled, trimmed, and barged to Honolulu, where Gil Ane, a former professional football player and wrestler who was then a waterfront union official, took over. He found a German freighter in port that was soon departing for Rarotonga and went to see the captain to request that he take the logs to Aitutaki, stopping there just long enough to give a blast on his horn and drop the logs overboard before continuing to Rarotonga. Just as the incredulous German captain was about to say no, a Cook Islander who had previously sailed on *Hōkūle'a* and who was serving aboard the freighter, reported to the captain. After greeting Gil and learning about his request, the crewman volunteered: "That's all right, Captain. I'll take care of it. Don't worry." The skipper shrugged and said okay.

Two weeks later the freighter dropped the logs into the sea off Aitutaki. The Aitutakians promptly came out in a powerboat and happily jumped into the ocean to embrace the logs. After giving them Aitutaki names, they towed the logs through the pass and hauled them ashore.

However, Nainoa's attempt to also help out on the canoe construction met with some resistance. Impressed by a new computer program for calculating how best to carve a log to yield the largest possible canoe hull, he offered to send the Aitutaki canoe builders detailed cutting instructions based on a computer analysis. The resultant "scuffle of communication," as Jon Jonassen phrases it, that passed between Honolulu and Aitutaki via his office ended when the head of Aitutaki's district council firmly said, "Tell our friends in Hawai'i that this is an Aitutaki canoe."[4] When he received the message, Nainoa immediately understood and thereafter concentrated on training the Aitutaki navigators along with their counterparts from the other islands. The navigators twice flew to Honolulu for lessons at the Bishop Museum's planetarium and aboard *Hōkūle'a*, and Nainoa made a round of their islands as well.

IN JUNE OF 1992 *HŌKŪLE'A* set sail for the Cooks via the Society Islands, the archipelago dominated by Tahiti that slants several hundreds of miles across the South Pacific. With respect to the southeast trades, Tahiti and its outliers form the windward group of the archipelago while the string of small high islands and low atolls that trail off to the west-northwest constitute the leeward group.[5] After touching on Tahiti, *Hōkūle'a* proceeded to Huahine, the first of the leeward islands. There the Hawaiians anchored to wait for the arrival of the Cook Island trainees, who were flying in from

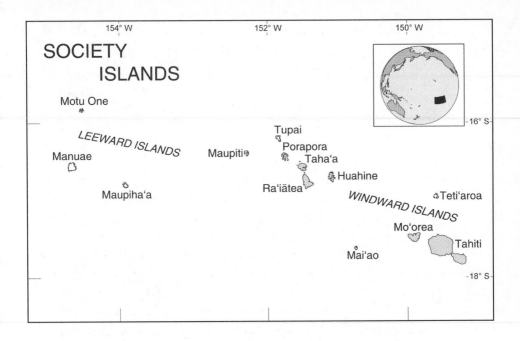

SOCIETY
    ISLANDS

154° W   152° W   150° W

Motu One

LEEWARD ISLANDS   Tupai
Manuae   Maupiti   Porapora
                                 Taha'a
                                 Huahine
Maupiha'a   Ra'iātea
                                      Teti'aroa
                   WINDWARD ISLANDS
                        Mo'orea
                                      Tahiti
                   Mai'ao

-16° S
-18° S

Rarotonga to join the crew and get some practical sailing experience on the way to the Cooks. From Huahine, the joint Hawaiian-Cook Island crew sailed *Hōkūle'a* to adjacent Ra'iātea, where they took part in a special ceremony at an ancient temple, and the trainee navigators reviewed their instructions for the crossing to the Cooks. After making one last stop in the Societies at Porapora (Borabora), a gem of an island dominated by a massive central peak but softened by sparkling lagoons and an atoll-like barrier reef, *Hōkūle'a* set off for the Southern Cooks, the nearest of which was about three days to the southwest.[6]

At Nainoa's request, I joined the crew at Porapora to document the trainees' navigation trials on the way to the Cooks, as well as their subsequent sail in the newly built double canoes from the outer Cook Islands to Rarotonga. I had become active again in the Polynesian Voyaging Society in the early 1980s, serving as a researcher and, whenever I could get away from teaching, as a crewmember on the long voyages. I had sailed on *Hōkūle'a* during the 1985–1987 voyage to Aotearoa and back, and was looking forward to serving again with the expert Hawaiian sailors and chronicling their uniquely educational mission.

Upon passing by Maupiti, a miniature high island just west of Porapora, Nainoa put the trainee navigators to work. First he set the course for Maupiha'a, a small atoll less than a day's sail to the west. As it was midday, Nainoa showed the trainees how to steer toward the unseen island by backsighting—looking astern and lining the canoe up

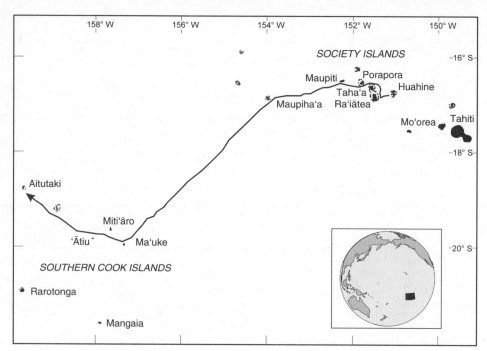

Route of Hōkūle‘a *from Huahine to Aitutaki, September 1992.*

so that Maupiti's twin peaks were in line with Porapora's central mountain, and then adjusting the heading a bit to the south in order to intercept Maupiha‘a exactly. Just before sunset, he had the students review the 32-point conceptual compass and also practice estimating the canoe's speed by judging how long it took for a wood chip to pass from the bow to the stern. Once night fell the trainees were able to switch to steering by the stars.

Early the next morning, the trainees were delighted to spot the tops of Maupiha‘a's palm trees breaking the horizon. After additional navigational tutelage, Nainoa gave them responsibility to guide the canoe to Ma‘uke, the closest of the Cook Islands, then about 240 miles to the southwest. Nainoa told them that he would stand by to answer any questions but would not volunteer any corrections. Captain Gordon Pi‘ianai‘a and I had the responsibility of tracking the canoe with a GPS receiver by plotting successive position fixes on a chart that was to be kept from the eyes of the trainees.

That night the trainees used the stars to keep the canoe on course, doing a fairly good job until a few hours before dawn when Nainoa, overriding his promise, intervened when he thought they were heading too far to the east of the course line. Nainoa and Chad Baybayan reset the course according to the rising sun and handed the steering back to the trainees. When the sun rose too high in the sky to yield an accurate bearing, Nainoa had them steer by the still-visible moon, which was slanting down toward the west-southwest. He also coached them on keeping oriented according to the dominant swells, in this case fairly regular ones coming from the east with occasional strong ones from the north.

When plotted on a chart, the canoe's GPS positions revealed that the Cook Islanders were right on target. A line drawn through the points and extended southwestward hit Maʻuke exactly, no easy feat since the island is only a few miles wide. At dawn, the island's outline appeared some ten miles ahead, immensely pleasing everyone.

Like its immediate neighbors in the Southern Cooks, Maʻuke is part volcanic and part coral. Its low central plateau represents the last stages of erosion of the island's volcanic core. Surrounding the core is a *makatea*, a ring of coral rock that was once a living reef. This had been thrust some fifty feet above sea level by tectonic movements to form a continuous cliff around the island. We sailed slowly along to the western side of Maʻuke, where a trainee from the island assured us that we could land through a narrow opening that had been blasted into the fringing reef and the raised *makatea* behind it. Since the island sloped so steeply into the sea that there was no anchorage, half of us stayed on board to sail *Hōkūleʻa* back and forth while the other half went ashore to inspect Maʻuke's newly built canoe and enjoy the local hospitality.

Going ashore in a battered aluminum boat powered by an outboard motor combined some of the thrills of surfing with the terror of smashing onto a coral reef. When our turn came, five of us clambered into the boat. The operator then nonchalantly buzzed over to the entrance of the narrow pass and waited for the right wave to come along. When one started peaking, he gunned the motor and surfed through the pass and into a shallow basin, grounding the boat with a jarring bang on a coral ledge. As the wave receded, we jumped out and scrambled for dry land before the next wave flooded the basin again.

By three that afternoon, everyone was back on board except Nainoa and a few others who were waiting to present our passports to an immigration officer scheduled to fly in from Rarotonga. Captain Piʻianaiʻa took advantage of the opportunity to coach Tura Koronui (Koro), the Chief Administrative Officer of ʻĀtiu and the navigator of the island's canoe, and several crew members of the Maʻuke canoe who had also come on board. First, he showed them how to steer to windward, pushing the steering paddle deep into the sea to hold the canoe off the wind and pulling it up when the bow moved too far off the wind. Then he had each novice take control of the steering paddle to get the feel of keeping the canoe sailing at just the right angle to the wind. Next he showed them how to wear the canoe around, that is, how to sail her onto the other tack by turning away from the wind as opposed to tacking, or putting the bow across the wind. This involved first closing the aft sail by bringing the boom up to the mast and then—

sailing just with the fore sail—slowly turning until the wind crossed the stern and the fore sail could be eased over to the other tack.

I marveled at Gordon's technique of showing the Cook Islanders this maneuver, having them verbally repeat the sequence of steps involved, and then patiently letting them try it again and again until they got it right. A graduate of the California Maritime Academy and an experienced sailor, Gordon was well qualified to teach sailing, and his experience as the head of Hawaiian studies at Kamehameha Schools also contributed to his knack for coaxing the best out of the trainees.

When we finally got underway just before dark, Nainoa was feeling extremely pressed. The original plan had been to stop at each of the outer islands, drop off that island's navigator and a Hawaiian crewman to serve as a sailing instructor, and then head for Aitutaki, where *Hōkūle'a* would anchor until the festival started. But we were already behind schedule, and the light shifting winds that settled in were not at all favorable for sailing to each and every island, so we instead headed straight for Aitutaki.

ACCORDING TO A LEGEND that is still vividly retold in dance and song, a heroic navigator named Ru led an expedition to settle Aitutaki. One version of this tale, published by a *tumu korero* in 1895, begins on an island called 'Avaiki, which could have been Ra'iātea, the island formerly called Havai'i (the Tahitian way of pronouncing 'Avaiki, Hawai'i, Hawaiki, etc.).[7] In another version published forty years later, the home island is called Tupuaki, which sounds like the Cook Island way of pronouncing Tupua'i in the Austral Islands, which is located several hundreds of miles south of Tahiti.[8] According to the latter version, Ru was a skilled navigator who became so worried about overpopulation that he decided to build a double canoe and set sail toward the setting sun to find a new land. But first he had to overcome the fears of his four younger brothers as well as his four wives by convincing them that he had the knowledge and skills to take them to a new land. Once that was accomplished, twenty young unmarried women also willingly agreed to join the expedition.

The canoe builders located two large trees and, after the proper rituals, they cut them down and hollowed them out with their adzes. The finished hulls were then hauled down to the beach where they were lashed together to make a double canoe named *Ngapuariki*, which the translator rendered as "The Two *Ariki*." He was not certain whether *ariki* referred to actual chiefs or metaphorically to the twin hulls, or both. Paddles were hewn and mat sails woven, and the crew spent much time paddling and sailing *Ngapuariki* to gain proficiency for the voyage. Then for two days, friends and relatives helped to gather enough food for the voyage. Large quantities of taro, *puraka* (a taro-like root), and *kuru* (breadfruit) were loaded, along with enough water for a long voyage.

The following morning the winds were favorable, and Ru decided to set sail. Once clear of the reef, the sails were hoisted and the canoe headed west before the trades. Ru took the steering paddle and Verituamaroa, one of his younger brothers, went forward to stand between the twin bows as the pilot. But the next day the sky clouded over, and the wind started blowing from the west, the direction toward which they were sailing. The heavily laden canoe was riding low in the water, and the sea was so rough that the men and women had to bail constantly. As the wind strengthened and the seas rose, Verituamaroa grew frightened and urged Ru to turn back. Ru refused, saying that he knew the sea and would bring them safely to land. As the waves broke over the canoe throughout the night, Ru could be heard encouraging his crew. But upon seeing the huge running sea at dawn, he too became afraid, though he still refused to turn back.

One of his brothers persuaded him to pray to the god Tangaroa for help. Here is what Ru said:

> *Tangaroa i te titi, Tangaroa i te tata,*
> *Eu eu ake ana te rangi,*
> *Kia tae atu te tere o Ru ki uta i te 'enua.*

Tangaroa, supreme on high, Tangaroa, supreme below,
Sweep away those angry clouds,
So that Ru's people can reach the land.

Soon the wind dropped and the sea grew calmer. Ru's brothers persuaded him to pray again. Not long thereafter, the clouds parted to reveal a guiding star, and the winds started blowing from the right quarter. After bailing out the hulls and resetting the sails, the men pointed the canoe back toward the west, sailing toward the star. After three days of good weather, Verituamaroa, who was still at his forward post, cried out that he could see land. They had reached Aitutaki.

HŌKŪLE'A'S JOURNEY to Aitutaki was nowhere near so dramatic. After squalls hit the canoe as we passed between 'Ātiu and Miti'āro, calms alternating with light variables slowed our progress so that it took another day and a half to make a dawn landfall on Aitutaki. We landed in the district controlled by the line of *ariki* (chiefs) called Tamatoa, the same title as that of the high chiefs of Ra'iātea. The current Ariki Tamatoa, a distinguished-looking yet informal gentlemen in his sixties, welcomed us and explained that we would be housed in the old mission house on the hill above, where the local people would provide us with all our meals.

There we were thrust into a way of life that had been developed over a century and a half ago, when missionaries of the London Missionary Society, fresh from converting the Tahitians, brought their brand of evangelical Christianity to Aitutaki. We lived within the thick, coral-cement walls of the Takamoa Mission House, saying grace before every meal and being startled awake before dawn every Sunday by the clang of a church bell, after which many of us attended services in the old coral church. Fortunately by this time many of the most rigid missionary dictates had been softened. And the huge meals of fish, shellfish, meats, taro, breadfruit, rice, and other staples that the "mamas" prepared and served were delicious. After dinner, visits to the local tavern down at the beach made our stay on Aitutaki all the more enjoyable.

A BIG SAILING SHIP arrived during our second week at Aitutaki. On the deck lay the disassembled components of a long outrigger sailing canoe that had just been built in the Marshall Islands of Micronesia. Because the canoe was not made for long distance travel, the builders had dismantled her and shipped the components aboard *Tole Mour*, a handsome schooner that regularly conducted medical tours around the atolls of the Marshalls. After being reassembled, the canoe would join the Cook Island vessels for the sail to Rarotonga.

Dennis Alessio, a young boatbuilder from my hometown of San Diego, was behind this reconstruction. Several years earlier he had sailed on *Tole Mour* to the Marshalls. But to his great disappointment he could not find any of the long and graceful ocean sailing outriggers that had so impressed the first Western explorers to reach these atolls. They were no more. The big canoes had apparently lasted into the mid-1900s, after which the Marshallese began to rely on boats made of plywood or aluminum and powered by outboard motors. Shocked that the Marshallese had abandoned their ancient craft for expensive and unreliable outboard-powered boats, and impressed by the success of *Hōkūle'a*, the idealistic boatbuilder vowed to revive the ancient art of building and sailing outrigger canoes.

Fortunately, there were still some men in the Marshalls who had, in their youth, built and sailed the big canoes. To rescue their knowledge and experience before it was too late, Dennis organized a project with the museum at Majuro atoll, the capitol of the Republic of the Marshall Islands. The aging masters worked with young apprentices to construct a series of sailing canoes on Majuro and several other islands, including the remote atoll of Eniwetok. There Dennis recruited a master canoe maker, Lombwe Mark, then 71, and his only slightly younger assistant, Hertes John, to reconstruct the long, slim outrigger canoe now resting disassembled on the beach at Aitutaki.

The two venerable craftsmen and eight young trainees fashioned the hull from several drift logs that had washed up on Eniwetok. With steel-bladed adzes they carved interlocking sections from the logs and then lashed them together to make a sleek, knife-edged hull that was a little over fifty feet long, yet measured less than two feet across at its widest point. A single outrigger float extended well out from the hull to counter the overturning force of the wind on the canoe's big lateen sail. Officially the canoe bore the name *Waan Aelon Kein* (Canoe of These Islands), but everybody called her *Walap*, which simply means "Big Canoe."

DEPARTURE FOR RAROTONGA from Aitutaki and the other outer islands was scheduled for October 9. All the canoes were to leave their respective islands that morning and sail all day and night to make landfall on Rarotonga sometime during the afternoon of the second day.

At the farewell ceremony the previous night, Nainoa took the occasion to compliment and encourage Clive Baxter and Dorn Marsters, the two recent graduates of Aitutaki's Araura College who would jointly navigate *Ngapuariki* to Rarotonga:

> We've sailed close to a thousand miles with Clive and Dorn. When we were requested to help train navigators, we said that we will do all that we can. But we can't do it all. We can only provide the training on land as well as the training at sea by using *Hōkūle'a*. But we can't make the students want to learn. We can't make the students be disciplined in their training. That's up to them. We've been training for over a year now, and I would like to say how proud I am about how well these two sons of Aitutaki have done. And I'm confident, looking at the condition of your canoe and knowing how skilled these individuals are on the ocean, that you will be more than proud when the canoes come together at Rarotonga.

Earlier, Nainoa had inspected the Aitutaki canoe, named *Ngapuariki* after its legendary forerunner. At 35 feet long, she was only a little over half the length of *Hōkūle'a*, but thanks to skillful carving of the pair of logs sent from Hawai'i, the resultant hulls gave her plenty of buoyancy. The Aitutaki had built a sound and seaworthy canoe and were justly proud of their achievement.

To everyone's great disappointment, the day of departure dawned cloudy with heavy showers and shifting winds. Whether starting from Aitutaki located almost due north of Rarotonga or from the other islands that lie to the east, the canoes needed easterly trade winds and fair skies to make the crossing. But the mixed, alternately calm and squally weather that plagued us on the way from Ra'iātea to Aitutaki was still hanging on. We learned on the shortwave radio at the Chief Administrative Officer's home that the 'Ātiu canoe had jumped the gun and already set sail only to capsize within sight of the island. Fortunately the yacht *Spirit*, which had been drafted to escort the canoe, was able to take the crew off and stand by, using the overturned vessel as a sea anchor, until a boat came to tow the canoe back to 'Ātiu. The Miti'āro canoe, which had reached 'Ātiu the day before, had set out right after the 'Ātiu vessel but turned back when the crew saw the bad weather coming. The crew of the Ma'uke canoe, which was approaching 'Ātiu just as the other canoes were leaving, also saw the dark clouds on the horizon and wisely ducked into the 'Ātiu anchorage for shelter. As rain hammered the corrugated iron roof of the administrator's house, Nainoa requested that all the crews stand down and wait until the weather improved.

The delay gave the Marshallese time to finish reassembling their canoe. An admiring crowd was attracted by the sight of the gray-haired canoe masters lashing the outrigger to the hull by a much more complicated system of cross beams, braces, and ties than that used by the Polynesians. But the real show came a few days later when the Marshallese launched the *Walap* and took her out for a test spin by sailing her out to sea through the narrow, winding channel.

Unlike Polynesian canoes that have a fixed bow and stern and must either tack or wear around, the double-ended Marshallese canoes are "shunted" from one side of the wind to the other by literally changing ends. The crew first luffs the single lateen sail, then pivots it around the short mast mounted at mid-hull. They then lash the tack of the sail to what was moments earlier the stern, but is now the bow. Once the sail fills and is sheeted in, the canoe sets off sailing on the opposite side of the wind. Even those of us familiar with this maneuver were amazed to see how deftly the Marshallese shunted their way out the narrow channel and through the pass, and then, after sailing back and forth offshore, easily worked their way back to the beach.

TRADE WINDS and clear skies did not return until Thursday the 15th. After radio checks of the weather at each of the islands, Nainoa gave the go-ahead for all the canoes to set sail for Rarotonga.

At Aitutaki, first *Ngapuariki*, then *Hōkūle'a*, and finally *Walap* worked their way through the pass. Once outside the reef, *Ngapuariki* took a tow to head east around the island in order to reach a position off the southern coast where Clive and Dorn could take advantage of the natural backsighting range provided by Aitutaki's central peak and an islet just offshore. By putting the canoe on a line mentally drawn from the peak through the islet, the sailors would be headed due south directly for Rarotonga. Although *Walap* started after *Hōkūle'a*, the lightweight racehorse of a canoe quickly pulled ahead of the much heavier double canoe and headed close into the wind for Rarotonga. Slowed by the light winds and unable to point as high as *Walap*, *Hōkūle'a* lagged way behind.

Tua Pittman, a tall, handsome Rarotongan who had sailed on two legs of the

Canoes Sailing from the Outer Islands to Rarotonga

Starting Island	Canoe Name
Aitutaki	*Ngapuariki*
Aitutaki	*Walap* (from Eniwetok, Marshall Islands)
Aitutaki	*Hōkūle'a* (from O'ahu, Hawai'i)
'Ātiu	*'Enua Manu*
Miti'āro	*Te Roto Nui*
Ma'uke	*Maire Nui*
Mangaia	*Te Rangi Ma Toru*

Voyage of Rediscovery, had the job of guiding *Hōkūle'a* to his home island. In order to head towards Rarotonga, he kept the canoe sailing as close to the wind as was possible in the light trades, keeping track of her heading by watching the sun and backsighting on Aitutaki. When the sun set and the stars appeared, Tua oriented himself and steered the canoe according to the star compass Nainoa had taught him. About midnight, however, a light squall came through, after which the sky remained cloudy and the wind blew fitfully, conditions that were to challenge Tua and the other navigators for the rest of the crossing.

During the remainder of the night, winds remained light and variable, and the skies were almost totally overcast. On the following day, Tua estimated that they had freshened enough to allow *Hōkūle'a* to point directly toward Rarotonga. Because of the overcast skies, he had been steering by swells rolling in from the southeast. That afternoon around three, the heavy clouds parted briefly to reveal the peaks of Rarotonga ahead. Despite far from ideal conditions, Tua was right on target on his first crossing as a solo navigator.

As *Hōkūle'a* neared the island, we spied the billowing sails of *Tole Mour* off to the northeast and then the single lateen of *Walap* ahead of her. Given *Walap*'s speed, we had thought the Marshallese canoe would be in port by then. Dennis Alessio later filled me in on what had happened. Because *Walap* sailed so much faster than *Tole Mour* in light airs, the Marshallese had to periodically heave to and wait for the big boat to catch up. Just before dawn, they were delayed further when steep seas hit the canoe, shattering the mast near its base. After spending several hours attempting to re-join the sections, they finally gave up. Jury-rigging the shortened mast with a reefed sail, they continued with reduced speed to Rarotonga.

I was particularly curious to learn how *Walap* had been navigated. The Marshallese are famed for a unique remote sensing system based on detecting islands before they can be seen by the way they distort the regular patterning of the ocean swells. *Walap*'s navigator, Toshiro Jokon, was considered to be one of the last masters of this almost-forgotten navigational method. According to Dennis, he started out steering on the dominant southeast swell and kept track of Aitutaki's position by monitoring how the island deflected the swells. The navigator's strategy was to sail to windward of the direct course to Rarotonga and as the canoe neared the island to gradually turn toward it. Around midnight, Toshiro began to feel the southwest swells that were bending around Rarotonga, and for the rest of the night and into the day, he used these to home in on the island. By early afternoon, he sensed from the angle and intensity of the swells that Rarotonga was near but did not actually see land until around 3 o'clock, about the same time Tua had spotted it from *Hōkūle'a*.

Since we had been sailing without using a radio, the first thing we did upon tying up at the government pier was to ask about the other canoes. We learned that only *Maire Nui* from Ma'uke had reached Rarotonga. According to Stephen Kornberg aboard *Kama Hele*, the Hawaiian yacht that had escorted *Maire Nui*, the canoe's navigator had done a fine job. After leaving 'Ātiu (where the canoe had stayed after the aborted start of the previous week) the navigator, a young police officer named Pe'ia Tua'ati, had combined backsighting on 'Ātiu with observations of the swells and the sun to keep the canoe on course until sunset. During the night, he steered by the stars and constellations that he knew from his training would be setting in the west or rising in the east on or near the same bearing as the course line. When the skies clouded over around midnight and it started raining, Pe'ia oriented on the swells and checked the heading by the rising moon whenever its glow could be seen through the cloud cover. The next day he sailed mostly by the swells until, like Tua Pittman aboard *Hōkūle'a*, he finally sighted the island late in the afternoon.

According to radio reports received from escorting yachts, the Miti'āro and 'Ātiu canoes, as well as Aitutaki's *Ngapuariki*, were still working their way towards Rarotonga. But the canoe from Mangaia was reported missing at sea. *Te Rangi Ma Toru*, at 45 feet, was the largest of the outer island fleet. All we could learn was that the navigator, Ma'ara Pearaua, and the younger members of the crew had set sail from Mangaia without the captain. Furthermore, they left before the government patrol boat, *Te Kukupa*, arrived from Rarotonga to supply the canoe with a radio and other required safety gear and to serve as an escort back to Rarotonga.

With one canoe missing, and three accounted for but still out at sea, it was hardly possible to sleep that night. Around midnight we learned that *Ngapuariki* had landed. After backsighting on Aitutaki to get their course line, co-navigators Clive and Dorn kept *Ngapuariki* sailing straight for Rarotonga, deviating only slightly from the course line. However, to avoid having the older crewmembers spend a second night exposed

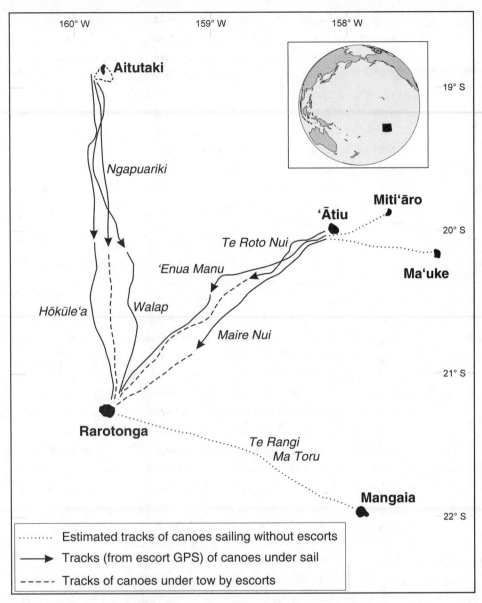

Aitutaki

19° S

Ngapuariki

Miti'āro

'Ātiu

20° S

Te Roto Nui

Ma'uke

'Enua Manu

Hōkūle'a   Walap

Maire Nui

21° S

Rarotonga

Te Rangi
Ma Toru

Mangaia

22° S

.... Estimated tracks of canoes sailing without escorts

⟶ Tracks (from escort GPS) of canoes under sail

----- Tracks of canoes under tow by escorts

Routes of canoes from outer southern Cook Islands to Rarotonga, 15–17 October 1992.

on the deck, as the canoe neared Rarotonga, the escorting yacht took her under tow and brought the at risk crewmembers aboard. Nonetheless, even while under tow, Clive and Dorn continued to navigate using a hand-held radio to transmit steering directions to the yacht ahead of them.

Just before dawn the next day, we went down to the harbor to move *Hōkūle'a* from the government pier in order to make room for *Te Kukupa*, the patrol boat returning after a fruitless search for the Mangaia canoe. But just as the patrol boat was entering the pass, it suddenly turned around and headed south around the island at full speed. From the marine radio on a neighboring ship, we learned that *Te Rangi Ma Toru* had been spotted off the eastern shore of Rarotonga and that *Te Kukupa* was speeding there to take her under tow.

While waiting for *Te Kukupa* to return with the canoe we heard that Ma'ara, the navigator of the Mangaia canoe, was in big trouble. It was said that because he didn't get along with the captain, a ranking elder who was also the island's mayor, Ma'ara had deliberately set sail without him in order to have a free hand in navigating to Rarotonga. Leaving before *Te Kukupa* had arrived to deliver the required radio and safety gear and then escort her to Rarotonga compounded the charge.

After the patrol boat entered the pass with *Te Rangi Ma Toru* in tow, the two vessels tied up along the government pier. Several policemen immediately boarded the canoe and led the dejected navigator away. It was all an accident, Ma'ara told them. He said that on the morning of departure, they had just gone out for a short training sail when strong easterly trades blew them west of the island and prevented them from tacking back. After drifting farther and farther away from the island, around noon they decided to make the best of the situation by heading for Rarotonga. But without a radio on board, they had no way to communicate their decision.

All had gone well for them until around 9:00 p.m., when the weather front hit, bringing strong winds and steep seas. Ma'ara decided it was too risky to continue sailing and so lowered the sails until the wind decreased. Later, navigating by the swells and glimpses of the moon through the overcast, Ma'ara reckoned he was able to keep the canoe on course through the rest of the night. At dawn he expected to spot the peaks of Rarotonga, but it was too rainy and overcast to see anything. Not wanting to proceed farther without sighting land, Ma'ara kept sailing the canoe back and forth until around 4:00 p.m. when he finally spied Rarotonga. The Mangaia crew then headed toward the island but arrived offshore well after sunset. As it was too dark to attempt a landing, they stood off the island all night. At dawn their flashlight signals were seen from shore, and just as a fishing boat was taking them under tow the patrol boat arrived.

At 11:30 a.m. the 'Ātiu canoe, *'Enua Manu*, entered the harbor, and an hour and a half later the last canoe arrived, Miti'āro's *Te Roto Nui*. Both canoes had been slowed by the bad weather and *Te Roto Nui* had been taken under tow by her escorting yacht in order to reach land safely. How the crews of *'Enua Manu* and *Avatapu*, the cargo vessel escorting her, worked together bears recounting. *Avatapu* was owned and captained by Nancy Griffith, an experienced sailor from Hawai'i who was under contract with the Cook Islands government to carry cargo and passengers around the Cooks. The ship just happened to be at 'Ātiu the day the canoes were to set sail for Rarotonga, and the people there asked Nancy if she would escort 'Enua Manu. She couldn't refuse, particularly since the 'Ātiu people had treated her and her crew so kindly a few years back when her previous ship had hit an offshore reef and sank.

Nancy and the navigator Koro were old friends, and they quickly established radio communications between the two craft. However, lest she wound the crew's pride in their seamanship, Nancy was hesitant to say anything to Koro about a problem with the canoe's rigging that she had spotted. A pair of backstays ran from the canoe's single mast to the stern crossbeam connecting the twin hulls. Unfortunately the crew had neglected to release the backstay on the lee side (the side away from the wind), which meant that they could not let the sail out very far before it hit the stay. Apparently that was the reason 'Enua Manu had capsized the week before. When the squall hit, the taut sail jammed against the stay and pushed the canoe over.

When 'Enua Manu encountered heavy winds during the first night of her second try to reach Rarotonga, the crew immediately lowered the sail to keep from turning over again. The following day, four of the older crewmembers who had suffered through the night in the wind and rain were taken on board Avatapu. At this point the sailors on Avatapu who were from Palmerston Island, an atoll in the Northern Cooks where everyone still knows how to sail, begged Nancy to let them intervene. After some hesitation, she agreed, and the sailors jumped onto the canoe, released the backstay, trimmed the sails and the joint crew happily set off to complete the voyage.

SEVERAL DAYS LATER, all the canoes gathered together at Awana Harbor in the Ngatangi'ia subdistrict. According to local traditions, several of the famous migration canoes that settled Aotearoa had set sail from Awana. The two big double canoes built on Rarotonga expressly for the festival were there to welcome the visitors and thereby uphold the honor of the island. Takitumu, a sailing canoe 53 feet long represented the Takitumu District, and Uritaua, an 87-foot long paddling canoe, represented the Ngati Uritaua, a small tribe that had built the imposing war canoe to press land claims against their larger neighbors as well to impress the voyagers coming from overseas.[9]

After being saluted by Takitumu and Uritaua, one by one the visiting canoes entered Awana harbor. Joining Hōkūle'a, Walap, and the outer Cook Island canoes were a number of vessels that had been shipped to Rarotonga. These included several small sailing canoes from Papua New Guinea and New Caledonia, as well as an ornately carved Māori war canoe, a single-hulled vessel that was broad enough to be stable without an outrigger. Once all the canoes were drawn up on the beach or anchored just offshore, a formal welcoming ceremony followed with speeches in English and a variety of Polynesian and other Pacific languages, interspersed with chants and songs from the nations represented.

As Prime Minister of the host nation, the recently knighted Sir Geoffrey Henry lauded the efforts of all those who had brought their canoes to the festival, and especially the navigators who had guided their craft to Rarotonga from neighboring islands or more distant archipelagos:

> They have already proven beyond a doubt that their ancestors explored and occupied the Pacific with both purpose and precision. If that were all that their voyages meant, they might as well stop, for they have proven the point. But, no, they will not stop. What appeals to them, and certainly to me, is the image of the Pacific navigator, standing near the helmsman, never fully resting, sensing the world around him, the feel of the wind, its force and direction, the pattern of the waves and their multi-origin rhythms, the temperature and the direction of the ocean currents, the ever changing cosmos.

More impromptu were the Prime Minister's remarks about Andrew Sharp, who had died in 1974, two years before we sailed *Hōkūle'a* to Tahiti. Sir Geoffrey talked about how, as a student in Aotearoa, he had been forced to sit through Sharp's lectures and study the historian's accidental settlement theory—and then regurgitate it on the exam. Now he did not hesitate to say how wrong the historian had been, adding:

> How I wish Andrew Sharp was alive today. I would have bought his ticket, given him free accommodation and bought all his food so he could see all the canoes sailing to Rarotonga using the old methods of star navigation.

Missing from the celebration was *Te Aurere*, the canoe from Aotearoa that was still at sea about 120 miles south of Rarotonga. The conditions east of Aotearoa were unusually cold and stormy that year, probably an aftermath of the previous year's eruption of Mount Pinatubo in the Philippines. After *Te Aurere* had been pummeled by several big storms, and further delayed by intervening calms, Nainoa had radioed the canoe from Aitutaki to urge the Māori sailors to take a tow from their escort yacht and head for warmer latitudes and calmer seas. Fortunately, as the battered sailors approached the Cooks they were sped along by favorable winds, and by the afternoon of the next day it was clear that *Te Aurere* would make it to Awana Harbor by that evening.

Toward sunset a crowd gathered at Awana. Just as the sun was setting, the Māori canoe dramatically entered the pass. When the crew stepped ashore, looking dazed from their stormy passage and the dash for Rarotonga, Sir Geoffrey greeted his *teina*, or "younger brothers," as he called them. (Since, according to Rarotongan traditions, Aotearoa was settled from or via the Cooks, Rarotongans do not hesitate to emphasize their seniority.) The Prime Minister, ever ready with a smoothly turned phrase, used the occasion to stress that by recreating their past canoes and voyages, Polynesians could contemplate the future with a new confidence:

> From this time on, we are not going to be the same anymore. This event has changed us all. We are on a new level of understanding now. We are on a new plane of knowledge. We are looking to the future with greater confidence than we have ever had before. The events of the past few days—the arrival from the outer islands of our people in their canoes, and your arrival through trials and tribulations to get here—have changed time completely for us. The future is no longer so frightening.

TWO DAYS LATER, the Hawaiians threw a party to celebrate the safe arrival of the canoes from the outer islands and to honor all those who had taken part in the adventure. Despite problems with the weather, and mishaps along the way, everyone was happy with the outcome—even the mayor of Mangaia, to whom the navigator Ma'ara had profusely apologized for having set sail without him.

Toward the end of the celebration, Nainoa addressed the Cook Islanders directly, telling them about the forthcoming voyage from Te Henua 'Enana to Hawai'i and challenging them to join in:

> Your crews have trained hard for two years, and they have accomplished their mission. And now we have to look toward the future. A culture does not remain alive unless it is practiced. To keep your voyaging tradition alive, you have to keep sailing. We need to take the next, further step in training and make a long voyage together. I would like to make a challenge: that we look towards a deep ocean voyage that we can all do together. In 1995 we will be sailing from the Marquesas to Hawai'i, and I have a vision of us sailing together with a Cook Island canoe.

The navigator's challenge could not be ignored. The Cook Islanders embraced it as did the Māori and later the Tahitians. What had originally been planned as a solely Hawaiian initiative would become a pan-Polynesian endeavor.

Chapter Three

The Sin at Awarua

DURING THE QUIET HOURS before dawn on March 18, 1995, voyaging canoes from around Polynesia began to gather off the coral reef fringing the southeastern end of Ra'iātea, a high volcanic island a day and a half's sail to the west-northwest of Tahiti. *Hawai'iloa* and *Hōkūle'a* had crossed the equator from distant Hawai'i. *Te Aurere* had come from the massive land of Aotearoa, well beyond the tropics far to the southwest. Elaborately carved *Tahiti Nui*—the longest canoe of the fleet at 75 feet—had sailed over from neighboring Tahiti. Swift *Takitumu* had made her way from Rarotonga. Three canoes would not make it on time. *Makali'i* from Hawai'i and Rarotonga's *Te Au o Tonga* were still at sea, and a second Tahitian canoe, *'A'a Kahiki Nui*, was not yet completed.

The sailors aboard maneuvered their canoes in the darkness, taking great care to keep clear of the reef outlined intermittently by white flashes of surf. Gradually the eastern horizon began to brighten, washing out the stars and bringing into focus the island's mountainous silhouette. The sun rising over Ra'iātea's green peaks turned the almost windless sea from black to a deep translucent blue. Taking up their paddles, the crews stroked toward the break in the reef known as Te Avamo'a, the "Sacred Pass." They were headed for Taputapuātea, a great temple rising just beyond the shore.

Aotearoa's aptly named *Te Aurere*, meaning "Flying Spray," led the procession. As her twin hulls entered the pass, a Māori elder named Te Ao Pēhi Kara began to chant. Addressing his ancestors as well as the living, he intoned these somber words:

> *Tiwha tiwha te Pō Tiwha tiwha te Ao*
> *He whare i mahue kau e He whare i mahue kau e*
> *Ka whatinga ake te kura o te marama*
> *Ka pahuka mai te moana in ngā tai e ngunguru nei*
> *Tēnei ko te toka kia tātou kua hinga rātou kua hinga*
> *Kua takoto i te ringa kaha o Aitua*

Dark is the night, gloomy the day
The house is left desolate and abandoned
A fragment of the moon is torn away
The sea froths as the waves rush ashore
This is our rock, the rock is left to us
For they have passed on
Laid low by the strong hand of death.[1]

Those who had been laid low were his tribal ancestors, cruelly murdered centuries earlier at the *marae* ("temple" in Tahitian) of Taputapuātea. But in his next utterance the elder signaled that his message was really about life, not death:

Tihei Mauri Ora!
Let there now be life!

As he continued chanting, Te Ao Pēhi Kara developed this theme, declaring that the disastrous breach between his people and those of Ra'iātea, Tahiti and their allies, and centuries of desolate solitude that had followed the heinous crime, were now ended. The *tapu* (taboo)[2] on long distance voyaging that prohibited canoes from Aotearoa and other distant lands from sailing to Ra'iātea had at last been lifted. Long-range voyaging could begin again, bringing the scattered Polynesian peoples together once more:

Tēnei te nihinihi tēnei te nana
Tēnei te wā hikitia ngā tapu
ō runga i tēnei kokoru ki runga
i ō tātou mātua Tūpuna
E tangi ake nei te ngākau
Turuturu o whiti whakamau kia tina
Tina! hui ē, taiki ē.

This is the neap tide and the raging tide
It is time to remove the *tapu*
from this bay onto our ancestors
The heart is moved
So let it be for all time
We are united

55

A bearded Tahitian, Raymond Graffe was waiting on board a paddling canoe just inside the Sacred Pass. He was wearing a tall headdress topped with the darkly iridescent feathers of the jungle fowl and a long cloak made of bleached bark cloth. After Te Ao Pēhi Kara finished his chant, his Tahitian counterpart stood up and declared in his own language that the *tapu* had been lifted.

As *Te Aurere* glided across the lagoon, a Raiatean man standing in the shallow water shouted out in Tahitian: "Come hither! Come hither o great canoe of Aotearoa!" Several women on shore, bedecked with garlands made from the long shiny leaves of the *tī* plant (*kī* in Hawaiian; *Cordyline terminalis*), followed with a chorus of welcoming come hithers: *Haere mai, haere mai, haere mai*. Then a masculine voice from the crowd commanded in Rarotongan that the conches be sounded: *Tangi Te pū!* The assembly of trumpeters from Rarotonga lifted spiraled conch shells to their lips and blew with all their strength creating a buzzing, throbbing roar that overlaid the welcoming come hithers and spread over the crowd massed along the shore.

After anchoring their craft in the lagoon, *Te Aurere*'s crew boarded a paddling double canoe fitted with a wide platform laid across the hulls. As they approached the narrow beach where the welcoming dignitaries were assembled, the Māori sailors were greeted by more come hithers, blasts from the conch shell chorus, and declarations that they had at last returned to Taputapuātea, the *marae pū* (central temple) of Polynesia. The crew waded ashore to be embraced by their hosts, who draped them with garlands made from scented leaves. The Māori sailors then formed ranks and acted out a vigorous *haka*, a challenge by which they displayed their strength and resolve with defiant gestures and threatening words.

Their Raiatean escorts led the sailors from the landing beach to an adjacent stone structure, a large open rectangle bounded by low walls. This was Hauviri, a temple of the Tamatoa dynasty, the line of chiefs that had ruled Ra'iātea for centuries. After being welcomed by the Tamatoa descendants, the crew was taken past the towering investiture stone, a basalt monolith before which new rulers were girdled with the *maro 'ura*, a broad woven belt emblazoned with bright red feathers symbolizing chiefly office.

To the accompaniment of blasts from conch shells and the beating of drums, the crew was then escorted inland over the "Road of a Thousand Flowers" to Taputapuātea itself. This grand temple is an open structure without walls. From a broad platform paved with volcanic stones rises a massive *ahu* or altar—a narrow rectangle over 140 feet long and in places twice human height faced with huge slabs of coral sandstone and filled with coral rubble.

Against this imposing backdrop, the Māori voyagers waited as each successive crew came ashore to be welcomed and then escorted to Taputapuātea. As the last of the sailors took their places, a spare Tahitian man in his early seventies began speaking.

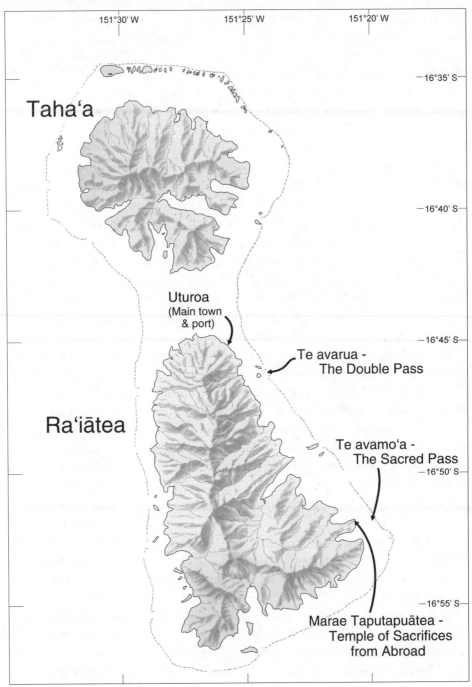

Ra'iātea and Taha'a within a single barrier reef.

Dressed in a wraparound *pareu* and a short, feathered cloak and headdress, he welcomed the voyagers onto the *marae* with more come hithers pronounced three times, first in Tahitian and then Tuamotuan, 'Enanan, and Hawaiian. He then told the assembled crews how "our mother," by which he meant Taputapuātea, is throbbing with maternal joy because "you, the children, the descendants" of those who centuries before had set sail from here have this day returned from the "four sides of the dark, dark sea of Hiva."

IN THE EARLY 1980s historians, anthropologists, and sociologists began paying attention to self-conscious efforts of cultural revival among peoples around the world. Many focused on rituals and practices that they judged to be consciously revived or created outright for political purposes. One of the most influential works was a collection of essays edited by British historians, Eric Hobsbawm and Terence Ranger, entitled *The Invention of Tradition*. They were interested in traditions that claimed or appeared to have been developed long ago but had really been more recently "invented, constructed and formally instituted," or had "emerged in a less easily traceable manner." Their examples included the creation of royal rituals and pageantry to increase respect for the British monarchy and the construction of a Highland Scots identity featuring tailored kilts, distinctive clan tartans, and other elements they considered to be of dubious authenticity.[3]

First a trickle and then a flood of articles began appearing in scholarly journals that explored how people from the many cultures of the Pacific were "inventing" or "socially constructing" their traditions and customs.[4] Although most of these publications were probably not read by those whose efforts and beliefs were being analyzed, a few such works caught the eye of native intellectuals. Prominent among these were: Jocelyn Linnekin's essay on how contemporary Hawaiian nationalists were deliberately formulating traditions for political ends; Allan Hanson's charge that the Māori have adopted cultural constructs that had actually been developed by foreign scholars during late 1800s and early 1900s; and Roger Keesing's claim that Pacific peoples were "creating pasts, myths of ancestral ways of life" that have little or no relation with the actual past as "documented historically, recorded ethnographically, and reconstructed archaeologically."[5]

That the subjects of these and similarly phrased writings might take exception is not surprising. In particular, foreign professors use of such terms as "invention," "social construction" and "myth-making" appeared condescending and insulting to those whose beliefs and actions were being so cavalierly analyzed. Māori critics denounced Hanson as shallow and uninformed. Haunani-Kay Trask, a native Hawaiian professor at the University of Hawai'i, castigated Keesing, Linnekin, and other foreign academics

Calling the canoes ashore to Taputapuātea.

for setting themselves up as authorities on Hawaiian and Pacific cultures, yet ignoring that indigenous people do base their cultural constructs on a deep knowledge and study of traditional ways.[6] The response made in the name of culture theory—that authenticity is a non-issue since traditions are invented in all cultures anyway—compounded the original insult. Arguing that traditions are neither genuine nor spurious but simply socially constructed, in effect, denies the possibility of expressing a cultural identity based on a remembered past.[7]

By singling out the works of a few anthropologists, I do not mean to imply that they alone are prone to such scholarly arrogance. Anthropologists trained to sift through ethnographical, historical, and archaeological evidence to reconstruct past cultures have a built-in bias toward privileging their analyses over what they might regard as ill-informed native beliefs. What these trained experts have to say may be well-grounded in their scholarship, but the way they say it, in particular when expressed with the latest academic buzzwords, can come across as rude and uninformed cultural criticism.

I cannot exempt myself from this tendency but would like to note that as my engagement with voyaging has deepened, I have tried to hold that bias in check and genuinely learn from the people whose cultures I study. Working alongside Hawaiians, Tahitians, Cook Islanders, and Māori over the last several decades has taught me how much they value their remembered past. They go beyond Santayana's dictum about the perils of ignoring history and actively look to their ancestors for inspiration in coping with present and future problems. For example, in an essay on cultural renaissance and identity in French Polynesia, educator Wilfred Lucas explains that his fellow Tahitians are "using the past to confront the future," gaining insights and strength from prior accomplishments to help them cope with the Nuclear Age into which they have been thrust. Similarly, the historian Lilikalā Kameʻeleihiwa writes that: "It is as if the Hawaiian stands firmly in the present, with his back to the future, and his eyes fixed upon the past, seeking historical answers for present-day dilemmas."[8]

Such a stance makes sense to those reconstructing ancient voyaging canoes and sailing them around the Pacific or taking part in the rituals of canoe launching, departure, and arrival. They feel that by reviving elements from their seafaring past, they are gaining strength and inspiration for their voyage into the uncharted seas of the future.

SELECTING IDEAS AND PRACTICES from the past and adapting them for present purposes is hardly limited to today's Pacific. Consider the cultural revival movement that Westerners call their Renaissance. Forgotten texts from ancient Greece and Rome were retrieved from old monasteries, Arab libraries, and Jewish scholars to become the basis for learning once more. Long-neglected ruins from antiquity were sketched and studied, and their features were included in new churches and other public buildings. Yet the architects of Europe's rebirth were obviously not trying to faithfully recreate all facets of ancient life. They revived those elements of classical wisdom, design, and practice that were consonant with their current needs and thinking, not those they considered to be out of step with current values.

To cite a more recent example of such selective inspiration, consider the revival of the Olympic Games late in the nineteenth century. When Pierre de Coubertin was seeking a classical model for bringing athletes of the world together, he chose the pan-Hellenic games, not the gladiatorial combat so bloodily celebrated in Rome's Colosseum. Furthermore, he did not seek to impose on the athletes of the new Olympic Games the ancient practice of competing in the nude.[9]

Today ethnic groups, nations, and would-be nations from around the world are engaged in selectively recalling their respective cultural heritages, bringing them forward, however altered, into the present. This is as much an age of cultural revival and identity as it is of globalization, particularly in those regions, such as the Pacific, where indigenous peoples are either still under foreign rule or find that the outside world and its influences are pressing heavily upon them. Reviving languages and other cultural elements has become a way to demonstrate cultural identity and worth in the face of lingering colonial structures and increasingly impinging globalizing pressures. It is no accident that the voyaging revival first took hold in Eastern Polynesia,[10] for their people were hit early and hard by the outside world. They have much to reclaim and a strong motivation for asserting their identity vis-à-vis their former or actual colonial overlords, as well as others who have settled in their islands or who now visit them in mass as tourists.

Continental diseases previously unknown in these islands ravaged their inhabitants, killing them outright and debilitating the survivors. For example, by the 1890s the number of Hawaiians had fallen to around 40,000, a catastrophic drop even using the conservative estimates of 250,000 to 400,000 Hawaiians living in 1778, when Captain Cook opened the islands to the outside world. If revisionist estimates of upwards of a million Hawaiians have merit, the population crash was even more horrific.

Colonizing Americans and Europeans developed a sugar industry in the islands, economically overwhelming the survivors. The plantation laborers they brought in from China, Japan, and other places around the world demographically swamped the native Hawaiians. Under the Kamehameha dynasty, the Hawaiians had earnestly tried to join the world community of nations as a sovereign kingdom, but in 1893, Western businessmen, sugar planters, and other opportunists staged a coup. With the help of armed U.S. Marines landed from an American warship, they overthrew the government and declared a republic. In 1898 they convinced an expansionist United States Congress to annex the islands. This left the Hawaiians a largely dispossessed minority in their own islands, which first became a U.S. Territory and, in 1959, a State of the American union. Despite recent progress, they remain the poorest educated, most afflicted by disease, and most frequently incarcerated of Hawai'i's major ethnic groups.

The Māori experienced a similar depopulation and occupation by foreign settlers coming predominantly from Britain. Although the Treaty of Waitangi, signed in 1840 by Māori chiefs and British representatives supposedly guaranteed most of the land to the Māori, after the wars of the 1860s, the British took over vast tracts, throwing open the country to colonial settlement. This soon relegated the Māori to the marginal position of a deprived minority in an overseas territory of a European power, which has since evolved into the predominantly European country of New Zealand. Those Tahitians and their cousins in the neighboring archipelagos who survived the biological onslaught of imported diseases saw their islands taken over piecemeal by France between 1842 and 1888 to form the overseas territory now called Polynésie Française (French Polynesia). Yet they were not so overwhelmed by foreign settlers and laborers as were the Hawaiians and Māori, and remained a majority in their own islands, keeping

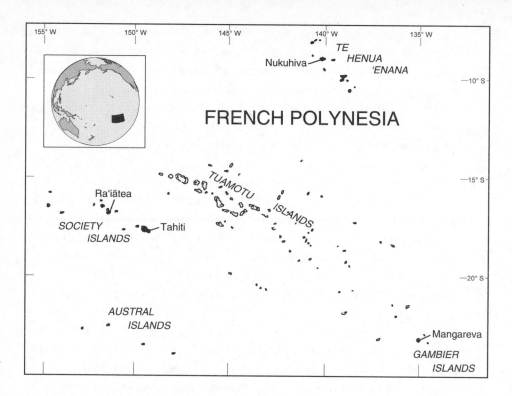

control of much of the land. Nonetheless, being ruled by a proud European power has had its costs as well as benefits, including the obligation to host France's nuclear testing program during the Cold War. Even the Cook Islanders, now sovereign in their own islands, have not escaped unscathed from their relatively brief and benign period of colonial rule, or their continued dependency on New Zealand.

THE TEXTUAL INSPIRATION for celebrating the voyaging revival at Taputapuātea came from a tale told around 1830 to John Orsmond, a British missionary, by a Raiatean chiefess named Tu'au. She had learned it from her grandfather, Tainoa, who was said to have been one of the last Raiatean sages fully conversant with the old learning. The text was not printed until 1928 when it appeared in *Ancient Tahiti*, a volume compiled and edited by the missionary's granddaughter, Teuira Henry.[11]

The story begins with the marriage of Pōiriri, a "prince" from the distant island of Rotuma located on the far western edge of Polynesia, and Te'ura, a "princess" from Porapora, the island immediately to the northwest of Ra'iātea. Their union led to the inauguration of the *Fa'atau Aroha*, a "Friendly Alliance" of islands from across Polynesia, centered on the Opoa district of Ra'iātea where Taputapuātea is located.

The islands of this alliance were split into two groups called *Te-ao-uri* and *Te-ao-tea*, terms that Teuira Henry translated respectively as "The Dark-land" and "The Light-land." In one of the few sections of her account given in Tahitian as well as English she quoted a song commemorating the alliance that begins with these lines:

Nā ni'a Te-ao-uri,	Above (east) is the dark-land,
Nā raro Te-ao-tea,	Below (west) is the light-land,
E tō roa te manu ē.	All encompassed by birds.

Actually, *nā ni'a* and *nā raro* probably meant being to windward and to leeward of Ra'iātea relative to the flow of the southeasterly trade winds. Tahiti and the islands to windward of Ra'iātea belonged to the Dark-land. The Light-land was composed of the islands to leeward of Ra'iātea, starting with neighboring Taha'a, Porapora, and the islets beyond, then continuing to Rarotonga and the other islands of the Cook group, and jumping all the way to Aotearoa and Rotuma.

According to the text, for many generations, "priests, scholars and warriors" from the two sides periodically set sail from their respective islands to meet at Taputapuātea and celebrate "great religious observances and international deliberations"—until a murder shattered the alliance. At the last of these reunions, a quarrel erupted between Paoa-tea, a high priest of the Light-land, and a high chief of the Dark-land, who slew the priest in anger. When the victim's fellow delegates learned of the murder, they struck down the killer, leaving him for dead (though he was later revived). They then took to their canoes and fled back to their islands in the west. But they did not sail directly out to sea through Te Avamo'a. Instead the aggrieved delegates fled through the deep waters of Ra'iātea's broad lagoon and struck out for the open ocean through Te Avarua, the "Double Pass," so called because an islet in the middle divides the channel. "Thus ended the friendly alliance which long had united many kindred islands." The great canoes from the distant islands of the Light-land never again sailed together to Ra'iātea.

Teuira Henry also cited oral traditions from Aotearoa and Rarotonga that corroborated this Raiatean account. These were brought to her attention by S. Percy Smith, the New Zealand scholar who founded the *Journal of the Polynesian Society* and who devoted much of his life to tracing Māori origins. In 1897, while traveling around Polynesia in quest of traditions that might indicate from whence the ancestral Māori had set sail, he visited Teuira Henry in Honolulu where she was preparing *Ancient Tahiti* for publication while teaching at Kamehameha Schools. Smith was particularly excited to learn about the Raiatean tradition of the murder at Opoa and the subsequent flight of the delegation, for in it he saw the key to the meaning of lines from an old Māori song which hitherto had been opaque to him:

Tenei ano nga whakatauki o mua—
Toia e Rongorongo "Aotea,"
ka tere ki te moana.
Ko te hara ki Awarua i whiti mai ai i Hawaiki.

These are the sayings of ancient times—
Twas Rongorongo launched "Aotea,"
when she floated on the sea.
Because of the sin at Awarua they crossed over from Hawaiki.[12]

Smith reasoned that the Hawaiki from whence the Aotea canoe "crossed over" the sea must have been Ra'iātea, since that island's ancient name was Havai'i, the Tahitian cognate of Hawaiki. Similarly, he realized that Awarua was identical with the Avarua of the Raiatean legend. Although the Māori tradition refers to multiple victims whereas only a single victim is featured in the Raiatean and Rarotongan accounts, Smith concluded that the "sin" in question must refer to the same murderous assault as that recounted in the Raiatean tradition. Teuira Henry also noted that the Māori canoe was called Aotea, the same as *Te-ao-tea* (less the definite article *te*), as well as the root of Aotearoa.[13]

The Rarotongan account of these events appeared in *A Narrative of Missionary Enterprises in the South Seas,* a best-seller among pious British and American readers of the nineteenth century written by the missionary John Williams. He recounted how after the people of Tahiti, Ra'iātea, and neighboring islands had been converted, he and his fellow missionaries of the London Missionary Society began to search out new islands to gain additional converts. He was particularly anxious to find Rarotonga, an important island that Raiateans told him lay to the southwest. After failing on his first try, Williams finally found the island, thanks to sailing directions provided by the inhabitants of neighboring 'Ātiu. When the Rarotongans learned that the missionary's native assistants were from Ra'iātea, they demanded to know why their ancestors had killed the Rarotongan high priest Paoa-tea, using the same name given in the Raiatean account. They also wanted to know what had happened to the great drum their priests had transported to Taputapuātea to present to the god 'Oro. They called it *Tangimoana* (Sounding-at-sea), which but for a single sound shift is identical to *ta'imoana*, the name employed in the Raiatean account for the big drums carried aboard the canoes making the pilgrimage to Taputapuātea.[14]

FROM STUDYING *ANCIENT TAHITI* and other writings that stressed the centrality of Ra'iātea and its famous temple in Polynesian history, Herb Kāne and I had concluded that *Hōkūle'a* should make a pilgrimage to Taputapuātea after reaching Tahiti on that first trip. We knew that the temple had supposedly been abandoned with the coming of Christianity and while it may have been used for secret rituals since then, it no longer played a formal role in Raiatean life. When I had visited Taputapuātea in 1962 while doing fieldwork in Tahiti, the stone structure lay deserted and crumbling, surrounded by rows of carefully laid out coconut palms, the nuts of which were used for the manufacture of soap, margarine, and other products. We therefore hoped that sailing *Hōkūle'a* to Taputapuātea might stimulate Raiateans to pay more attention to this ancient center.

Judging from the scene that greeted the canoe as she anchored offshore the *marae* in 1976, *Hōkūle'a*'s coming indeed spurred the Raiateans to action. Upon hearing of her impending visit, they cleared the temple's stone pavement, cleaned the grounds, and repaired some of the worst damages to the long altar. On arrival day, upwards of a thousand islanders massed at the temple to greet their cousins from across the equator.[15]

But midway through the welcoming ceremony, a short, balding man demanded to speak. The orator—who we learned later was known as Parau Rahi (Big Talk)—began by telling the assembled crowd how learning that *Hōkūle'a* was coming to Ra'iātea had made him recall a prophecy he had heard when he was a small boy. Long ago a migratory canoe called *Hotu Te Niu* had set sail from Ra'iātea carrying a selection of the most qualified people from Ra'iātea and neighboring islands—the best sailors, farmers, healers, and the like, as well as fertile women skilled in domestic crafts. No family groups departed together, just individuals especially selected for migration. Parents who had to give up a son or daughter, as well as the husbands or wives of those who had been chosen, had been forced to accept that they would never see their loved ones again. As the years passed with no word about the expedition, a great sadness descended over Ra'iātea and the neighboring islands. This caused the aggrieved parents, spouses, children, and other kin to declare a *tapu* on any further overseas voyaging that would be lifted only when a canoe bearing the descendants of those long-lost migrants returned to Taputapuātea.

Parau Rahi then told the enthralled crowd how excited he had become when *Hōkūle'a* reached Tahiti, and he heard that it would continue on to Taputapuātea. Given the linguistic identity of Hawai'i and Havai'i, he thought that the Hawaiian canoe must be carrying the descendants of those who had left so long ago. This filled him with joy, said the orator, explaining that the coming of *Hōkūle'a* would lift the voyaging *tapu*. Then, after a long pause, Parau Rahi's expression changed completely. Glowering at the visitors from Hawai'i, he shouted out: "But you have ruined everything! You made a terrible mistake! You did not come in through the Sacred Pass!"

Instead of consulting Raiatean elders about how visiting canoes should approach

Taputapuātea, we had followed the instructions of the Tahitian maritime officials to sail directly to Ra'iātea's official port of entry, Uturoa, register there, and then proceed to the temple. This meant that instead of entering the lagoon through Te Avamo'a, *Hōkūle'a* had sailed through Te Avarua, the pass through which the survivors of that fateful attack of centuries ago are said to have had fled. Then in order to reach Taputapuātea expeditiously, we had the canoe towed from Uturoa through the lagoon. If we had known the correct protocol of entering the lagoon, we would have gladly sailed back out to sea and then re-entered through the Sacred Pass. By the time we realized our error, it was too late. Even sailing *Hōkūle'a* smartly out the Sacred Pass upon leaving that evening for Tahiti did not set things right for Parau Rahi and those who had been impressed by his speech.

DESPITE PARAU RAHI'S criticism and the outrage expressed by some Protestant pastors about reviving "pagan" ceremonies at Taputapuātea, *Hōkūle'a*'s coming had stimulated Raiatean leaders to think seriously about the importance of the temple in their history and what role it might play in the future. A key person in this process was Pierre Sham Koua, a school administrator and sometime vice-mayor of Uturoa whose name reflects his European, Asian, and Polynesian ancestry. As a former Catholic seminarian with a strong sense of history, Pierre had long been interested in Taputapuātea and its ancient role as a religious center. But he did not realize how important voyaging was to Taputapuātea until *Hōkūle'a* first arrived in 1976, when he personally welcomed the Hawaiian crew ashore. Soon thereafter, he discovered that the voyaging connection could directly serve the cause of historic preservation. By citing the cultural importance of the site as manifest by *Hōkūle'a*'s pilgrimage from Hawai'i, Pierre was able to squash a plan to bulldoze the temple and turn the grounds into a soccer field.

Pierre's vision of the role Taputapuātea could play in contemporary Ra'iātea further evolved as he again welcomed *Hōkūle'a* to the *marae* in 1985 while on her way to Aotearoa, and once more in 1992 when the canoe called there en-route to the Pacific Arts Festival in Rarotonga. He came to envision the *marae* as something more than an ancient temple where "folkloric" ceremonies could be reenacted. He wanted it to become a vital cultural center that would bring together people from around Polynesia for cultural exchanges, workshops, and scholarly meetings. When Pierre heard that all the voyaging canoes would rendezvous at Tahiti before proceeding to Te Henua 'Enana, he campaigned to get them to call first at Taputapuātea.

The indigenous Government of French Polynesia (which controls internal affairs in the territory) got behind the joint visit to Taputapuātea and allocated funds to rebuild the temple and adjacent structures, and clear the surrounding grounds in order to open the complex to public view. Specialists from the Ministry of Culture and the Museum of Tahiti and the Islands joined with Pierre and other Raiatean leaders to develop a scenario for the visit. Despite differences in detail between the three accounts of the assault on the delegates from the Light-land, the organizers followed Teuira Henry in concluding that they all referred to the same event. They interpreted the Māori tradition as meaning that the assaulted delegates had come from Aotearoa, and, reflecting Parau Rahi's reasoning, proposed that if the tribal descendants of those who had suffered would formally forgive the assault, the *tapu* on voyaging could at last be lifted. (The fact that *Hōkūle'a* had supposedly removed it by properly sailing through Te Avamo'a in 1985 and again in 1992 was conveniently forgotten.) This would be an ideal way, they thought, to symbolize the revival in Polynesian voyaging, as well as reestablish Taputapuātea as the sacred center of a reconstituted Friendly Alliance of voyaging peoples.

At a planning meeting held in Rarotonga in late 1994, the organizers approached Hector ("Hec") Busby, the builder and captain of *Te Aurere* canoe who is also known by his Māori name of Heke Nukumaingaiwi Puhipa. Hec, a large rough-hewn man then in his early sixties, had retired from his bridge-building business a few years earlier in order to construct *Te Aurere*. He told the organizers that he had never heard about the "Sin at Awarua." But he willingly agreed to look for an elder who knew about the tradition and who could chant the words of reconciliation needed to lift the *tapu*. Hec's search led him to Te Ao Pēhi Kara, a scholarly retired headmaster who was also a leader in Aotearoa's *Kōhanga Reo* movement to reverse the decline of the Māori language by means of special pre-schools taught entirely in that language. Yes, the scholar told Hec, he had heard the tradition about the murderous assault at Hawaiki on crewmembers of the Aotea canoe, and would be honored to compose and chant the needed *karakia* (incantation).

JOINING THE CREWS assembled before the long altar of Taputapuātea were officials, elders, orators, dancers, chanters, and others from the respective islands represented. In addition, a cultural association from 'Uapou, one of the islands of Te Henua 'Enana, was on the *marae*, along with a group representing Rapa Nui, the lone island 2,000 miles to the southeast of Tahiti that is known to the outside world as Easter Island. Neither group had a voyaging canoe, but both wanted their respective islands to be part of this celebration. The 'Uapou delegates had come to express their solidarity with the voyaging revival. They also requested that the canoes pay a call on their island as well as Nukuhiva when they sailed to the Marquesas. The Rapa Nui delegates, most of whom were actually from an immigrant community long established on Tahiti, had come as would-be voyagers. Although they had only recently heard about this event, they managed to construct a makeshift outrigger canoe. As a historical gesture, they covered it with reeds to recall the reed rafts their ancestors made after Rapa Nui had been deforested. After shipping the canoe to Raʻiātea on the deck of an inter-island ferry, they paddle-sailed her from the harbor to Taputapuātea, arriving to claim their place on the *marae* just as the ceremonies were starting.

Each island delegation was given the opportunity to express their thoughts and sentiments, which they enthusiastically did through prayers, chants, songs, and speeches. Central to their presentations were recollections of the exploits of the voyaging heroes and migratory canoes of the respective islands. Many speakers also stressed how the history of their own islands was bound up with that of Taputapuātea. For example, Larry Kimura, a professor of Hawaiian language at the University of Hawaiʻi's Hilo branch, spoke about how his people were linked to Taputapuātea through ties of ancient kinship and spilled blood:

> *No laila mākou e huli hele nei hoʻi i ke alahula i alahula hoʻi iā mākou i o ko mākou mau kūpuna i o kikilo a hiki maila hoʻi mākou i o ʻoukou i kēia ʻāina, ko mākou ʻāina ia ʻo ko ʻoukou ʻāina hoʻi ia. ʻO ko mākou ʻāina kupuna e moe maila hoʻi ko mākou ʻiewe i kanu ʻia i loko o ka honua o kēia mau paemokupuni. I hiki maila hoʻi mākou no ka hoʻōia ʻana hoʻi i ko mākou koko ʻo ko ʻoukou koko he hoʻokahi nō ia. ʻAohe nō mea e hoʻokānālua ai. Ua ʻike ʻia hoʻi ua kahe hoʻi ke koko o kūpuna o kākou i ola hoʻi ke kapu o kēia marae nei a kākou e kū nei.*

This is our return in search of the well-traveled pathways that have become so familiar to us because of our ancestors of antiquity. And now we have arrived before you at this place which is ours as well as yours. These are our ancestral lands where our afterbirth remains still, where it has been buried in the earth of these island archipelagos. We have come to affirm our blood ties with yours as one. There can be no question about this. It is recognized that the blood of our ancestors has flowed to bring life and sanctity to this *marae* we now stand upon.[16]

With each delegation taking their time to express themselves, the ceremony went on and on. By late morning, the participants were suffering visibly from the blazing sun. This led to a breakdown of the strict protocol that called for their complete isolation from the surrounding crowd. Green drinking coconuts, plastic bottles of water, and cans of soft drinks were being passed onto the *marae* to relieve the thirsty, heat-struck participants.

Nonetheless, the presentations proceeded smoothly until almost noon, when

Hawaiian crewmembers before the ahu *at Taputapuātea.*

Gaston Flosse, the part-European President of French Polynesia, stepped onto the *marae* to join the host delegation. Early that morning when Pierre Sham Koua and I drove to Taputapuātea, we had been met at the entrance to the grounds by earnest Tahitian youths wearing bright headbands and draped with the long dark-green leaves of the *tī* plant. They were members of the youth brigade of the pro-independence political party, *Tāvini Huira'atira nō Porinetia* (usually translated in English as "Servant of the People"). They politely but insistently passed out a brochure printed in Tahitian, English, and French addressed to all their "cousins in the Pacific." It denounced the collaboration of local politicians with France and the testing of nuclear bombs in the nearby Tuamotu Islands. But they stayed in the background—until President Flosse joined the Tahitian delegation on the *marae*.

Brigade members then gathered at the inland end of the platform and suddenly unfurled banners condemning Flosse for selling the motherland to the French and their nuclear bombs. This display caused a stir among the crowd of spectators, but the canoe crews and delegates did not overtly react—not even the Cook Islanders, the closest neighbors downwind of the testing site. Flosse himself, an experienced politician who supported France's right to use Moruroa for testing their nuclear weapons, also did not pay attention to the commotion and went on with his speech.

The ceremony continued without further incident, closing with three rituals. Selected crewmembers from each canoe drank *'awa* together to seal the re-establishment of the Friendly Alliance. Others deposited heavy stones carried from their home islands

69

on the *marae*. Then their Raiatean hosts bundled together lengths of sennit from each canoe and buried them under the paving to assure a safe voyage to Hawai'i.

PROTESTS AGAINST nuclear testing. Plastic water bottles and bright red cans of Coca-Cola on the sacred temple. Dozens of professional and amateur photographers along with several film teams fighting for clear shots. Electronically amplified chants and speeches, and even the utterance of a Christian prayer begging Jehovah's forgiveness for holding this event on a pagan temple. The ceremonial process that morning was obviously not a slavish reconstruction of the ancient way delegates from the islands were said to have entered the Sacred Pass, landed ashore, and conducted their rituals.

Among other things, there were no human sacrifices. Taputapuātea was dedicated to the war god 'Oro who demanded human offerings. Indeed, Teuira Henry translates Taputapuātea as "sacrifices" *(taputapu)* "from abroad" *(ātea)*. According to her text, at the gatherings of the Friendly Alliance, these offerings were delivered through the Sacred Pass by the canoes coming from the islands belonging to the alliance. The narrative of that delivery starts out with a wide angle view of "the long canoes in the wind" *(te va'a roa o te mata'i)* heading for the Sacred Pass, streaming behind them long pennants colored dark or light depending upon which side of the alliance they represented:

> Upon approaching the sacred passage of Te-ava-moa, just at daybreak, the canoes united in procession, and out from the horizon, as if by magic, they came in double file, each representing a separate kingdom. To the north were those of Te-ao-tea, to the south those of Te-ao-uri, approaching side by side, the measured strokes of the paddles harmonizing with the sound of the drum and occasional blasts of the trumpet.[17]

Then, the focus shifts to a close-up of the canoes and the macabre cargo carried on their decks:

> Across the bows connecting each double canoe was a floor, covering the chambers containing idols, drums, trumpet shells, and other treasures for the gods and people of Raiatea; and upon the floor were placed in a row sacrifices from abroad, which consisted of human victims brought for that purpose and just slain, and great fishes newly caught from fishing grounds of neighboring islands. They were placed upon the floor, parallel with the canoe, alternately a man and a cavalli fish, a man and a shark, a man and a turtle, and finally a man closed in the line.

Once "this terribly earnest procession" came ashore at Taura'a a Tapu (Landing Place for Sacrifices), the warriors, chiefs, priests, and other dignitaries greeted the voyagers. Together they silently set to work, suspending the sacrificial victims in the trees, stringing them up with long sennit ropes that ran through the temples of their lifeless skulls. Still more bodies were employed as rollers, over which the canoes were drawn onto the land.

Though well aware of this ancient protocol, the organizers of this gathering of reconstructed voyaging canoes certainly had no intention of recreating such a gruesome spectacle. Instead, they focused on the idea of symbolically renewing inter-island ties by ceremonially lifting the voyaging *tapu* believed to have been imposed when the Friendly Alliance broke up after the assault on delegates from the Light-land. The organizers and the visiting canoe crews and delegates had gathered at Taputapuātea to celebrate their rediscovery of voyaging, not to recreate past practices in their entirety. To do so they drew upon historical precedents, but selectively choosing only those they wanted to recall.

This is not to say that the preparations for the event, as well as its execution, went smoothly. The whole process of reviving voyaging has been rich with controversy over such issues as which canoe design best represents an ancient form, who has the right to sail the canoes, and what protocols to follow at the various ritual turning points. In this problematic area of indigenous authenticity and authority, consider the comments of Herb Kāne about a controversy among Hawaiian cultural leaders over the *'awa* (kava) drinking ceremonies that had come to be regular features of canoe launchings and departures in Hawai'i since *Hōkūle'a* was built.

In an article in the August 1993 issue of *Ka Wai Ola o OHA*, the monthly newspaper of the Office of Hawaiian Affairs, reporter Jeff Clark juxtaposed opposing views about how Hawaiians were serving and drinking this soporific infusion of the pounded root of the *'awa* plant (*Piper methysticum*, known elsewhere in the Pacific as *kava*, *yaqona*, etc.). Kamaki Kanahele, a trustee of the Office of Hawaiian Affairs, had asserted that there was no such thing as a formal *'awa* ceremony in traditional Hawaiian culture, and the organizers of today's ceremonies appeared almost to be making up the ritual as they went along. In response, Parley Kanaka'ole and Sam Ka'ai, who had frequently presided over these ceremonies, argued that they had not invented them and that they were following distinctive procedures for the ritual drinking of *'awa* learned from their elders.[18]

In a subsequent issue of the newspaper, Herb Kāne strongly supported the belief that Hawaiians did have formal *'awa* ceremonies before the missionary era, and argued for the legitimacy of the particular practices followed by Kanaka'ole and Ka'ai. But he did admit that knowledge of the specific chants and other details of the pre-missionary ceremonies had been lost with the virtual disappearance of 'awa drinking among Hawaiians. Furthermore, he added that contemporary Hawaiian 'awa ceremonies have been heavily influenced by practices from Western Polynesia, where the drink has continued to be consumed without any hiatus caused by missionary or other foreign pressures. Kāne traced this Western Polynesian influence to an 'awa ceremony he had conducted at Hōkūle'a's launching in 1975:

> This ceremony was offered to us as a gift from a hānai [adopted] member of the royal family of Tonga, including the use of the largest tanoa (kanoa bowl) in existence, and there was no pretense about it being Hawaiian. We felt honored by the offer. To decline would have appeared ungracious. Moreover the idea appealed to the cultural purpose of Hōkūle'a as an instrument that might help bring all Polynesians closer together—an active symbol of a shared ancestry.[19]

That subsequent 'awa ceremonies celebrated by Hawaiians might combine remembered Hawaiian practices with those of their cousins from Western Polynesia did not bother Kāne:

> We may also be experiencing the dawn of a new (or simply rediscovered) "Pan Polynesian" cultural development as a result of the increasing frequency of cultural exchanges among all Polynesians. When meetings occur between Hawaiians, Tahitians, Maori, or Western Polynesians, much enjoyment is derived from exploring the astonishing similarities within the basics of their respective languages, customs and traditions. From such similarities, bridges of communication and bonds of friendship are being created; out of these will grow cultural traditions that will be understood by all Polynesians. The Hawaiian 'awa ceremony as interpreted by Ka'ai and Kanaka'ole, because they express the fundamentals universal to the Polynesian concept of good manners, may be counted among these traditions.

IN CONTRAST, DANI CARLSON, a longtime Tahitian friend who had studied with me at the University of Hawai'i in the 1970s, is wary of some of the revived practices in her home islands. For example, she avoided the ceremony at Taputapuātea—even though as an oral tradition specialist at the Museum of Tahiti and the Islands she helped plan the event. Instead she stayed at her family home on the adjacent island of Taha'a, where she and local leaders organized a low-key, community-oriented reception for the canoes when they called there a few days later. Like a number of other thoughtful students of Tahitian culture, she is disturbed by the practice of staging reenactments of supposedly ancient ceremonies such as the elaborately costumed and choreographed chiefly investiture held annually for tourists at Tahiti's Arahurahu *marae*. Indeed, she might agree with the comment of anthropological historian Greg Dening that such "re-enactments tend to hallucinate a past as merely the present in funny dress."[20]

Although the gathering at Taputapuātea might be similarly dismissed as so much folkloric play-acting, I found it qualitatively different from such tourist-oriented events as the Arahurahu ceremonies. Those who had sailed the canoes to Taputapuātea were largely performing for themselves, and many were profoundly affected by their pilgrimage.

Compare, for example, the experience of Hector Busby with that of his late countryman Te Rangi Hiroa, when the latter visited Taputapuātea in 1929, the year after Teuira Henry's *Ancient Tahiti* had been published in Honolulu. Although trained as a physician and noted for his public health work in Aotearoa, Te Rangi Hiroa was also famed for anthropological research among his fellow Māori as well as the Cook Islanders and Samoans. Later he was appointed the Director of Hawai'i's Bishop Museum, Professor of Anthropology at Yale University, and knighted, using his European name, as Sir Peter Buck.

For years this distinguished scholar had wanted to make a pilgrimage to Taputapuātea. From his tribal traditions, he reckoned that some of his ancestors had come from Ra'iātea, and he felt that much of Māori theology had emanated from the island's famous temple. In 1929 he had his chance. While conducting fieldwork on the atoll of Tongareva in the Northern Cooks, a passing British warship bound for Ra'iātea offered him passage. After landing at Uturoa, with great expectations he took a small boat through the lagoon to Opoa, the district where the temple is located. When, however, he at last saw Taputapuātea, Te Rangi Hiroa was utterly devastated by the deserted temple and brusquely left after a cursory inspection. Later he explained his disappointment:

> I had made my pilgrimage to Taputapu-atea, but the dead could not speak to me. It was sad to the verge of tears. I felt a profound regret, a regret for—I knew not what. Was it for the beating of the temple drums or the shouting of the populace as the king was raised on high? Was it for the human sacrifices of olden times? It was for none of these individually but for something at the back of them all, some living spirit and divine courage that existed in ancient times of which Taputapu-atea was a mute symbol. It was something that we Polynesians have lost and cannot find, something that we yearn for and cannot recreate. The background in which that spirit was engendered has changed beyond recovery. The bleak wind of oblivion had swept over Opoa.

Foreign weeds grew over the untended courtyard, and stones had fallen from the sacred altar of Taputapu-atea. The gods had long ago departed.[21]

Sixty-six years later, Hector and his crew aboard *Te Aurere* experienced Taputapuātea in a very different way. Sailing through the Sacred Pass to remove the *tapu*, then being greeted by an expectant crowd on the restored *marae*, greatly uplifted these contemporary representatives of the Light-land. Hec had been excited to learn that Te Ao Pēhi Kara knew a Māori version of this tradition and would compose the chant of reconciliation to lift the voyaging *tapu*. When *Te Aurere* entered the pass and Te Ao Pēhi Kara began chanting, Hec says that he fell into a trance and personally felt the pain of the assault on his ancestors long ago. When the chanting ceased and the *tapu* was formally lifted, he came to, feeling totally exhilarated at having left the ancient tragedy behind.[22]

Chapter Four

A Fleet of Canoes

WHEN *HŌKŪLE'A* REACHED Aotearoa in December of 1985, the Hawaiians were welcomed onto the historic Waitangi *marae* located deep in the Bay of Islands on the northeast coast of the North Island. After the silver-haired Māori elder Sir James Henare warmly greeted and generously praised the Hawaiians, he turned to his fellow tribesmen and urged them to respond to *Hōkūle'a*'s visit by building their own voyaging canoe and sailing to Hawai'i.

Hector Busby took Sir James' exhortation to heart and started thinking about carving a voyaging canoe. The bridge builder had long been associated with *Ngatokimatawhaorua*, the 117-foot long *waka taua* (war canoe) that had been constructed in the late 1930s for the centennial of the 1840 Treaty of Waitangi.[1] As a boy, Hec had watched her being built and launched, and in 1973, he led an effort to repair and relaunch the centennial canoe. Over the years, he has taken her out on numerous ceremonial missions, including greeting *Hōkūle'a* as the Hawaiians entered the Bay of Islands. Yet despite his long association with the big war canoe, Hector knew very little about sailing canoes.

At the time of Western contact, most Māori canoes appear to have been paddling craft, though some used auxiliary sails. Although drawings and descriptions of sailing canoes exist, including some double-hulled ones, active knowledge about building and sailing such vessels does not seem to have survived, at least not in the Northland where Hector lives.[2] Therefore, when he began looking into how to make a voyaging canoe, Hec naturally turned to Nainoa for advice. The two were already good friends, more like father and son given their age difference. Hector had hosted Nainoa when the Hawaiian flew down to Aotearoa to ask permission to sail *Hōkūle'a* into the Bay of Islands and call upon the Waitangi *marae*. While discussing the details, Nainoa had stayed at Hec's house on the shores of Doubtless Bay, where the navigator spent night after night out in the cold, studying the stars as they appeared at that southerly latitude. Nainoa was therefore more than happy to share his knowledge about sailing canoes with Hector, and he gave him a preliminary design for *Hawai'iloa*.

One advantage that Hec and his colleagues had over the Hawaiians when it came to building voyaging canoes was the *kauri (Agathis australis)*, probably the best tree in all of Polynesia for carving big canoes. Although these forest giants do not reach the great heights of *koa* and spruce, their smooth, cylindrical trunks grow considerably thicker. Furthermore, *kauri* resists splitting and can be virtually knot-free for the first 60–70 feet. The old canoe carvers hollowed out these massive logs to make ultra wide, single-hull paddling canoes that did not need a stabilizing outrigger float. They also joined sections carved from several *kauri* logs end-to-end to make truly enormous canoes, such as *Ngatokimatawhaorua*, which had been constructed from the dugout sections of three trees scarfed together.

However, by the twentieth century, the great *kauri* forests that once covered much of the Northland had almost all been cut to erect ships, buildings, and to clear the land for farming and grazing. Fortunately, some remaining stands had been protected, although this meant that Hector had to lobby hard to gain permission to cut down a pair of mature *kauri* to make *Te Aurere*.

In January of 1992, I flew down to Aotearoa as part of a Polynesian Voyaging Society delegation that was presenting a Hawaiian *ki'i* (i.e. *tiki*, a statue or image) to be displayed on the grounds of the Waitangi *marae* to commemorate *Hōkūle'a*'s 1985 visit. Afterwards, we drove to Hector's home at Doubtless Bay. There he and a group of young Māori apprentices (who were supported through a government training program for unemployed youths) had shaped the two *kauri* logs into a pair of dugout hulls 57 feet long and were just then joining them with crossbeams and a central platform. Although the partly finished craft was similar to the original plan for

Voyaging Canoes Scheduled for Te Henua 'Enana Voyage

Canoe	Nation	Date	Length	Hull Base Materials
Hōkūle'a	Hawai'i	1975	62 feet	Framing & plywood
Te Aurere	Aotearoa	1992	57 feet	*Kauri* logs
Takitumu	Cooks	1992	53 feet	Framing & plywood
Hawai'iloa	Hawai'i	1993	57 feet	Spruce logs
Te Au o Tonga	Cooks	1995	72 feet	Framing & plywood
Makali'i	Hawai'i	1995	54 feet	Fiberglass
Tahiti Nui	Tahiti	1995	75 feet	*Tōtora* logs
'A'a Kahiki Nui	Tahiti	1995	45 feet	*'Uru* logs

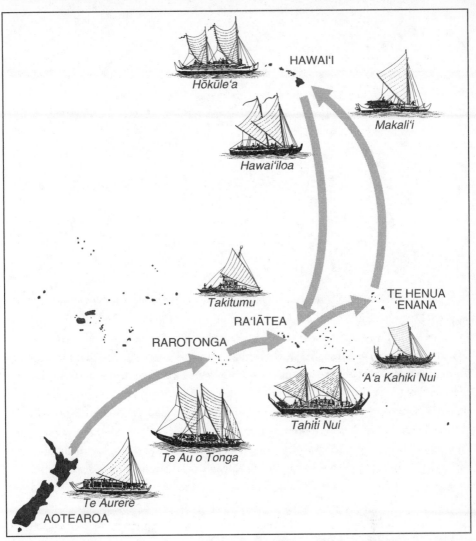

Voyaging canoes from Aotearoa, Rarotonga, Tahiti, and Hawai'i shown to scale.

Hawai'iloa, Hector had incorporated some distinctively Māori features. Instead of making the hulls smooth, he had given them a scalloped finish, which he explained was a Māori way for reducing drag. Hec had also sculpted a pair of striking prow pieces *(tauihu)* modeled on an ancient canoe prow that had been excavated not far from his property and now is displayed in a museum in Auckland. This sole decorative touch gave *Te Aurere* a more archaic appearance than the elaborately carved canoes of the more recent Classic Māori period.

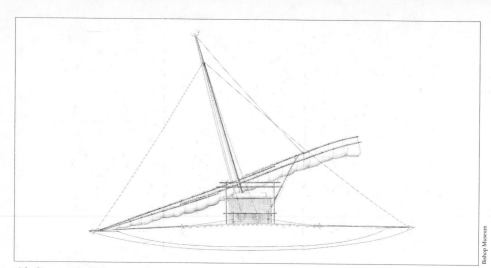

A kalia canoe of Tonga.

THE COOK ISLANDERS already had *Takitumu*, the 53-foot long double canoe that Sir Thomas Davis had built to uphold the nation's honor at the Pacific Arts Festival. *Takitumu* was light, fast, and controversial. Papa Tom, as Sir Thomas is known locally, advertised that she was a scaled-down replica of the original *Takitumu* that the Tahitian high chief Tangi'ia had sailed around the South Pacific many centuries ago. He also claimed that she better represented the archaic voyaging canoes of Eastern Polynesia than did *Hōkūle'a*, a claim that Herb Kāne objected to because *Takitumu* was actually modeled on a relatively recent *kalia* type of canoe developed in Western Polynesia and Fiji some 300 years ago. Tongan voyagers, using Fijian trees and employing Samoan carpenters, had innovatively combined the lateen sail and double-ended shunting configuration of Micronesian outrigger canoes with the Polynesian double canoe form to come up with a vessel that outsailed earlier types of double canoes.[3]

However, for the journey to Hawai'i, the Cook Islands government wanted to build a larger, sturdier, and more typically Cook Island canoe. Nothing was really done until early 1994, when Sir Thomas again stepped into the breech and announced that he would build a new voyaging canoe to be called *Te Au o Tonga*, after a canoe of that name sailed centuries ago by Karika, a Samoan high chief who fought his rival Tangi'ia, but later became his ally.[4] This time Papa Tom sought to emulate a distinctively Cook Islands sailing vessel. But he quickly realized that there were no drawings of large sailing canoes from the Cooks, as by the time Western explorers reached the islands, the era of voyaging had long passed.[5] That didn't stop him. He reasoned that since the Cook Islanders and Tahitians are closely related he could legitimately borrow a Tahitian design. After examining drawings of Tahitian canoes made by the draftsmen and artists

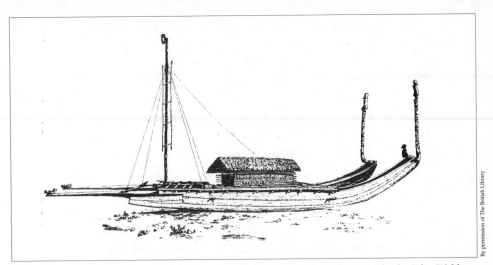

A Tahitian tipaerua *double canoe drawn up on shore. Pen, wash, and watercolor by John Webber.*

on Cook's voyages, Papa Tom selected the *tipaerua*, a type of double canoe that featured very low prows and high arching sterns.

Particularly since the Cook drawings clearly showed that *tipaerua* hulls were pieced together rather than dugout from single logs, Papa Tom had no compunctions about building the hulls *Hōkūle'a*-style with milled lumber framing covered with plywood. Besides, he reasoned that even if Rarotonga had trees large enough to make dugout hulls he would not have sacrificed them, as too much timber would have been wasted in the hollowing-out process. Regardless of the materials used, the hastily built craft turned out to be an impressive canoe. Whereas the longest of *Takitumu*'s unequal hulls (a feature of the *kalia* design that further sets it off from earlier canoe types) was 53 feet long, both of *Te Au o Tonga*'s hulls were 72 feet long. Moreover, they were very deep and wide, enabling the canoe to accommodate a large complement of crew and passengers along with plenty of food, water, and other supplies for a long journey.

THE SAGA OF *TAHITI NUI*, the official Tahitian entry, is much more complicated. During our 1976 stay in Tahiti, we were hosted by the Tainui Society, an organization formed to welcome *Hōkūle'a* and afterwards build a Tahitian voyaging canoe to sail to Hawai'i. In being such generous hosts, however, the society spent almost all the money they had raised for building their own canoe. After returning to Hawai'i, I sent *Nālehia* to Tahiti to provide the Tainui members with a double canoe to sail while raising additional construction funds and building their own craft. Unfortunately, by the time *Nālehia* arrived, they seemed to have lost their enthusiasm about canoe sailing. She was little used, and the Tahitians forgot about building their own canoe and sailing to

Hawai'i. After years of lying neglected in a small boat harbor, the Hawaiian double canoe was destroyed in a hurricane.

In the late 1980s a young Māori carver named Matahi Whakataka (AKA Greg Brightwell) decided to build a big double canoe to sail from Tahiti to Aotearoa, following the legendary migration route of his tribal ancestors. He cut down a pair of *tōtora* (*Podocarpus totora*). As these were nowhere near as big around as *kauri* trees, he carved them to make the keel sections of a pair of hulls that would have to be built up with planking. However, when he couldn't get enough support in Aotearoa to finish the canoe, Matahi flew to Tahiti to seek additional funding.

There he met Francis Cowan, an experienced sailor who had crewed with Eric De Bisshop on the French adventurer's ill-fated 1956 attempt to sail a bamboo raft from Tahiti to South America as a sort of reverse *Kon-Tiki*. Later in Tahiti, Francis built a Tahitian outrigger sailing canoe, and then started work on a double canoe he intended to sail to Hawai'i. Late one night, however, the unfinished canoe caught fire, a mysterious event that abruptly ended the project. Perhaps because he saw something of himself and his early dreams in the young Māori, Francis agreed to aid Matahi and helped him obtain funds from the French Polynesian government to ship the partially shaped logs to Tahiti and complete the canoe.

The 72-foot long canoe was completed in 1990 and christened with the Māori name of *Hawaikinui* (Great Hawaiki), in reference to Hawaiki, the legendary Māori homeland that many think was Tahiti or nearby islands. Each hull was composed of a dugout base made from a single *tōtora* log, onto which two levels of planking had been added to gain displacement and freeboard. Matahi embellished these and other parts of the superstructure with Māori carvings that, along with the tall curving sails patterned after those used on ancient Tahitian canoes, made for a striking craft.

Hawaikinui was not easy to handle—she tracked well but was difficult to turn— perhaps because the keels of the twin hulls were virtually flat, instead of gradually curving upward at each end to give them the desired rocker profile needed for maneuvering. Moreover, the builders had trouble getting the Tahitian-style sails to work properly and eventually replaced them with Western-style yacht sails. Despite these problems, Matahi, Francis, and three others sailed *Hawaikinui* from Tahiti to Rarotonga, and on to Aotearoa to fulfill the Māori carver's dream.[6]

Because of the financial aid received, *Hawaikinui* belonged to the government of French Polynesia. Despite dockside demonstrations by hundreds of Māori who had come to consider the canoe their own, she was shipped back to Tahiti. Once there, *Hawaikinui* was exhibited under a great tent on the grounds of the Museum of Tahiti and the Islands. But after a hurricane ripped the tent away, she began to deteriorate rapidly from exposure to sun, wind, and rain. Within a few years, the once beautiful craft was rotting away—except for the sturdy *tōtora* bases of the hulls.

In early 1994, when President Gaston Flosse finally released funds to build a new voyaging canoe, government officials turned to *Hawaikinui* in hopes that she could be rebuilt. However, upon discovering the canoe's sorry state, they decided to salvage only the insect-resistant keel sections of her twin hulls. After the boatbuilders cut off the rotten superstructure and hull strakes, they built up the hulls by inserting ribs and attaching plank upon plank of heavy Fijian hardwood. The finished ultra deep and narrow hulls, each 75 feet long, were then joined closely together with crossbeams, over which was laid a long platform.

At her launching just two weeks before the ceremony at Taputapuātea, the completed canoe was christened *Tahiti Nui* (Big Tahiti), a name that normally refers to the largest of the two volcanic cones that make up the island of Tahiti. (The smaller one is known as *Tahiti Iti*—Little Tahiti.) At the time, President Flosse was talking about changing French Polynesia's name to *Tahiti Nui*, meant in the sense of a "Great Tahiti" composed of all five of the territory's archipelagos. The canoe was therefore called *Tahiti Nui* to symbolize this new nation in the making. As part of that effort, the outer flanks of her twin hulls were carved with bas-reliefs, featuring traditional designs from each island group. The canoe also flew the huge flag of the territory, which featured a double canoe with five stick figures standing on deck symbolizing the constituent archipelagos.

However grand *Tahiti Nui* looked, as a sailing canoe she left much to be desired. When the sails were raised immediately after launching, the canoe drifted backwards. The builders, who were used to making paddling canoes and powerboats, had placed the canoe's second mast way too far aft. At the urging of the Hawaiian sailors newly arrived on *Hawai'iloa* and *Hōkūle'a*, the mast was moved forward to achieve the proper relationship between the center of effort of the wind upon the sails and the center of lateral resistance of the canoe's hulls. Even so *Tahiti Nui* did not sail very well, probably because the hulls were so deep and narrow. In smooth water, the canoe could sail forward, but in the open sea she hobby-horsed badly as the twin bows and sterns alternately plunged deep into the swells, and then abruptly rose up when they had finally displaced enough water to gain buoyancy.

Apparently it had never occurred to anyone to study the old drawings and engravings of the ancient Tahitian canoes from the Cook expeditions and then copy one of the designs, as Papa Tom had so adroitly done. Instead they ignored traditional Tahitian naval architecture and built a strangely shaped craft that could not really sail. The chief victims of this mess were *Tahiti Nui*'s captain and crew. They were professional seamen, but on power vessels, not sailing craft. As employees of the government's public works division, their job was to run the ships used to transport workers, equipment, and construction materials around French Polynesia for building roads, schools, medical clinics, and other government facilities. Despite their lack of sailing experience, they had been saddled with the virtually impossible task of some-how making *Tahiti Nui* ready for the voyage.

'A'A KAHIKI NUI was Tahiti's second—albeit unofficial—entry. The 45-foot long double canoe was the creation of Karim Cowan, Francis Cowan's nephew who had attended some of the navigation and sailing classes held at the Bishop Museum planetarium and aboard *Hōkūle'a*. He had a canoe maker carve him a modest double canoe from a pair of breadfruit trees (*Autocarpus altilis*), called *'uru* by Tahitians, and *'ulu* by Hawaiians. When well-meaning advisors pointed out that his canoe did not have enough freeboard and carrying capacity for sailing all the way to Hawai'i, Karim built up the hulls in the style of *Tahiti Nui*. But adding several layers of planking resulted in an ungainly craft that lacked needed structural strength. After nearly foundering during the first sea trial, Karim regretfully withdrew his canoe.

MAKALI'I, the third Hawaiian canoe, represented the island of Hawai'i, the so-called "Big Island" of the archipelago. Although the Polynesian Voyaging Society included crewmembers from all islands on *Hōkūle'a*'s voyages, and visited these islands on educational cruises, many outer islanders wanted voyaging canoes of their own. A Maui group had built *Mo'olele*, a *wa'a kaulua* similar to *Nālehia*, and was sailing her around Maui and adjacent islands with great success. But no one from the outer islands had attempted to build a long range voyaging canoe, until late 1993 when a new group called *Nā Kālaiwa'a Moku o Hawai'i* (The Canoe Builders of the Island of Hawai'i) started work on *Makali'i*.[7]

The nucleus of the group had first come together to build *Mauloa*, a small outrigger sailing canoe that, under Mau Piailug's supervision, was roughly carved out of a short, thick *koa* log with stone adzes, and then finished with steel adzes. To construct *Makali'i*, the canoe builders, led by *Hōkūle'a* veterans Milton ("Shorty") and Clay Bertelmann, started with a pair of fiberglass hulls that had been originally fabricated to make a Hawaiian *wa'a kaulua*, but had lain unused for years after the project collapsed. Raising the freeboard of the hulls by adding side strakes, connecting them with crossbeams, and developing the sail rig, resulted in a fast and lively single-masted, 54-foot canoe. What *Makali'i* lacked in terms of traditional materials, was more than made up for by her fine sailing characteristics, and the tremendous spirit of her crew and their many Big Island supporters. More than two dozen of the latter flew down to Tahiti to greet the canoe and her sailors and later see them off for the voyage home. Their enthusiastic chants and dances greatly enlivened the welcoming and departing ceremonies.

AS THE HAWAIIANS had conceived the joint voyage, and trained the navigators from Aotearoa and the Cooks, it was only natural that they develop a plan for how the journey should be conducted. However, the captains and navigators from all the canoes did not have a chance to discuss it as a group until the meeting held in Rarotonga in late 1994, just a few months before the canoes were to set sail from their respective islands. Nainoa particularly welcomed this meeting as an opportunity to go over safety procedures. Foremost in his mind was the requirement that each canoe should be followed by an escort vessel that could assist a dismasted or otherwise disabled canoe, and, in a worst case scenario, could rescue the entire crew.

Nainoa's insistence on using escort boats stemmed from the tragic attempt to sail *Hōkūle'a* back to Tahiti in 1978. Whereas the yacht *Meotai* had followed the canoe in 1976 to provide a safety net as well as track her for the navigation experiment, in 1978, *Hōkūle'a* set sail without an escort boat. Those in charge felt that relying on another vessel clashed with their vision of the voyage and that the canoe had already proven its seaworthiness on the first trip to Tahiti. In case of an emergency, *Hōkūle'a* carried a short-wave transceiver, and a new device, an EPIRB, an emergency locator beacon that transmitted distress signals to be picked up by passing aircraft and satellites.

After a long, drawn-out ceremony at Honolulu's Ala Moana Beach Park, *Hōkūle'a* departed at dusk, with gusty north-northeasterly winds blowing and small craft warnings in effect along the coast. The crew barely had time to raise the twin masts, sails, and booms of the Hawaiian rig before it was dark. A number of crucial tasks were left undone, including putting the EPIRB in a secure place and lashing it down.

As Honolulu lies 500 miles to the west of the meridian of Tahiti, any vessel headed there has to slant hard into the easterly trades in order to gain enough easting while moving south. In 1976 we initially gained a couple of hundred miles of easting by tacking into the trades around the north coast of Maui and the Big Island, a slow process that took us five days to finally clear the archipelago. This time the sailors welcomed the strong northerly winds blowing that evening, apparently hoping to sail directly southeast to get past the Big Island in a couple of days, rather than having to tack slowly northeast around it.

Sailing swiftly, *Hōkūle'a* soon reached the infamous Ka'iwi Channel between O'ahu and its eastern neighbor Moloka'i. The wind and seas funneling between the two volcanic masses had really started to pick up, and the Coast Guard had posted storm warnings. At that point, the crew should have lowered *Hōkūle'a*'s sails to the deck for safety. Yet they left them up to gain maximum easting. By around midnight the canoe had crossed the channel, but the seas began heaping up even more. *Hōkūle'a* was then sailing in the comparatively shallow water covering Penguin Bank that extends southwest of Moloka'i. Under pressure of the wind, the canoe was heeling way over and breaking seas were sweeping over the depressed lee (downwind) hull.[8]

The ocean had found the canoe's weak point. When sailing hard to windward, *Hōkūle'a* heels over, exposing the lee hull to boarding seas. In 1975, while sailing from Kaua'i to O'ahu in much more benign conditions, the lee hull of the canoe had suddenly swamped. Afterwards we built compartments into the hulls and developed a method of wedging the hatch covers closed to prevent boarding seas from seeping in, as well as procedures for regularly checking and bailing out the compartments. Though not at all ideal, the system worked during the 1976 voyage.

During preparations for the 1978 voyage, these procedures seem to have been ignored or were simply forgotten. Only thin bungee cords attached from inside the compartments held the hatches loosely in place. At this critical moment, they were no match for the seas now washing over the hull. Compartment after compartment flooded rapidly, causing the canoe to heel over at an even more perilous angle. The wind pressure on the sails had to be relieved immediately by releasing the sheets, the lines controlling the sails. But these had been tightly lashed onto wooden cleats and left untended, instead of being looped over the side rail and hand held with a quick-release friction grip, as Kāwika Kapahulehua had taught us to do during heavy weather on the 1976 trip. Crucial seconds passed while the crew futilely groped in the darkness. Before anyone could untie or cut the sheets free, an extra-strong gust blew the heavily listing canoe over completely, dumping everyone into the angry sea.

At that point, an escort boat could have taken the survivors on board and radioed for help. But *Hōkūle'a* was alone in the sea, and to their horror, the crew found they could not send a distress signal. The short-wave radio was headed for the bottom, and the locator beacon, an early model that did not automatically start transmitting when immersed in water, apparently drifted away before anyone had a chance to turn it on.

The next day, after several failed attempts to draw the attention of passing aircraft with flares, the captain finally gave in to the earnest pleas of Eddie Aikau that he be allowed to paddle his surfboard to Lāna'i, the nearest island. Eddie, a great surfer and lifeguard famed for rescuing both fellow surfers and wayward tourists from the huge winter seas off O'ahu's North Shore, grabbed his board and paddled off. He soon disappeared over the mountainous seas, never to be seen again. As he was already thoroughly chilled by having been semi-immersed in the ocean and buffeted by cold winds and breaking seas for more than twelve hours, Eddie probably fell victim to acute hypothermia before he could reach land.

As dusk approached, the situation looked even more desperate. The canoe was drifting southwest away from the islands and from the sea and air lanes connecting them. Some crewmembers, barely clinging to the capsized hull, looked as though they might not make it through another night. Then came a miracle. The last flight of the day from Kona on the Big Island to Honolulu was late and had been diverted farther south than usual, putting it on a path almost directly over the disabled canoe. Just as the plane was about to pass far overhead, the pilot happened to glance down as a flare arched skyward. The pilot notified the Coast Guard whose helicopters soon flew out to rescue the surviving crewmembers.

From that bleak moment on, the Polynesian Voyaging Society made safety a first priority. Perhaps most importantly, they mandated an escort boat on all long voyages. During the Tahiti sail in 1980, *Hōkūle'a* was escorted by *Ishka*, a motor-sailer built and captained by Alex Jakubenko. *Dorcas*, a Canadian yacht skippered by Dan and Peggy White, escorted the canoe during the 1985–1987 Voyage of Rediscovery. For the 1992 expedition to Rarotonga, Alex Jakubenko returned to duty with a brand new motor-sailer, *Kama Hele* (Hawaiian for "Traveler"), built especially for escorting *Hōkūle'a*. On the forthcoming voyage, *Kama Hele* would be escorting *Hawai'iloa*.

WITH THIS EXPERIENCE in mind, Nainoa came to the planning meeting at Rarotonga, determined that each vessel sail north to Hawai'i with its own escort boat. Some delegates were uncomfortable with the idea. They had neither been through a capsize nor had experienced the loss of a fellow sailor and seemed to be confident about sailing without an escort. Probably out of respect for Nainoa, no one raised any objections until the august and sometimes imperious Sir Thomas Davis forthrightly rejected the plan. Instead he proposed that they should provide their own security:

> If we are going to talk about safety, one of the greatest things we can do is to look after each other. Yet we are willing to go off with escort boats following us in case anything goes wrong, when traditionally we looked after one another. We've somehow accepted that foreign vessels are infallible, and that our canoes are fallible.[9]

He wanted the canoes to sail together in a compact fleet so that every vessel was always within sight of at least one or two others. In case any canoe ran into trouble, others in the fleet could come to the rescue.

Nainoa politely but firmly disagreed with his senior colleague. The issue, he insisted, was safety, not tradition. He argued that the canoes could not look after one another simply because they would not be able to keep sailing together as a tightly clustered group:

> For seven canoes that have not trained together, that have different performances, different speeds, different maneuvering capabilities, different rigs,

that will perform differently in different weather conditions—trying to keep those seven canoes together in my mind would be near impossible. Our ancestors may have been able to do that. I don't think this table should assume that we're now in a position in our growth to do that.

He was too polite to say so, but Nainoa was particularly worried about the canoes from Tahiti and the Cooks that were still being built. The rendezvous at Taputapuātea was scheduled for mid-March, just three and a half months away—hardly enough time to complete the canoes, test and troubleshoot them, and train their crews. Nainoa was more than a little afraid a fatal accident might occur during the voyage. At one point he even went so far as to declare that if one person dies, the whole voyage dies. Yet instead of singling out the unfinished canoes as the ones most needing escorts and other safety measures, he began talking about *Hōkūle'a* and *Hawai'iloa*:

> Our canoes in Hawai'i are seaworthy, our crews are trained, and yet we who have had the most experience will no way sail without an escort boat. I've not only sailed, I've dove, I've worked on boats my whole life. I've buried friends at sea who've maybe been negligent, and those who weren't, who were lost by accident. We've made mistakes and we've paid dearly for them. We're not in a position to make them again and repeat history.

Although Papa Tom had much less experience in canoe navigation than Nainoa, he spoke with some authority stemming from sea adventures spanning more than a half century. Furthermore, the tall, 78-year-old figure had pursued several distinguished careers as a physician, public health expert, consultant to government and industry, and, more recently, as his nation's Prime Minister.

In his engaging autobiography, *Island Boy*, Papa Tom writes about his childhood on Rarotonga. He loved to paddle a tiny outrigger canoe out to sea, trying the impossible—to go far enough to lose sight of Rarotonga's peaks, yet have enough time left to paddle back home for supper. As a teenager, he experimented with small sailing canoes, learning basic principals of hull design that he says were later useful in building *Te Au o Tonga*. He earned a medical degree at Otago University in Aotearoa's South Island and spent several years as a medical officer back in Rarotonga during the late 1940s. Then he took to the sea again, this time sailing a yacht halfway around the world to Boston.[10]

There the physician enrolled in the Harvard School of Public Health. After earning a masters degree, he remained in the United States, working in public health and medicine and serving as a consultant with the renowned firm of Arthur D. Little.

Among other things, he had a key role in the U.S. Army's program of rocketing monkeys into space to gain physiological data needed for sending humans into space.

In 1971 Rarotonga's long-absent native son returned to the Cooks to stand for Parliament, the start of a long political career, as leader of the opposition, and for nine years as Prime Minister. Along the way, he was knighted by Queen Elizabeth, took the title of Pa Tuterangi Ariki and married Pa Tepaeru Ariki, the Paramount Chief (some say "Queen") of Rarotonga and President of the House of Ariki (traditional chiefs). After leaving politics, Papa Tom devoted his time to a variety of projects. Aside from building *Takitumu* and *Te Au o Tonga*, he wrote his autobiography and also published *Vaka, Saga of a Polynesian Canoe*, a fictional biography of the legendary canoe that first bore the name *Takitumu*.[11]

Having two such experienced sailors disagree so completely over how to conduct the voyage cast a pall over the meeting. The Cook Island navigators were particularly torn. They had trained with Nainoa and trusted him, yet were to serve aboard *Te Au o Tonga* under the authority of Captain Sir Thomas Davis, Pa Tuterangi Ariki. Despite their suggestions and those offered by others, no compromise could be reached. The meeting ended without any resolution.

NAINOA'S FRUSTRATIONS over the escort boat issue and other safety concerns were never fully laid to rest. Right after the long ceremony at Taputapuātea, he was eager to get all the captains and navigators gathered at Ra'iātea to go over safety procedures and discuss how the joint sail would be coordinated. Instead, Tahitian cultural officials convened a surreal meeting to discuss their proposal for a Pacific-wide association of voyaging societies. While they went on talking about such organizational details as how the association's secretariat would rotate among member nations, Nainoa futilely tried to discuss issues of preparedness and safety for the voyage at hand.

After the canoes made their way from Ra'iātea to Tahiti, a meeting was held to go over the plans for the sail to Nukuhiva. Despite some useful discussion about weather conditions, radio frequencies and the like, too much time and energy again went into debating fleet versus escort boat approaches to safety. Papa Tom raised the same issue at the final meeting held in Te Henua 'Enana just a few days before leaving for Hawai'i. He asserted his objections to escort boats, forcing the now thoroughly exasperated Nainoa to restate his case. This was unnecessary as a compromise was actually in the making. All the canoes would sail separately with individual escorts, including a pair of cruising yachts that had just been pressed into service. This would allow the navigators to work independently as they had been trained. Yet the canoes would also sail together as a highly dispersed fleet in which each vessel would be electronically linked to the others by means of twice-daily radio calls.

Chapter Five

The Native Land

IN 1595 SPANISH SHIPS sailing west from Peru chanced upon a sprinkling of volcanic islands. Alvaro Mendaña de Neyra, the expedition's leader, collectively named these Las Marquesas de Mendoza to honor his patron, Don García Hurtado de Mendoza, the Viceroy of Peru and the Marquis of Cañete. Almost two centuries later, in 1791, American and French merchant ships independently sighted several other high islands just to the north of those seen by the Spanish. Western cartographers eventually grouped these islands—Fatuiva, Tahuata, and Hiva'oa in the south and Nukuhiva, 'Uahuku, and 'Uapou in the north, plus several much smaller ones—as a single archipelago they called the Marquesas Islands.[1]

But why should we continue to call the archipelago after the noble title of a long-forgotten colonial administrator when its Polynesian inhabitants call it Te Henua 'Enana in the northern dialect and Te Fenua 'Enata in the southern dialect? To honor those who first settled these islands, as well as their living descendants, I have been using Te Henua 'Enana rather than the Marquesas Islands, choosing the form from the northern group because the canoe fleet was scheduled to call on its main island of Nukuhiva before sailing to Hawai'i. In addition, I employ *'Enana* to refer to the archipelago's native inhabitants, and *'Enanan* for the language and as an adjective.[2]

The usual English translation of Te Henua 'Enana as "The Land of Men" misses a crucial point. "The Land" accurately translates *Te Henua*, but the ambiguous English plural noun "Men," whether thought of in the sense of humans in general or males in particular, does not really reflect the specific way I hear *'Enana* being used. The people call themselves *'Enana* (the equivalent of *kanaka* in Hawaiian, *ta'ata* in Tahitian, *tangata* in Māori, etc.) to distinguish themselves as native to the land, in contrast to those foreign to the land, the *hao'e* (compare *haole* in Hawaiian, which originally meant "foreign"). Hence, I prefer to translate Te Henua 'Enana as "The Native Land" in order to stress how the people identify their island world in terms of themselves.[3]

WHENCE CAME THE HAWAIIANS? In 1959 Bishop Museum archaeologist Kenneth Emory tried to answer this question. He proposed that they had come from Tahiti, meant in the larger sense to include the other Society Islands as well as Tahiti proper. Kenneth backed up his answer by citing inquiries into Hawaiian traditions made during the early 1800s by a missionary and a native Hawaiian scholar, as well as his own research.[4]

In 1823, William Ellis, a British missionary who had been stationed in the Society Islands for several years, made an extended tour of Hawai'i. He stopped for some time in Kailua, the village on the Kona coast of Hawai'i Island which then served as that island's capital. Because of his fluency in Tahitian, he was able to talk at length with Governor Kuakini and other Hawaiians about their origins. Although Ellis complained that, like the Tahitians, the Hawaiians could not give him precise details as to their origins, he did learn that they considered the question in two different ways:

> The general opinions entertained by the natives themselves, relative to their origin, are, either that the first inhabitants were created on the islands, descended from the gods, by whom they were first inhabited; or, that they came from a country they called Tahiti.[5]

Ellis went on to explain that according to the priests of Tane, Tanaroa, and other gods, "the first man was made from Haumea, a female deity," whereas other informants supposed that "the chiefs were descended from Akea, who appears to have been the connecting link between the gods and men." These mythical progenitors are known widely in Polynesia: Haumea (alternatively called Papa), who personified earth stratum; and Ākea (or Wākea), her male counterpart who personified vast space. However, the missionary also noted that whereas descent from these primordial figures explained the origin of the chiefly lines, among the common people accounts of ancestors arriving in canoes from Tahiti were "far more general and popular."

Although Ellis spelled the name of this legendary homeland as Tahiti, other early visitors wrote it down as Kahiki. Depending on their ear or the local dialect, the initial and penultimate consonants sounded to foreigners as either a /k/ or a /t/. When American missionaries standardized the Hawaiian alphabet, they chose /k/ over /t/, and so Kahiki became the preferred form. Although Kahiki was obviously cognate with the South Seas Tahiti, the Hawaiian form had a more general meaning of an overseas land or lands and even sectors of the sky. Ellis tried to reconcile these diverse meanings by proposing that whereas in the distant past, Hawaiians had used the term to apply to the island of Tahiti (or less specifically to Tahiti and its neighbors), they generalized the term after contact between Hawai'i and Tahiti ceased.

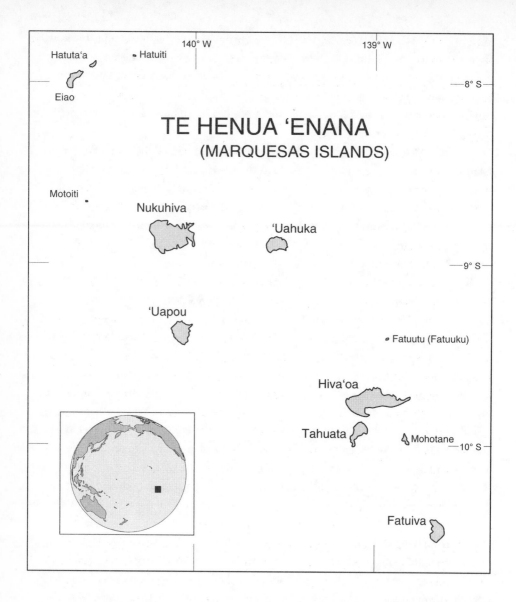

TE HENUA 'ENANA
(MARQUESAS ISLANDS)

A generation after Ellis, the Hawaiian historian David Malo considered the issue of Hawaiian origins in his book-length manuscript *Mo'olelo Hawai'i,*which was unfortunately not published until 1903, when it appeared in translation as *Hawaiian Antiquities.*[6] Like Ellis, Malo reported that he had not learned much in detail by directly asking people where their ancestors were from. (Neither Malo nor Ellis seem to have heard the Hawai'iloa legend, or at least they did not write about it.) Malo's attempt to search the Kumulipo and other ancestral Hawaiian genealogies for islands where the first ancestors previously lived was equally frustrating. Although he found place names that appeared to be foreign, such as Lolo-i-Mehani, where it was said Papa and Wākea had once lived, he was not able to match any of these names with islands known to lie beyond Hawai'i. This is not surprising. By trying to extract migration history from accounts about primordial ancestors, Malo was mixing two different approaches to origins.

When Malo focused on the treasury of Hawaiian chants, prayers, and legends, he readily found a likely candidate for the Hawaiian homeland. He noted that the name Kahiki was often mentioned as a homeland in these traditions and cited in support of the then-growing belief that the first Hawaiians had come "from near Kahiki and from Kahiki itself." Although Malo was certainly aware that Kahiki had other meanings, he was obviously using the term to refer to the South Seas Tahiti.[7]

EARLY ARCHAEOLOGICAL and linguistic research also pointed to Tahiti as the leading candidate for the homeland of the first Hawaiians. During the mid-1920s, Kenneth Emory, a young Bishop Museum researcher, surveyed ancient *marae* and other stone structures throughout Tahiti and its neighbors. During the 1930s, he expanded his archaeological surveys to the Tuamotu atolls and the high island of Mangareva at the southeast end of that chain. Comparing these surveys with those he had conducted in Hawai'i suggested that the Hawaiians had come from southeastern Polynesia, most likely Tahiti. Kenneth's later comparison of Hawaiian with other Polynesian languages for his Ph.D. dissertation reinforced his belief that Tahiti was the Hawaiian homeland.[8]

In 1950 Emory started a revolution in Hawaiian archaeology. Up to this point he had studied only surface remains and had not conducted any systematic excavations. Like most of his colleagues, he did not think the islands had been settled long enough for deep deposits containing artifacts to have accumulated. Nonetheless, in need of funds to supplement his meager Bishop Museum salary, in 1950 Kenneth readily accepted an offer from the University of Hawai'i to teach a new course in archaeological field methods focusing on excavation techniques. The field site, a rock shelter at Kuli'ou'ou on O'ahu's southern coast, had been well chosen. He and his students were happily surprised to find that its soil was deeply stratified and yielded ancient fish-hooks, adze fragments, and even a few rare tattoo needles.[9]

While the Kuli'ou'ou excavation was in progress, Willard Libby, a physicist from the University of Chicago, announced he had developed a method of dating archaeological specimens of biological origin by measuring the ratio of decaying radiocarbon atoms (^{14}C) to stable carbon atoms (^{12}C). Kenneth quickly sent off a sample of charcoal taken from a fireplace at the lowest level of human occupation at Kuli'ou'ou. This first radiocarbon date from the Pacific indicated that the cave had probably been first occupied sometime between A.D. 766 and 1126.

Such exhilarating success on his first attempt at modern archaeology stimulated Kenneth, his students, and his volunteers to find and excavate a variety of other sites around the Hawaiian Islands. He recruited Yosihiko Sinoto, a skilled young Japanese archaeologist with considerable experience in excavating rich mound sites in Japan. After several years of intensive work, Yoshi was able to establish a radiocarbon-dated archaeological sequence based on over 4,000 fishhooks of shell, bone, and wood excavated from thirty-two sites around the islands. Since the form of these hooks varied significantly over time and space, they provided a valuable index to trace cultural movements and developments within Hawai'i.[10]

The next step was to test the theory that Hawaiians came from Tahiti by applying the new archaeological techniques there. In early 1960, Kenneth and Yoshi flew down to Tahiti and, with great expectations, began their search for sites that would yield sequences of fishhooks to compare with those from Hawai'i. In the more tropical and humid Societies, they couldn't find any large dry rock shelters with deep cultural deposits. And they had trouble working in the lowlands because burrowing land crabs had churned up the soil. Although the team eventually managed to locate a few recent sites with fishhooks and other artifacts, without any evidence that reached far into Tahiti's past, they could not test the Tahitian homeland theory.[11]

Fortune smiled when they returned to Tahiti in 1962. Just a few days after their arrival, a medical officer from Maupiti—at the western end of the Society chain—came to see them carrying a stone adz, and a pair of whale-tooth pendants. These had been unearthed by a farmer preparing ground for planting. The archaeologists immediately recognized that the pendants resembled those found in early Māori sites, suggesting they dated back to a time when Tahitians were migrating to Aotearoa. Yoshi immediately took a boat to Maupiti. There he uncovered more artifacts similar to those found in early sites in Aotearoa, but differing from later Tahitian and Māori forms.[12]

Kenneth realized that these finds, along with recent discoveries from Te Henua 'Enana, required that he revise his thinking about the Hawaiian homeland. Robert Suggs, a young archaeologist from Columbia University, had just published reports of his pioneering excavations conducted on the 'Enanan island of Nukuhiva during the late 1950s. These challenged the long-held view of Tahiti's primacy in Polynesian history, elaborated most fully by Te Rangi Hiroa during the 1930s and 1940s. Whereas the Māori scholar proposed that Polynesians first settled in the Societies about 400 A.D., and from there spread over Polynesia, Suggs hypothesized that Te Henua 'Enana had been settled directly from Western Polynesia as early as 200 to 100 B.C., and that the archipelago had subsequently served as an independent center for population dispersal to the eastern Tuamotus, Mangareva, and Rapa Nui. After examining Suggs' evidence,

Kenneth concluded that early Hawaiian artifacts looked closer to those of Te Henua 'Enana than to early Tahitian ones and that therefore Te Henua 'Enana was the "more likely homeland of the first Hawaiians than the Society Islands."[13]

Kenneth and Yoshi's subsequent reexamination of fishhooks from the three archipelagos led them to conclude that whereas early Hawaiian hooks closely re-sembled the archaic Marquesan hooks, late Hawaiian hooks were more like the late Tahitian hooks they had found in excavations and in private collections. They therefore proposed a "dual settlement" model: Hawai'i had been settled first from Te Henua 'Enana around 500–750 A.D., while about 1250 A.D. influential Tahitian voyagers arrived and partially Tahitianised the culture.[14]

Linguistic evidence for first settlement from Te Henua 'Enana turned out to be even more persuasive than that from archaeology. Roger Green, an archaeologist equally at home in linguistics, classified Hawaiian as a member of the Marquesic sub-group of Polynesian languages, a language grouping separate and distinct from the Tahitic sub-group. Moreover, Samuel Elbert, co-author (with Mary Kawena Pukui) of the standard *Hawaiian Dictionary*, discovered a number of words shared uniquely by 'Enanan and Hawaiian, and not by any other Polynesian language. For example: *'anahu* ('Enanan) and *lānahu* (Hawaiian) for charcoal, and *he'ua* ('Ena.) and *lehua* (Haw.) for the flower of the *'ōhi'a* tree *(Metrosideros macropus)* and the tree itself. More recently, linguist Jeffrey Marck argued that Hawaiian and 'Enanan uniquely share a number of sporadic sound changes indicating they were once a single language. Perhaps the simplest way to account for this linguistic evidence is to say that the people who first settled Hawai'i spoke a language from Te Henua 'Enana that evolved into Hawaiian, and later incorpo-rated words from Tahitian.[15]

WITH THE FORTHCOMING VOYAGE being talked about as a re-creation of the first expedition to reach Hawai'i, the issue of the Hawaiian homeland became more than academic. Early in 1993, NHCAP Director Lynette Paglinawan asked me for advice. Lynette, whom I had known since our days studying at the University of Hawai'i in the late 1950s, wanted to know just how well Kenneth and Yoshi's hypothesis—that the *'Enana* had first settled Hawai'i and the Tahitians came later—had held up over time. I warned her that it had been challenged by a number of archaeologists. Some argued that it failed to consider that the correspondences in artifact forms highlighted by Kenneth and Yoshi could have been the result of independent invention in Te Henua 'Enana, Tahiti, and Hawai'i rather than phased migration between them. Others proposed that at the time Hawai'i was first settled, the cultures of Tahiti, the Cooks, Te Henua 'Enana, and other archipelagos of southeast Polynesia were so alike that it would be impossible to select one and declare it the Hawaiian homeland.[16]

Nonetheless, I told Lynette that considering all the evidence from legends, language, and archaeology, I thought that the model of initial settlement from Te Henua 'Enana followed some centuries later by contact with Tahiti remained the leading hypothesis of Hawaiian origins.[17] But since the issue of who exactly reached Hawai'i first was not yet fully settled, I suggested it might be better not to claim that *Hawai'iloa* would re-create *the* original voyage to Hawai'i. I recommended instead she simply say that *Hawai'iloa* would commemorate the discovery and settlement of Hawai'i by sailing there from Te Henua 'Enana, the leading candidate for the original Hawaiian homeland. Lynette seemed relieved and was happy to leave it to others to identify the precise origin of the first Hawaiians.

TE HENUA 'ENANA is favorably located for sending canoes to Hawai'i because it lies southeast of the chain and well upwind with respect to the trade wind flow. Canoes can therefore easily sail to Hawai'i by broad reaching (sailing with the wind abaft the beam, i.e., greater than 90°) across the southeast trades of the Southern Hemisphere, and then reaching (sailing with the wind abeam, i.e., around 90°) across the Northern Hemisphere's northeast trades.

This favorable alignment does not, however, address the question of why one or more canoe-loads of *'Enana* would have sailed so far to the north-northwest when the overall trend of the Polynesian advance had heretofore been eastward. Perhaps this change of migration direction came after the awful realization that there were no more empty lands to eastward. Explorers who headed east from Te Henua 'Enana would have been sorely disappointed, for empty ocean stretches over 3,000 miles until the Galapagos Islands and then South America rise out of the sea. In contrast, voyagers who dared to sail several compass points to the west of north would have had a good chance of intercepting the Hawaiian chain. Yet exploring that far downwind with respect to the trades would have been chancy, for if no islands were found, beating back home would have been difficult. Why, then, would anyone have set off in that direction?

Could migrating land birds have tempted *'Enana* to sail to the north-northwest? Several species of migratory shorebirds fly back and forth between Alaska and Eastern Polynesia: the Pacific golden plover (*Pluvialis fulda*, *kōlea* in Hawaiian), the bristle-thighed curlew *(Numenius tahitiensis, kioea)* and the ruddy turnstone *(Arenaria interpres, 'akekeke)*. After breeding during the northern summer along the shores of northern Alaska, these birds fly south to winter on tropical islands. Although many land in Hawai'i, some travel farther south to Te Henua 'Enana, the Tuamotus, and the Societies. During the northern spring, they fly back to the Arctic to breed, and then return to the tropics at summer's end. As islanders recognize that these are land birds, they would have concluded that the birds are coming from and returning to some unknown land to the north. Perhaps some adventurous 'Enana converted their flight paths into a star compass bearing and sailed to the north in hopes of finding new lands.[18]

Although a direct bearing from Te Henua 'Enana to Alaska passes east of Hawai'i, strong northeast trades and accompanying currents might have pushed a canoe toward Hawai'i. Alternatively, if birds migrating from Te Henua 'Enana headed first toward Hawai'i, and after stopping there or overflying the islands, turned north to fly directly to their breeding grounds, voyagers who followed the birds' initial bearing could have intercepted the long Hawaiian chain.

Herb Kāne and Abraham Pi'i'anai'a—a geographer and extremely popular professor at the University of Hawai'i who was the first director of its Hawaiian Studies program—offered another hypothesis to account for their ancestors' discovery of Hawai'i.[19] They suggested that once 'Enanan voyagers sailing northwest crossed the equator, they would have spotted a strange star that behaved differently from all the others. This is Polaris, the North Star, known in Hawaiian as Hōkū Pa'a (Fixed Star) because it doesn't appear to move across the sky. According to their scenario, this fixed star would have so fascinated the voyagers that they turned north to sail toward it. Since by this time, their northwest heading would have brought them to a point south of Hawai'i, turning north would have put them on course for the chain.[20]

But their hypothesis does not consider the slow wobble in the axis of the earth's rotation, the so-called "precession of the equinoxes." At present, Polaris does not stand perfectly still in the sky. It makes a tiny, barely noticeable circle as it seemingly revolves around the North Celestial Pole, a projection of the Earth's axis of rotation. Because this wobble waxes and wanes in a 26,000 year cycle, when Hawai'i was first reached some 1200–1500 years ago, Polaris made a much larger circle around the North Celestial Pole. Nonetheless, one of the other circumpolar stars that then orbited closer to the North Celestial Pole might have served as a more enticing guiding star.

IN 1813 THE YOUNG AMERICAN REPUBLIC was once again at war with Great Britain. Captain David Porter of the USS Essex had been hunting British ships in the Pacific and brought three prizes of war into Taiohae Bay on the south coast of Nukuhiva, the main island of Te Henua 'Enana's northern group. When not bullying the 'Enana and trying to get their chiefs to sign a petition to James Madison to have the American president become their chief of chiefs, Porter wrote in his journal about the island and its people. Included in his entries were tales about some 'Enana who were still setting out in search of new islands. These and similar accounts from that period provide graphic examples of migration under threat of war and famine. Although they may not directly apply to voyages made much earlier, when Te Henua 'Enana was probably less crowded and perhaps more peaceful, they nonetheless provide rare glimpses of Polynesians setting out to sea under duress and enticed by shamanic visions of lush, unoccupied islands.[21]

For example, Porter wrote that the grandfather of Keatonui, a leading chief of Taiohae whose name he spelled "Gattanewa," had:

> sailed with four large canoes in search of land, taking with him a large stock of provisions and water, together with a large quantity of hogs, poultry, and young plants. He was accompanied by several families, and has never been heard of since he sailed.

The captain also recounted that just two years before his arrival, another chief and his whole tribe:

> had many large double canoes constructed for the purpose of abandoning their valley, and proceeding in search of other islands, under the apprehension that they would be driven off their land by other tribes; but peace took place, the canoes were taken to pieces, and are now carefully deposited in a house, constructed for the purpose, where they may be kept in a state of preservation to guard against future contingencies.

Porter also reported that a beachcomber named James Wilson had heard that "more than eight hundred men, women and children" had left Nukuhiva and other islands of the group "in search of other lands" in recent years. None were ever heard of again except for a woman who had been dropped off at a small island just north of Nukuhiva and was later picked up by bird feather hunters. Wilson also told Porter about the role of "priests" in promoting such voyages:

> Three or four days after the departure of the canoes, on these voyages of discovery, the priests come lurking to the houses of the inhabitants of the valley, whence they sailed, and in a squaking and affected voice inform them that they [the emigrants] have found a land abounding in bread-fruit, hogs, cocoa-nuts, and every thing that can be desired, and invite others to follow them, pointing out the direction to sail, in order to fall in with the desirable spot. New canoes are constructed, and new adventurers commit themselves to the ocean, never to return.

These priests—male or female—were called *tau'a*, a word related to the Hawaiian *kāula*. They were distinct from the other religious specialists called *tuhuna* (roughly

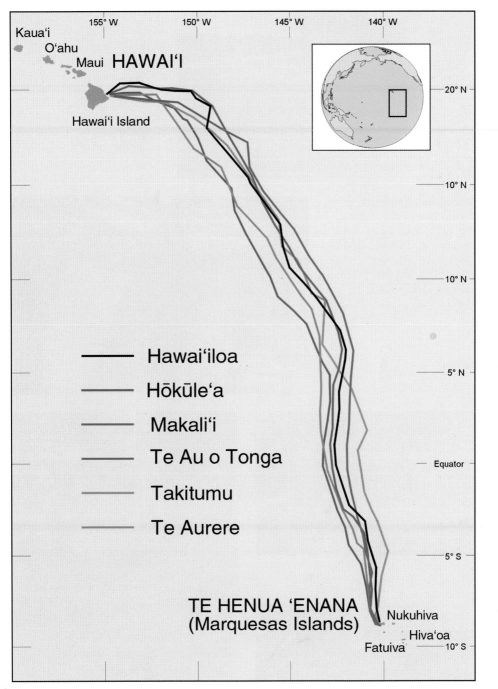

Despite being navigated independently, the six Polynesian voyaging canoes demonstrate remarkably similar courses during the 1995 voyage over the two thousand mile journey north from Nukuhiva to Hawai'i.

A long and fruitless search of Hawai'i's depleted koa forests yielded no logs large enough to create voyaging canoe hulls. Through the generosity of the native Alaskans, two huge spruce logs arrive at Bishop Museum where they will be carved into double hulls of the voyaging canoe Hawai'iloa.

Bishop Museum

Master canoe builder, the late Wright Bowman, Jr. (left) prepares to make a horizontal cut using a custom jig for his chain saw. "Bo" was ultimately responsible for the successful creation of Hawai'iloa.

Bishop Museum

Bishop Museum

Sketching during the Hawai'iloa construction process.

© Moana Doi

Traditional butterfly patches across a crack in a koa sidestrake (mo'o).

Applying varnish on Mauloa.

Bishop Museum

Hawai'iloa *on a crew training sail along the Windward coastline of Moloka'i.*

The Wayfinders

In 1976 Mau Piailug, a traditional navigator from the atoll of Satawal in Micronesia, guided Hōkūle'a from Hawai'i to Tahiti using only his knowledge of the natural signs of the heavens and seas around him. A young Hawaiian, Nainoa Thompson, worked with Mau to absorb his methods and successfully navigate the canoe throughout Polynesia. Nainoa then created a course to train new navigators from Hawai'i and around the Pacific. In 1995, five of the six canoes were guided by wayfinders who had learned from Nainoa.

Pius "Mau" Piailug.   *Nainoa Thompson shaping* Mauloa.

Longtime sailor Chad Baybayan
served as both captain and navigator
aboard Hōkūle'a on the voyage
north from Te Henua 'Enana.

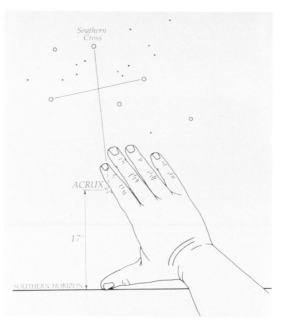

Estimating a canoe's latitude by
using one's hand to measure the
angular height of Acrux, the
bottom star in the Southern Cross,
from the southern horizon. Since
Acrux is 27° above the horizon at
the equator, when the "reading"
indicates 17°, the observer must be
located at 10° north of the equator.
This is an example of how Nainoa
combines traditional and Western
navigation methods in his
wayfinding techniques.

Bruce Blankenfeld served
in the dual roles of captain
and navigator aboard
Hawai'iloa on the 1995
journey.

Synthetic and sennit
lashings on Hawai'iloa
during sea trials.

Bruce Blankenfeld and Wally
Froiseth.

Testing a woven lauhala *sail on* Hawai'iloa.

The Six Voyaging Canoes

First came Hōkūle'a. Built by the newly formed Polynesian Voyaging Society, she sailed from Hawai'i to Tahiti in 1976. The Hawaiians have continued plying the Pacific, sailing the canoe over 70,000 nautical miles to stitch together the islands of the Polynesian Triangle and establishing their ancestors' role in the greatest feat of settlement in the ancient world. Hōkūle'a has also inspired countless individuals and groups. In 1995 the fleet of six canoes pictured below sailed over the ancient migration route from Te Henua 'Enana to Hawai'i to commemorate the discovery of the Hawaiian Islands.

Hawai'iloa • Hawai'i • 57 feet

Hōkūle'a • Hawai'i • 62 feet

Makali'i • Hawai'i • 54 feet

Takitumu • Cooks • 53 feet

Te Au o Tonga • Cooks • 72 feet

Te Aurere • Aotearoa • 57 feet

Father and son voyagers of modern Hawai'i: Myron "Pinky" Thompson (left) and his son Nainoa. Pinky Thompson was one of the most influential citizens in modern Hawai'i. A tireless man of enormous humility, he created a number of critical social and educational programs for Hawaiians. Through his mastery of the ancient techniques of Polynesian voyaging, Nainoa has followed his father's example in creating a pride and determination of people in Hawai'i and throughout Polynesia. He has used the voyaging canoe as a symbol to teach self-reliance, sustainability, and Hawaiian values.

Sailing Hōkūle'a wing-on-wing.

Anchored in Nukuhiva's Taiohae Bay, the 75-foot double canoe Tahiti Nui flies a huge flag of French Polynesia.

Makali'i is an inspirational community project of Na Kālaiwa'a Moku o Hawai'i *from the Island of Hawai'i. Under the aegis of longtime* Hōkūle'a *sailors Chad and Shorty Bertelmann, the canoe has been used for educational projects around her home island. Shorty navigated* Makali'i *north from Te Henua 'Enana. Since that voyage, the canoe took Mau Piailug on a triumphant island tour culminating in his arrival home on Satawal in Micronesia.*

Mau, Nainoa and other canoe navigators can indirectly sense when they are nearing land by disruptions in the ocean swells, greenish reflections cast by shallow lagoons onto the undersides of clouds, and the sight of seabirds (such as this Fairy Tern) flying out to sea at dawn to fish and then returning to their nests to feed their young.

Mau Piailug (left) and Tava Taupu hafting stone adz blades to begin the creation of Mauloa, *a small koa outrigger canoe. Built at Pu'uhonua o Hōnaunau on the Big Island, she was finished with steel adzes. Earlier Tava and Nainoa had searched in vain for koa logs large enough for* Hawai'iloa's *twin hulls.*

equivalent to *kahuna* in Hawaiian). More precisely they could be called prophets, shamans, or inspirational priests, as possession by a god or spirit was the hallmark of their profession. When possessed they made demands of the people, pronounced on the guilty, foretold the future, cured the sick, and pointed the way to fertile, well-watered lands waiting to be settled.[22]

Edward Robarts, who jumped ship and lived in the islands during the late 1700s and early 1800s, was pessimistic about the fate of those *'Enana* who had been driven from their land by drought or bellicose neighbors, or had been enticed into the ocean by *tau'a* visions of rich, empty lands lying just over the horizon.[23] He recorded in his journal that he had seen a number of canoes set off on such desperate expeditions, some with 30 or 40 souls jammed so close together in their leaky craft that they could barely stir. He imagined that as the people became more and more benumbed and exhausted, they eventually gave up bailing and could only watch in horror as the water rose higher and higher in the hulls until the canoe foundered, and they descended to the depths. "Thus terminates," Robarts wrote, "their truly pitiable and untimely fate."

After penning this lurid passage about the dangers of native seafaring, Robarts appears to have crafted the following passage to impress future readers with his great solicitude:

> Several families offered me their daughters in marriage to conduct them to the promised land. I have told them with tears what they might expect. Nothing could change them. It has often griev'd [me] to the heart to see a handsome young lady weeping with her neighbours a few days before her departure. It happens sometime, when a family thus leaveing is belovd by their neighbours, the canoe gets broke to atoms and they [are] led back to their houses. Some-times this step has the desired effect and sometimes not; for they will hire a small canoe and go over to another Isle and build a canoe for their purpose and come over unexpected in the night time and take on board all that is concearnd.

Some nautically informed writers thought more highly of the 'Enanan craft. For example, Porter wrote that the double-hulled canoes used for inter-island sailing within the archipelago were "capable of resisting the sea for a long time" and that those "formed for the sole purposes of going in search of lands" were even larger and sturdier in construction.[24]

Although many *'Enana* may have gone to their death in leaky, overcrowded canoes during the drought-plagued years of the early 1800s, it does not necessarily mean that all those who set sail in earlier centuries to search for new lands also foundered at sea in inadequate craft. Polynesian traditions recalling an earlier age when voyaging was more widespread are now getting some support from archaeologists. Barry Rolett, my colleague from the University of Hawai'i, has found evidence of a progressive decline in both the inter-island circulation of adzes and offshore fishing suggesting that 'Enanan deep-sea sailing capabilities waned as their societies matured.[25]

Changes in 'Enanan social structure may have played a role in this decline. Building, sailing, and maintaining voyaging canoes was (and still is) expensive, difficult, and time-consuming. Judging from oral traditions, it was primarily the chiefs who used their high position to organize people and resources for building large voyaging canoes and undertaking planned voyages of exploration and settlement. Yet chiefly power in Te Henua 'Enana apparently diminished over time and came to be rivaled or surpassed by that of the *tau'a* shamans.

Archaeologist Patrick Kirch and historical anthropologist Nicholas Thomas relate the decline of chiefly power to environmental limitations. They propose that the absence of coastal plains plus rugged interior landscapes inhibited the unification of each island, or large sections thereof, under a single chief. In addition, the scarcity of permanent streams and rivers may to have hampered the development of irrigated *taro* agriculture that, elsewhere in Polynesia, played an important role in agricultural intensification and the rise of chiefly power. With each island broken into small, warring chiefdoms, the power of the *haka'iki*, as 'Enana called their chiefs, declined, while the influence of their prophets rose. Squawking *tau'a* urging people to take to their canoes were surely no substitute for powerful chiefs able to direct the construction of large seaworthy canoes and to organize well-planned and stocked expeditions.[26]

AFTER STOPPING FOR REPAIRS and supplies at Pape'ete, Tahiti's main port, all the canoes except *Tahiti Nui* proceeded to the rural Tahitian district of Tautira. The *Hōkūle'a* family and the Tautirans have a continuing relationship. The Hawaiians host the Tautirans when they visit Hawai'i to compete in canoe races or go shopping in the big chain stores, and the Tautirans generously take in *Hōkūle'a*'s crew and supporters whenever they stop at Tahiti. On this trip the Tautirans were outdoing themselves by hosting the crews and supporters of five voyaging canoes.

We were hoping that steady trades coming from the southeast (or better yet, from the south-southeast), would enable us to cross the 750 miles from Tautira to Nukuhiva in a week or less. But the combination of variable winds punctuated by spells of stormy westerlies characteristic of the Southern Hemisphere summer that should have faded away were still lingering. As April began, we had light winds coming mostly from the east, and worse yet, from the northeast, the direction toward which we had to sail in order to reach Nukuhiva directly.

With hopes that the weather would improve, Nainoa set the departure for April 4. But that day turned out to be rainy with variable winds. As the next day dawned clear with light east-southeast trades, *Hawai'iloa, Te Aurere, Takitumu, Te Au o Tonga,* and *Makali'i* set sail. *Hōkūle'a* departed the following day, and *Tahiti Nui* left Pape'ete a day or so after that.

I was sailing aboard *Gershon, Hōkūle'a*'s escort commanded by Stephen Kornberg. We would have preferred to report that all the canoes enjoyed strong and steady trades that speeded them to Nukuhiva in time for the arrival ceremonies, optimistically set for April 12. But the winds remained fickle, teasing the sailors with intermittent spells of southeasterlies that only briefly allowed them to hoist their sails. Most of the time the wind blew lightly out of the east and northeast, forcing the escort boats to tow their charges in order to maintain the required pace. Towing was boring and distasteful. But we did not have enough time to wait for ideal winds or tack laboriously into the light headwinds plaguing us. Besides, this leg of our odyssey was simply to position the canoes for the all-important crossing to Hawai'i, not to investigate how to sail from Tahiti to Te Henua 'Enana.

Hawai'iloa and *Te Aurere* managed to reach Nukuhiva on April 12, thanks to the powerful diesel engine of Alex Jakubenko's *Kama Hele,* which towed both vessels at once. However, as the rest of the canoes were far behind, the Nukuhivans put off the arrival ceremony at Taiohae until the 14th, and the two lead canoes were directed to anchor off Taipivai, a deep valley just to the east of Taiohae, until the day of the ceremony. The crews had an opportunity to hike through this fabled valley that had been made known to Western readers by the writings of a young sailor named Herman Melville. Over a century and a half ago, he had deserted a whaling ship at Taiohae and sought refuge in Taipivai. He later elaborated on his adventures in *Typee,* an autobiographical novel that became an archetype of the South Seas romance novel.[27]

On April 13th *Takitumu*'s escorting yacht suffered an engine failure. Nainoa radioed a request that *Gershon* drop *Hōkūle'a* and head south to take *Takitumu* under tow. While *Hōkūle'a* sailed slowly toward Nukuhiva, then some 45 miles away, we motor-sailed back to *Takitumu* and found her becalmed under a starry sky. Since Nukuhiva was too far away for us to make it there in time for the ceremony on the 14th, we instead towed *Takitumu* to the island of 'Uapou to honor the request for a visit made by 'Uapou delegates at Taputapuātea.

THANKS TO AN AUDIOTAPE made for me by Ka'au McKenney, one of my former students who was serving on *Hawai'iloa,* I was later able to review the speech Georges "Toti" Teikiehu'upoko, the president of the cultural association Motu Haka, gave to welcome the voyagers who reached Taiohae in time. He spoke clearly and slowly in

'Enanan so that speakers of other Polynesian languages could follow his words. English and French translations of his speech were read afterwards so others could appreciate what he was saying. Toti began by greeting the sailors:

Mave mai e te puke Toa he'e tai. Ka'oha nui e to mātou tau hua'a mei te Moana Nui a Hau.

Eia mai nei kōtou i Te Henua 'Enana, i 'inei te tihe'ia mai o nā 'Enana 'omua ana 'oa a 2000 'ehua i tēnei, epō mai te hano atu hakato'o i tahipito tau henua kē atu mei ke'ika kōtou iho, i koute'e ai i vāveka o tēnei ava tai rui no te hua haka'ua mai, e to mātou tau mata hua'a.

Ko'utau i tēnei ā no mātou pe'au haka'ua'ia in te puke hua'a o te Moana Nui a Hau (Patitifa), Ka'oha, Talofa, Kiaora kōtou, Iaorana, Aloha, Tena Kōtou.[28]

Welcome valiant navigators, greetings to our relatives from the vast Pacific.

You are here in the Land of Men, "Terre des Hommes," where the first *'Enana* disembarked more than two thousand years ago, before your ancestors left to discover your lands, from whence you have ventured upon the ocean to come here and enable us to meet you as our distant relatives.

Bless this day when we can say to our Pacific relatives: *Ka'oha, Talofa, Kiaora Kōtou, Iaorana, Aloha, Tena Kōtou.*[29]

Next Toti spoke about where Te Henua 'Enana fit in the ancient history of Polynesia as he understood it from Te Rangi Hiroa, Emory and Sinoto, Suggs, and other researchers. He reviewed the movement from Southeast Asia to Sāmoa and Tonga, and the subsequent settlement of Te Henua 'Enana followed by the spread to other islands of Eastern Polynesia. Wisely, he left the door open for new discoveries and interpretations, as Suggs' early settlement date for Te Henua 'Enana has recently been challenged by archaeologists who argue that the archipelago was not settled until 400–700 A.D.[30]

Toti then outlined 'Enanan traditions of how their ancestors had sailed from such distant places as Vavau (which could be Vavau in the Tongan archipelago, or Vava'u, the ancient name for Porapora in the Societies), and after a long struggle had found Te Henua 'Enana. He also honored such great Polynesian voyagers of legend as Aotearoa's Kupe, the Cook Islands' Te Erui, and Hawai'i's Hawai'iloa, as well as widely-shared

Polynesian heroes central in 'Enanan mythology as Māui, who snared the sun and fished up the islands, and Tiki, the first man. Finally he spoke about the common Eastern Polynesian tradition of Hawaiki as both the legendary homeland of the Polynesians and the underworld to which the souls of the dead return. Toti concluded his speech by again saluting the voyagers:

> *Kaoha Nui ia kōtou i 'uka o te motu of Tiki. Te Henua 'Enana te*
> *puta o Havaiki, te Henua o Maui.*

> *Ka'oha* from the archipelago of Tiki, the land of the *'Enana,*
> the entrance to Hawaiki, the land of Māui!

TOTI'S SPEECH AND THE ENTHUSIASM of the Nukuhivans gave no hint of how much the *'Enana* had suffered during more than four centuries of Western contact and domination. When Mendaña chanced upon Te Henua 'Enana, his expedition was headed for the Solomon Islands—which the Spanish had "discovered" in 1567 and apparently named in hopes that the rich mines which supplied the biblical King Solomon with so much treasure were actually located on these islands. With gold and other precious commodities at stake, few among the explorers felt constrained to treat the people they encountered along the way with diplomacy and kindness. Although the gregarious *'Enana* who swarmed over Mendaña's ships may have at times appeared threatening to the Spanish, especially when they started pilfering pieces of iron, their seemingly menacing looks and petty theft hardly warranted the killings that followed. So thought Pedro Fernández de Quiros, the expedition's chief pilot who lamented in his journal that the expedition's soldiers had slaughtered two hundred people: "Their evil deeds are not things to do, nor to praise, nor to allow, nor to maintain, nor to refrain from punishing if the occasion permits."[31]

After a reprieve of 179 years, during which there is no record of other foreign vessels visiting Te Henua 'Enana, encounters between Westerners and *'Enana* resumed with Cook's brief visit to the southern group in 1774. More explorers followed and then waves of sandalwood traders and whalers broke over the islands. Protestant and Catholic missionaries also appeared as did armed warships. Porter's temporary and unauthorized occupation of Nukuhiva in 1813 was but a harbinger of the French takeover of the islands in 1842 by Admiral Dupetit-Thouars and his black warships. Sporadic fighting between the occupiers and their unwilling subjects continued for a decade or two, while the missionaries sought to destroy 'Enanan religion and culture in order to implant their own faith, and muskets obtained from visiting ships made inter-tribal warfare all the more deadly.[32]

All the while, the population was falling precipitously, primarily from such introduced diseases as smallpox, dysentery, and gonorrhea. This catastrophic depopulation was also accelerated by social disruption caused by traders and whalers, naval bombardments and occupying troops, missionaries, and other intruders. The first population estimates made in the late 1700s indicated that some 90,000 'Enana lived in the archipelago. By 1863 the 'Enana numbered only nine or ten thousand. By the mid-1920s, only a little over two thousand dispirited survivors were left. Not until 1929 in the northern group and 1933 in the southern group, did births begin to exceed deaths. This gave the 'Enana the unenviable distinction of being the last major Polynesian group to begin their demographic recovery after a horrendous decline following exposure to the outside world and its diseases and guns.[33]

When I first visited Te Henua 'Enana in 1956 on board the trading schooner *Vaitere*, the population had recovered somewhat from the low point of a quarter-century earlier. Nonetheless, the 'Enana seemed unusually dour and resentful about their isolation and poverty. The archipelago was truly a colonial backwater. The French administration was putting very little money into roads, schools, and medical facilities. Moreover, the low prices 'Enana received for copra and other local products in contrast to the high prices they had to pay for cloth, kerosene, galvanized steel roofing sheets, and other imported goods seemed to be the result of a particularly insidious conspiracy. Within French Polynesia (then known by the ponderous title of Les Établissements Françaises du Pacifique), virtually all import and export goods passed through Tahiti's port of Pape'ete. Freight charges between the port and Nukuhiva were said to be greater than those between Tahiti and France.

In 1995 we saw a much reinvigorated Te Henua 'Enana with a growing population of over 7,000. Some of the material prosperity stemming from France's nuclear testing program had flowed to the archipelago. Whereas thirty-nine years earlier I had seen only a few short roads in and around the main settlements, there were now networks of roads over each major island. Some political realists said the French had funded the building of roads, as well as wharves, schools, medical clinics, and other public facilities, to buy votes. They needed the support of the predominately Catholic electorate of Te Henua 'Enana to oppose Protestant Tahitian politicians who were seeking increased autonomy or outright independence from France. Whatever the case, the benefits from these expenditures were very real to the people. In addition, through grants and loan programs, well-paying local government jobs, and savings brought home from working on Tahiti or at nuclear testing facilities in the Tuamotus, many people were able to build substantial houses equipped with running water, electricity, and other conveniences.

Yet the 'Enana still felt relatively isolated compared to the Tahitians and other

Polynesians. For example, whereas cultural groups, sports teams, and tourists frequently traveled from Tahiti to Hawai'i, the Cook Islands, Aotearoa, and other parts of the Pacific, and delegates from these and other island nations often visited Tahiti, the *'Enana* remained largely outside of this traffic. More to the point of this chapter, neither *Hōkūle'a* nor any of the other modern voyaging canoes had previously visited the archipelago. This was not for want of trying. On the return leg of the Voyage of Rediscovery, the Hawaiians had waited in vain at the Tuamotu atoll of Rangiroa for the right winds that would allow them to sail back to Hawai'i via Te Henua 'Enana.

Nukuhiva's dynamic mayor, Lucien "Ro'o" Kimitete, told us at Nukuhiva that this was why the coming of the canoes in 1995 meant so much to his people. The voyagers from faraway archipelagos reminded them that they were part of a larger whole, a widespread family of seafaring peoples. Six weeks later in Hawai'i, he repeated his remarks at a reception to honor the newly arrived canoe voyagers held at the residence of Hawai'i's Governor Ben Cayetano. Leaders from each of the island nations represented were asked to speak about what the voyage meant to their people. When it was Te Henua 'Enana's turn, Ro'o took the floor and explained (speaking in French, followed by his wife Debora's English translation) how much the people of Nukuhiva had gained from being the gathering point of the canoes before they sailed for Hawai'i. After telling the crowd how they have been isolated from the rest of Polynesia for so long, he shared what he had felt as he watched the canoes entering Taiohae Bay: "When I saw their sails appear on the horizon, I knew that we were no longer alone."

Chapter Six

Getting Underway

NUKUHIVA RISES ABRUPTLY out of the sea. Long ocean swells slam into her sheer cliffs—some more than a thousand feet high, but broken by several spectacular bays. It is as though the coral reefs, beaches, and coastal flats of an island like Tahiti or Rarotonga had all been submerged, leaving only a mountainous core punctuated by drowned valleys turned into bays.

Taiohae, on the south shore, is the most spacious of Nukuhiva's bays. The canoes and escorts had plenty of room to anchor, with space left for the constant stream of cruising yachts as well as the small freighters and government ships that call there. A collection of homes, stores, government buildings, and a few hotel bungalows lie scattered along the crescent bay's narrow shore. Beyond, the land rises steeply to commanding crests. Rough roads lead out of this amphitheater to the well-watered but steeply sloped valleys to the east and to the dry uplands of the island's western half.

Unfortunately, there was little time for sightseeing. After the welcoming ceremony, the sailors went to work taking on stores, including fresh fruits and some specially preserved native foods for a diet experiment. And there were the constant details: checking sails, rigging, and hulls; and fixing anything that needed attention. The navigators who were to guide the canoes to Hawai'i studied star charts, checking route maps and mentally rehearsing each successive stage of the voyage ahead. Just before sailing, they would put all their charts and papers away, and at sea use only their mental maps of the sky, the route and the location of the islands.

AFTER THE VOYAGE OF REDISCOVERY, Nainoa began teaching canoe navigation to selected crewmembers, including Chad Baybayan, Bruce Blankenfeld, and Shorty Bertelmann, who now were slated to guide *Hōkūle'a*, *Hawai'iloa*, and *Makali'i*. In the early 1990s, he began training candidates from Aotearoa, the Cook Islands, and Tahiti, as well as new recruits from Hawai'i. Nine of the navigators he trained—seven men

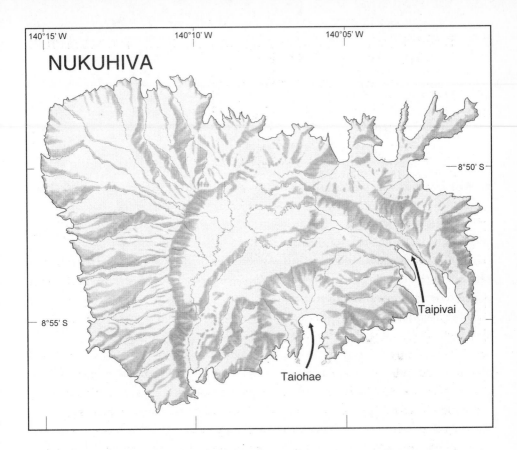

140°15' W   140°10' W   140°05' W

NUKUHIVA

8°50' S

8°55' S

Taipivai

Taiohae

and two women—were about to apply their hard-earned skills by guiding the three Hawaiian canoes, along with *Te Au o Tonga* and *Te Aurere*, to Hawai'i. (As neither *Tahiti Nui* nor *Takitumu* had trained canoe navigators on board, they were to be guided with modern instruments.)

Although the navigators were not going to use any charts or instruments on the voyage, the system they had been taught included some modern concepts and techniques that Nainoa grafted onto a traditional base, a process which began during his apprenticeship to Mau Piailug. When the master navigator began preparing Nainoa for the 1980 voyage to Tahiti, he found the young Hawaiian to be an excellent pupil. Not only did he have a tremendous drive to learn, but he had already spent countless nights studying the stars in the heavens as well as their images projected in Bishop Museum's planetarium under the careful guidance of astronomer Will Kyselka. Nainoa readily grasped Mau's 32-point compass and how to orient and steer on the stars and constellations that rise and set at or near these points. With more effort, he learned how to switch to other stars higher in the sky when clouds or haze obscured the horizon and also how to use the sun and moon. Learning to discriminate regular ocean swells from confused seas, and using them for orientation and steering whenever the sky was overcast or at midday when the sun was high in the sky, was much more difficult. However, not enough time remained for Nainoa to learn Mau's sophisticated method of dead reckoning.[1]

Dead reckoning (D.R.) refers to the process of estimating the changing position of a vessel at sea. Although the term is peculiarly English, it describes a universal function that, for example, the French and Spanish simply call "navigating by estimation." Earlier Western navigators estimated their position by throwing astern a float attached to a line knotted at precise intervals, and then timing the passage of the knots as the line unreeled. That gave them their speed in "knots," which now refers to nautical miles per hour. Multiplying this figure times hours spent on a compass bearing yielded their estimated track since their last actual or estimated position. When drawn on a nautical chart, the end point of this track gave them the current D.R. position in terms of a latitude and longitude intersection.

Mau dead reckons in an entirely different way. He mentally tracks his canoe moving along the course line to his destination, visualizing when the bearing to a reference island located to one side of the course line shifts from one point of his conceptual compass to another as the canoe approaches, draws parallel to, and then sails past the reference island. By mentally projecting each star compass bearing back across the course line, he cuts that line into segments that he calls *etak*. The image of completing successive segments gives him a mental map of the progress of the voyage until, finally, if his calculations are correct, the target island comes into view. If that doesn't sound confusing enough, consider also that the reference island, typically a low atoll, is always too far away to be seen from the canoe! In effect, Mau employs it as an invisible prop to estimate course and distance sailed by means of shifting star bearings.

To master such a method takes considerable time. Mau studied with his grandfather from age five to eighteen before he was allowed to navigate solo from one atoll to another. Nainoa had but a few months to learn this seemingly arcane method, and then apply it on the long voyage to Tahiti. Accordingly, Mau and his pupil worked out a more easily learned way of dead reckoning that combined traditional and contemporary concepts and procedures.

For example, to prepare for the voyage to Tahiti, Nainoa analyzed wind and current records (in place of lost traditional knowledge) in order to estimate the conditions that the canoe would encounter. He then matched the estimated conditions with *Hōkūle'a*'s sailing characteristics to draw a reference course line on a nautical chart, a sort of ideal course line to follow and against which he could mentally plot *Hōkūle'a*'s progress. As no charts, tables, or other aids were to be used at sea, Nainoa memorized the course line, along with the locations of the islands and the wind zones to be crossed.

Once underway, Nainoa guided *Hōkūle'a* by reference to his memorized course line and Mau's 32-point compass. To keep track of where the canoe was sailing, twice a day he estimated the direction (in compass points) and distance (in nautical miles) sailed by the canoe—initially from the departure point, and then successively from his last position estimate. He derived these figures by estimating the canoe's heading, gauging its speed by counting the seconds it took a wood chip to pass from bow to stern, and then factoring in estimated current drift and leeway.

To make a record of his dead reckoning positions without writing them down or charting them, each day Nainoa spoke into a tape recorder at sunrise and sunset, specifying how far in nautical miles and toward which star compass point he reckoned the canoe had sailed over the preceding 12 hours. After the voyage, we converted Nainoa's position approximations into latitude and longitude fixes and plotted them on a chart to indicate where Nainoa estimated *Hōkūle'a* had sailed.

Comparing the canoe's estimated track with her actual track (derived from position fixes obtained remotely by the ARGOS satellite tracking system[2]), enabled us to resolve a major controversy over navigational error. Andrew Sharp and others had argued that naked-eye course setting and steering by the stars, sun, moon, and ocean swells were inherently inaccurate, as was estimating current drift and leeway. In their way of thinking, just one degree of error each day for a month would throw the navigator's calculations off by 30 degrees. But such reasoning assumes that error accumulates in one direction. The 1980 figures showed that in the mind of a good navigator errors (or perhaps better said, "misestimates") tend to be random and therefore cancel each other.[3]

NAINOA HAS CONTINUED TO ADD to Mau's teaching. One night while Mau and I were drinking beer in Tahiti just before leaving for Nukuhiva, out of the blue he said to me: "You know Ben, that Nainoa, he knows hundreds of stars. Me, I only use thirty-four." Although exaggerating some, Mau was expressing a real contrast. Nainoa has built upon Mau's teachings to develop a system, which, though based on traditional wayfinding methods, uses many more stars and involves a number of novel ways of observing and analyzing them.

Nainoa has thus made canoe navigation much more accessible to contemporary students, precisely because he employs measures, concepts, and simple mathematical procedures already familiar to them. Max Yarawamai, Mau's distant relative who was scheduled to sail to Hawai'i on *Hawai'iloa*, made this point to me one evening at his Big Island home. He described how, while attending Nainoa's navigation classes and talking with the local students, he came to realize how much it was easier for them to

Canoe Navigators from Nukuhiva to Hawai'i

Canoe	Navigator
Hawai'iloa	Bruce Blankenfeld
Hōkūle'a	Chad Baybayan assisted by Moana Doi & Pi'ikea Miller
Makali'i	Milton "Shorty" Bertelmann
Te Au o Tonga	Tua Pittman & Pe'ia Tau'ati
Te Aurere	Jacko Thatcher & Piripi Evans

learn Nainoa's way of navigating than one based on *etak* and other concepts and methods that were utterly alien to them.

ON SUNDAY APRIL 16th, the Nukuhivans held a departure ceremony that began with rousing chants and dances. Presiding was Ro'o Kimitete. Dressed only in a purple *pareu*, a cloth wrap-around worn by men as well as women, the charismatic, strongly built mayor vigorously led a group of young Nukuhivans through a series of impressive performances. The crews from the canoes responded in kind with their respective ways of using body and voice to mark the fleet's departure.

The pace shifted when Keli'i Tau'ā, the *kahuna pule* (prayer expert) from Maui, stepped forward. First he introduced his acolytes, who chanted—shouting to the heavens—to the *akua* and *'aumākua*, the gods and guardian spirits, beseeching them to grant the canoes and their crews a safe and swift passage to Hawai'i. Then Keli'i himself began chanting a *ko'i honua*, a genealogical chant, but not one dedicated to a high chief as is the normal practice. Instead he had composed the *ko'i honua* to honor *Hawai'iloa*. In a soft, almost conversational tone, he recounted the ancestry of the canoe, beginning with the creation of the trees and their conversion into canoe hulls. Raising his voice, he then chanted about finishing the canoe and the voyage's unfolding, including in his verbal portrait the backgrounds of the key persons and groups that planned the voyage, built the canoe, and were sailing her.

Finally, came the *'awa* (kava) ceremony to bind the canoe crews together. With Keli'i presiding, his assistants mixed pounded *'awa* root with water in a large wooden bowl to make the ritual drink. Hawaiian youths—walking crouched over with knees bent—carried coconut cups of *'awa* to each of the crewmembers sitting cross-legged on the grass in a big circle. With some eighty sailors, the ceremony proceeded slowly, but despite the hot sun and the quivering thigh muscles of the sweating bearers, no effort was made to hurry. Each crewmember partook in turn of the *'awa*, and key persons among them had plenty of time to express to the assembly their *mana'o*, their thoughts, about the forthcoming voyage.

DURING THE CEREMONY, cool puffs of wind coming from the east-southeast began to penetrate into Taiohae Bay, cooling everyone and hinting that conditions would soon be right for sailing to Hawai'i. But last minute problems kept the canoes from leaving for several more days.

Everybody was anxious to depart, particularly Nainoa. *Hawai'iloa* had to be in Honolulu Harbor on May 19, a month hence, to be loaded aboard a Seattle-bound freighter to fulfill his promise to bring the canoe to the Native Alaskans. From Seattle the crew would sail her up Alaska's Inland Passage, stopping at villages and towns along the way to show the canoe to the people who had provided the spruce logs for her construction and to thank them for their gift. *Hōkūle'a* was also scheduled to be on the freighter to fulfill an earlier commitment to bring the canoe to the many expatriate Hawaiians living along the West Coast. The schedule was a little tight, but with good winds it wouldn't take more than three weeks to reach Hawai'i.

Of course it would have been more challenging to sail the canoes to North America. This could have been done by first heading north-northwest across the trades, then turning east upon reaching higher latitudes to sail before the prevailing westerlies.[4] But preparing for and undertaking such a long, roundabout voyage would not have left enough time to complete the Alaska and West Coast missions by the end of summer.

FINALLY ON APRIL 19th, *Te Aurere, Hawai'iloa,* and *Makali'i* set sail at two to three hour intervals. On the 20th, *Te Au o Tonga, Takitumu,* and *Hōkūle'a* left in that order at the same intervals. Staggering the departures over the course of two days would enable the navigators to do their jobs without being disturbed by the sight of other canoes.

But one canoe was missing from the fleet: *Tahiti Nui.* The Tahitians had been the last to reach Nukuhiva. Soon thereafter an official of the French court system seized the yacht that had towed *Tahiti Nui* from Tahiti, because in leaving Tahitian waters the owner had violated the terms of his lease-purchase contract. Discouraged, but not willing to give up, the Tahitian sailors prepared for a final make-or-break sea trial. Just as the first canoes were getting underway on the 19th, a government boat towed *Tahiti Nui* out to sea to test if she could sail well enough to head for Hawai'i. Sadly, there was no miracle. From a distance, it looked like the giant canoe was slowly losing ground as the crew attempted to slant her into the light trade winds.

Nonetheless, the fleet—now reduced to six canoes—was at last underway, heading for Hawai'i over a seaway that centuries before is thought to have been pioneered by the first people to find and settle Polynesia's northernmost islands.

Chapter Seven

North-Northwest to Hawai'i

FRESH EASTERLIES GREETED the canoes as they emerged one by one from Nukuhiva's wind shadow. After being bottled up in Taiohae Bay, the sailors welcomed the cool, if light, trade winds. *Hōkūle'a* and her escort, the yacht *Gershon* on which I was serving, were the last to leave Taiohae on the second day. At dawn the following morning, all we could see of Nukuhiva off to the south were the tops of her mountains piercing the horizon. By then we were drawing abeam of Eiao, a small volcanic island that, along with two even tinier islets, marks the northern limits of Te Henua 'Enana. Fine, particularly hard basalt from Eiao was once employed throughout the archipelago for making adzes, chisels, and other tools. This volcanic outcropping now lay deserted. The *'Enana* no longer have any need for stone tools, nor do they have any sailing canoes capable of reaching the island. When Eiao slipped below the horizon later that day, there were no more islands to be seen. Almost 2,000 miles of unbroken blue water lay ahead of us before the peaks of Hawai'i would rise out of the sea.

Nainoa was sailing on *Hōkūle'a*, but not as the navigator. He had handed that job over to Chad Baybayan, who was also serving as the captain. Chad, who had been sailing aboard *Hōkūle'a* since the late 1970s, was assisted by apprentice navigators Moana Doi and Pi'ikea Miller, two of the three women sailing in the fleet. Nainoa's role was to coordinate all the canoes, using a single-sideband transceiver to keep in contact with them and their escorts. This was why he launched *Hōkūle'a* last, casting the veteran canoe and himself in the role of *kahu*, guardians following the flock.

As we trailed *Hōkūle'a*, I fell into a routine. In addition to standing watch, steering, and doing chores, I spent hours listening to the short-wave radio getting news of the fleet. At sunrise and sunset, the canoe navigators would report to Nainoa, each giving his dead reckoning (D.R.) position, speed, and heading, along with details on wind, sea state, cloud cover, and rain. Then at 8:00 a.m. and 8:00 p.m. the captains of the escort vessels would report their respective positions as derived from Global Positioning

System (GPS) fixes, as well their speed, heading, and local weather data. These reports, plus radio discussions between Nainoa and the captains and navigators of the canoes and escorts provided me with an overall perspective of the unfolding voyage.

As *Hawai'iloa* was my focus, I also needed to gather more detailed information on how she was being sailed and navigated, as well as what was happening on board. Rather than conduct radio interviews with those sailing on *Hawai'iloa*, I counted on Cliff Watson, a television cameraman who was covering the journey for NHCAP. His videotapes of daily life aboard the canoe, and his twice-daily interviews with Bruce Blankenfeld, the canoe's navigator and captain, were to prove invaluable for portraying what the navigator-captain and others on board were doing and thinking. In addition, post-voyage interviews, particularly those conducted by filmmaker Gail Evenari, helped fill out the picture.

BRUCE BLANKENFELD, a Hawaiian stevedore in his late thirties, was making his first long voyage as the sole navigator. He was in high school when *Hōkūle'a* was being built, and didn't get a good look at the finished canoe until just before she sailed for Tahiti in 1976. Bruce recalls feeling that he was looking at something "out of the past," yet "important for the future." As a waterman who fished, paddled racing canoes, scuba-dived, and surfed, he was naturally drawn to *Hōkūle'a*, and also admits to being "awestruck that the canoe was a real community effort."

When *Hōkūle'a* returned from Tahiti, he started going on day sails and served on the ill-fated 1978 voyage. After the capsize Bruce stuck with the project, helping to rebuild the canoe and get her ready for a second attempt. He sailed on the 1980 voyage, and on the subsequent Voyage of Rediscovery, during which he and I served together on the leg from Rarotonga to Aotearoa. When Nainoa began training a new generation of navigators, Bruce gladly volunteered and was able to exercise his new skills on the 1992 return of *Hōkūle'a* from Rarotonga to Hawai'i, which he jointly navigated with Kimo Lyman. Now he was guiding *Hawai'iloa* entirely on his own.

NHCAP had asked Cliff Watson to make audio recordings of Bruce's twice-daily navigation reports, as well as to videotape scenes of everyday life aboard *Hawai'iloa*. But he could not resist expanding the assignment by interviewing Bruce in depth. The navigator had a good idea just what people wanted to know about voyaging from serving as an instructor on educational cruises and was happy to share his thoughts on voyaging as well as on how he was applying his training and skills to the tasks at hand.

DURING HIS FIRST INTERVIEWS, Bruce explained how the reference course line was designed to bring the canoes safely from Nukuhiva to Hawai'i's O'ahu Island. Heading straight for O'ahu might seem the most logical way to go. However, since canoes taking

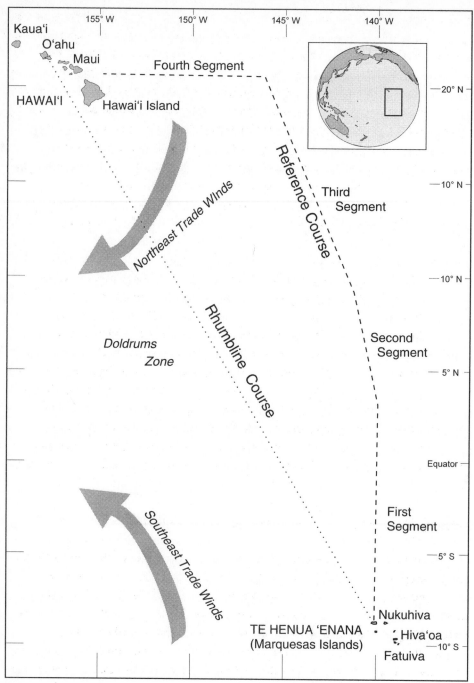

Reference course from Nukuhiva to Honolulu.

a direct route would pass Hawai'i Island on its southwestern, leeward side they would risk getting stuck in the long wind shadow cast by the island's great bulk cutting off the trade winds. Hawai'i is dominated by two great volcanoes which rise almost 14,000 feet above sea level. Mauna Kea (White Mountain, as its peak is often covered with snow in the winter) stands to the northwest, and the still-active Mauna Loa (Long Mountain) is in the southeast. Any canoes becalmed in the lee of Mauna Loa would probably drift far to the west before they were finally out of the wind shadow. By then they would be leeward of O'ahu and would have to tack to that island against the trade winds—no easy feat if the trades were strong.[1] To avoid such a predicament, Nainoa constructed an indirect, dogleg course designed to bring the canoes from Nukuhiva to a point parallel to Hawai'i Island, but well on its eastern (windward) side. Then they could safely turn downwind, heading west to make landfall on the Big Island and sail around it to O'ahu.

Following Nainoa's model, Bruce divided *Hawai'iloa*'s reference course into four segments. From Nukuhiva—located at 9° south latitude—the line extended due north to 3° north latitude (180 miles north of the equator, since one degree of latitude equals sixty nautical miles). The second segment, which ran from 3° to 9° north latitude, covered the Intertropical Convergence Zone between the trade wind belts that sailors usually call the doldrums, a term inspired by the dulling, boring effect of being stuck in the hot, humid calms common there. Bruce set the reference course line in this segment one "house" (*hale*, or compass point of 11° 15') to the west of north, a heading Nainoa calls *Haka Ho'olua* (north by west). The third and longest segment extended from 9° to 20° 30' north latitude, slanting across the northeast trade wind belt at an angle of two houses west of north (*Nā Leo Ho'olua* or north-northwest). Although the course line gives up considerable easting at this angle, it is nonetheless conservatively angled to be sure that *Hawai'iloa* ends up well to the east of the Big Island when it reaches its latitude. At that point, the crew would turn *Hawai'iloa* due west and sail carefully downwind while searching for the sight of Mauna Kea, the 13,825 foot peak that is Hawai'i's tallest mountain.

Bruce used his memorized image of the course line as a guide for course setting and for keeping track of where *Hawai'iloa* was sailing. Working from his estimates of course and speed made good, at each sunrise and sunset he mentally calculated how many miles *Hawai'iloa* was east or west of the course line and her latitude phrased in terms of degrees and minutes. Where the two estimates intersected served as a D.R. position that summarized where he thought the canoe was at the time. By plotting each successive D.R. position along with the GPS fixes from the canoe's escort, I was able to see at a glance the canoe's actual and estimated track.

DURING THE FIRST SEGMENT, the wind blew favorably from the east and east-southeast, enabling Bruce to head *Hawai'iloa* more or less directly north. But several days out, it began coming more out of the northeast, forcing the canoe to fall off two houses to the west of north. This didn't worry the navigator as the reference course had been so conservatively set that the canoe could give up some easting at this point and still stay well to the east of the Hawaiian chain. However, the GPS fixes from *Hawai'iloa's* escort, *Kama Hele*, indicated that Bruce was beginning to place the canoe slightly to the east of her actual position.[2] In contrast, his latitude estimates, which were based on his judgment of the canoe's speed as well as star sights, more closely reflected the canoe's northward progress.

Excitement grew as the canoes approached the equator. Late on April 23, *Hawai'iloa* crossed the line first. Three canoes made it across on the 24th and the remaining two crossed over during the pre-dawn hours on the 25th. Comparing the GPS positions of the escort boats with the D.R. positions of the canoes indicated that the navigators were doing a fairly good job of dead reckoning, although some were underestimating their latitude, that is, their northward progress. This probably reflected a common tendency to slightly underestimate sailing speed.

Next came the doldrums. If global wind flows were exactly symmetrical, the transition zone from the southeast to the northeast trades would be centered on the equator. But in the Eastern Pacific the southeast trades usually extend north across the equator, pushing the doldrums zone to between 3° and 9° north. There the spread, intensity, and duration of the doldrums can vary wildly. Whereas we got stuck in calms and light airs for a week during the 1976 Tahiti crossing, when *Hōkūle'a* and *Hawai'iloa* sailed to Tahiti on this trek they didn't experience any real calms, only a band of light easterlies that took a day and a half to cross. Everyone thus wondered whether the fleet would be delayed only a few days by light winds or become mired in extended calms.

As the canoes headed north, the brisk easterly winds that had taken them across the equator and into the Northern Hemisphere showed no signs of faltering. But during the evening of April 24th, the skies clouded over and it began raining. Without a star to be seen, *Hawai'iloa's* crew had to stay on course by steering on the wind and the swells. Later that night, what Bruce called the "mother of all squalls" hit, forcing the crew to lower the entire sail rig—masts, booms, and sails. Though disappointed with the weather change, Bruce was not at all surprised for at sunrise he estimated the canoe had almost reached 3° north, right where such transitional weather can be expected.

Fortunately, although it remained cloudy, the easterly winds picked up a little during the day, enabling the canoe to keep heading slightly west of north at four to five knots.* *Te Au o Tonga*, then sailing just out of sight and slightly behind *Hawai'iloa*,

---

* One knot is 1.00 nautical mile per hour, or a little over 0.5 meters per second.

reported similar conditions. The moderate easterlies held up during the night and into the morning of the 26th. However, hopes for a quick passage through the doldrums sagged that afternoon when the wind began to falter. During the sunset radio session, the other canoes reported that they were either becalmed or were sailing slowly in very light easterlies.

THEN NAINOA DROPPED HIS BOMBSHELL. He had just learned from Honolulu that the May 19th deadline to ship *Hawai'iloa* and *Hōkūle'a* to Seattle had been moved forward five days to the 14th. The navigator—whose careful nature leads him to always consider worst case scenarios—warned us that unless the canoes could get through the doldrums quickly, and then have steady winds the rest of the way, they might miss the deadline, causing the Alaska and California cruises to be cancelled.

After stressing the cultural importance of these missions, Nainoa urged each captain and crew to consider having their escort boats tow them through the doldrums, or, if they had an auxiliary engine, to motor through them. Although Nainoa told the captains that it was up to each of them to decide whether or not to use a power assist, he made it clear that he hoped the whole fleet would go along with his proposal. After consulting with their crews, the captains reported back, acknowledging the crisis and raising no objections to Nainoa's plan. In fact, the skippers of *Te Aurere* and *Takitumu* reported they had already cranked up their outboard motors.

The doldrums turned out to be fairly mild. The canoes were seldom totally becalmed for more than a few hours at a time. Very light easterlies prevailed, enabling them, particularly those with a power assist, to make fairly steady but slow progress to the north. Only *Hōkūle'a* transited the zone without assistance. Aboard *Gershon* we admired how Chad Baybayan and his crew kept the canoe sailing and avoided the temptation of taking a tow. *Hawai'iloa* took a tow only once when an oily, flat calm left the canoe dead in the water for several hours.

Te Au o Tonga shot way ahead of all the other canoes during this period, quickly exiting the doldrums and reaching 12° 38' north by the evening of April 29. This put her ahead of the other canoes by between two to four degrees of latitude (120 to 240 miles). Although *Te Au o Tonga* had left Nukuhiva on April 20, a day after *Hawai'iloa*, her speed enabled the Cook Islanders to gain on the Hawaiian canoe and overtake her on the 26th just as the doldrums were settling in. Once out of the doldrums, she sped off well ahead of the other canoes.

Sir Thomas credits *Te Au o Tonga*'s speed to the genius of the ancient Tahitian naval architects who first developed the *tipaerua* design that he had recreated in plywood. This design features low slim bows and high curving sterns extending well aft of the waterline. According to his analysis, the slim entry of *Te Au o Tonga*'s hulls allows them to slice through the water without raising much of a bow wave, thereby lessening drag, the enemy of speed. Papa Tom also theorized that the way the canoe's arched sterns extended well past the waterline levered the bows up, keeping them from digging into the sea.

Some credit for the canoe's speed must also go to its Hawaiian sail rig. After the ceremony at Taputapuātea, a squall had dismasted *Te Au o Tonga* on the way to Tahiti. When the disabled canoe tied up in Pape'ete Harbor, Wally Froiseth and several sailors from the Hawaiian canoes quickly removed the remains of *Te Au o Tonga*'s original sail rig and in a few days made a new set of masts and booms and rigged them with a spare set of *Hōkūle'a* sails. With her new rig, *Te Au o Tonga* was a winner.

But there was another reason why the big Rarotongan canoe transited the doldrums so quickly. Papa Tom was proud of *Te Au o Tonga*'s speed and was determined to reach Hawai'i before all the other canoes. He had chafed at having to leave Nukuhiva on the second day of the canoe departures, and he was not going to let the doldrums deter his quest to be first. Right after Nainoa requested that the canoes take a tow or turn on their engines, Sir Thomas fired up *Te Au o Tonga*'s powerful diesel engine.

Few people in the fleet were aware that *Te Au o Tonga* had such a powerplant. When I went aboard the canoe at Ra'iātea, one of the sailors asked me to take a look inside the starboard hull. When I asked him why, he just grinned and said to take a peep. Deep inside the hull, I spotted a bright blue Volvo marine engine. A drive shaft led aft, disappearing into a metal tube that penetrated the stern below the waterline. Nestled in the tube was a retractable propeller that when extended could drive the canoe at a good clip.

Later, while having dinner at Nukuhiva with Sir Thomas and the Paramount Chief of Rarotonga (his late wife's daughter), I asked him about the engine. He assured me that it was only used for getting in and out of harbors and through passes. Having the engine was certainly prudent, as big voyaging canoes cannot be easily maneuvered in confined waters by sail and paddle alone. And using the engine to power through the doldrums was, of course, in line with Nainoa's request. Yet when the other canoes were reporting over the radio that they were under tow or had turned on their outboard motors, we learned only indirectly that *Te Au o Tonga* was also under power. During the first reports from the escort boats as the fleet entered the doldrums, Peter Giles, the Canadian skipper of the yacht escorting the big canoe, drolly reported that he was motoring north to keep up with *Te Au o Tonga* because she was caught in a strong "Swedish current." Later in Hawai'i, the sailor who back in Ra'iātea had told me to take a peek inside *Te Au o Tonga*'s starboard hull, complained about how he and his mates had to put up with the noise and fumes of that "bloody engine" for 18 hours as they motored north.

SOON AFTER THE CANOES emerged from the doldrums and caught the northeast trades, *Takitumu* raced ahead of its escorting yacht, *Pozzuolana*, and disappeared in the darkness. Attempts to raise her on the radio failed, and when the sun rose the next morning, *Takitumu* was neither to be seen nor heard. Something like this had happened earlier when the yacht *On the Way* had lost sight of her charge, *Te Aurere*, and could not raise her on the radio. That crisis was soon resolved when *Te Aurere*'s crew recharged their dead batteries and restored radio and then visual contact. However, *Takitumu*'s disappearance was more alarming because she was so lightly built and her enthusiastic crew lacked much deep-sea experience.

Terepai Maoate Jr., the young Cook Islander who had led the effort to gain permission to sail *Takitumu* to Hawai'i, was serving as her captain and navigator. Junior, as everyone called him, had some sailing experience, including service on *Takitumu* when Tom Davis took the canoe from Rarotonga to Tahiti and back in 1993. However, he had not been trained in canoe navigation, and apparently didn't have any formal instruction in modern methods either. He was therefore using a magnetic compass, charts, and a GPS unit to guide *Takitumu*. Yet as the fleet proceeded northward, and Junior heard all the other canoes reporting their positions according to Nainoa's system, he became more and more curious about how his counterparts were navigating. Finally, he asked Nainoa to give him a crash course on canoe navigation over the radio. Nainoa obliged, and for several nights, we could listen to this unique example of distance learning at sea.

Despite the young Cook Islander's enthusiasm for learning navigation, he did not seem to fully grasp the need for cooperating with the other vessels in the fleet, and above all, his own escort boat. From the start of the voyage, Junior had been complaining about being saddled with an escort that was much slower than his canoe. Earlier, we had heard him bragging over the radio about how *Takitumu* could "really take off," leaving *Pozzuolana* far behind. When the winds picked up a few days out of Nukuhiva, he began sailing so far ahead of his escort that the yacht's skipper had to radio him repeatedly to slow down. After one incident in which the canoe was out of sight for hours, the skipper complained to Nainoa who in turn lectured Junior about not running away from his escort.

As the morning wore on without any radio contact with the lost canoe, worry grew that *Takitumu* might have capsized or been dismasted. If she were not found soon, the other canoes would have to start sailing back and forth in an organized search pattern. But before any such action had to be taken, we heard a faint call for help on an international distress channel. An anxious voice was calling from *Takitumu*. The canoe had somehow gone off the regular frequency for communicating with *Pozzuolana*, and the radio operator had been desperately cycling through the channels appealing for help.

When two-way radio contact was reestablished, Junior expressed great concern that the escort boat had lost them. After giving *Takitumu*'s GPS position, he said that he would wait there for *Pozzuolana* to catch up. When *Pozzuolana*'s skipper got on the radio, he proposed that they hasten their rendezvous by each sailing to a midway point on converging courses plotted by his GPS. Junior refused and without explaining why reiterated that he would wait for *Pozzuolana*. After some hemming and hawing over the airways, he finally confessed that his canoe couldn't sail because she had been dismasted.

As the young skipper later admitted, he had been driving *Takitumu* as fast as she would sail, trying to catch up with *Te Au o Tonga* and take the lead away from the big canoe. While racing ahead, the yard (the spar along the top of *Takitumu*'s lateen sail) suddenly shattered under the strain. The sail dropped into the water, and the drag snapped the mast off at its base, leaving the canoe helpless.[3] Once *Pozzuolana* reached the canoe, the shortened mast was jury-rigged, and the canoe's lateen sail raised with a spare boom. With her somewhat chastened crew, *Takitumu* set sail again, though at a more moderate pace.

ON THIS VOYAGE both Bruce Blankenfeld and Chad Baybayan combined the roles of captain and navigator on their respective canoes. Although we don't know for sure if early Polynesian sailors did the same, the broad meaning of the Hawaiian term *ho'okele wa'a* suggests just that. The Pukui-Elbert dictionary translates it as: "steersman; helmsman; navigator and to sail or navigate as the master of a ship."[4] Moreover, to take a living example, we know for sure that Mau and other *palu* from his part of Micronesia are in effect the captains of their canoes as well as the navigators.

Being a canoe navigator, particularly one also in charge of the running of the canoe, is not at all easy. Among other things, in order to keep precise track of their canoe's position always in mind navigators hardly sleep. Once when one of Mau Piailug's admiring fans asked him: "Who navigates when you sleep?" he replied tersely with a smile: "I no sleep, I'm a navigator." Yet he and the other navigator-captains cannot let their round-the-clock duties and lack of sleep weigh them down and make them irritable. Above all, they always have to treat their crew fairly and with tact.

In an interview conducted just before *Hōkūle'a* and *Hawai'iloa* left for the South Pacific, Mau outlined the difference between good and bad *palu*, focusing on leadership style rather than navigational competence:

> There are some who are good, and some who are not good. People in general
> look at the navigators and see how they act and how they treat their crew.
> People can observe the bad navigators, those who are bad in character, and

don't want to sail with them. They can also see the good navigators, those who treat their crew well, and they want to sail with them.

On board *Hawai'iloa*, Bruce discussed with Cliff how he was striving to be a good leader by treating each crew member fairly and with respect, and by encouraging them to learn their jobs well and always try to do the best they can:

> As far as leadership goes, it's important to make people feel competent in what they are doing. If you recognize that crew members are not doing things right, you just kinda of urge them on, nudging them towards getting it right. You don't just take over and order them to do this or that. You just say, "how about it if you do it this way." And then when they try and succeed, they feel that they are really contributing and they feel good about themselves.

Bruce considered *Hawai'iloa*'s crew top-notch and did not hesitate to compliment them on their efforts. For example, right after exiting the doldrums and entering the northeast trades, Bruce told the crew:

> You guys have done a great job. Everyone who comes on watch has been doing an awesome job. Myself, I have no problems with anything. I'm so comfortable with you guys, you are doing such a great job, that I do not feel that I have to keep on top of you, telling you to steer up or steer down.

The navigator-captain also made a special effort to keep everybody informed about the canoe's progress and what was happening elsewhere in the fleet. In addition, to mark the transition from one segment of the trip to the next, he had key crewmembers give a *pule* (prayer), followed by a short talk. Kimo Lyman, an accomplished yachtsman and longtime *Hōkūle'a* sailor serving as first watch captain, gave an uplifting prayer upon completing the first segment of the voyage. Then he complimented the crew on getting *Hawai'iloa* across the equator so quickly and outlined the challenges that lay ahead in the doldrums. At the next transition, second watch captain Gary Yuen, an excellent seaman and a fine cook, gave his *pule*, and talked about how the crew had worked together to get through the doldrums and about what was to be expected in the northeast trades.

Bruce also had those crewmembers with special assignments talk about their areas of concern. Archie Kalepa, a lifeguard from Maui who was the canoe's safety officer, spoke about using safety harnesses and what to do if anyone fell overboard. Kimo Lyman and Ka'au McKenney briefed the crew on using the shortwave radio and the

EPIRB unit. And physician Nate Wong talked about emergency medical procedures as well as day-to-day health concerns.

In addition, Bruce instituted a series of informal sessions designed to boost morale. On long ocean crossings, it is all too easy to get bored and then depressed. As crewmembers turn inward, they often become irritable. Teamwork suffers, squabbles become common, and full-blown fights may break out. Although brief, the hot and tedious tow from Tahiti to Nukuhiva had tested the crews. Bruce thought that *Hawai'iloa's* crew had gotten along well in part because of the efforts of Colonel Donna Wendt, an army nurse who was serving as the medical officer before Dr. Nate Wong joined the crew in Nukuhiva. Before the voyage, Donna had read a lot about the Tuamotu atolls and Te Henua 'Enana. On the way to Nukuhiva, she volunteered to give a series of talks about these islands and their people. Bruce noticed how her talks seemed to fascinate everyone and to boost their spirits, which led him to think about having everyone on board give some sort of presentation during the leg to Hawai'i.

HAWAI'ILOA CREW FROM NUKUHIVA TO HAWAI'I

Name	Island	Profession
Bruce Blankenfeld	O'ahu	Stevedore
Wally Froiseth	O'ahu	Pilot boat captain
Terry Hee	O'ahu	Stevedore
Archie Kalepa	Maui	Lifeguard
Kimo Lyman	O'ahu	Firefighter
Ka'au McKenney	O'ahu	Teacher
Cliff Watson	O'ahu	Television cameraman
Nathan Wong	O'ahu	Physician
Wallace Wong	Hawai'i	Computer engineer
Max Yarawamai	Hawai'i	Landscape gardener
Gary Yuen	O'ahu	Shipyard worker

As *Hawai'iloa* headed north from Nukuhiva, he called a meeting every day or so at which a crewmember would give an informal talk about himself, how he became interested in canoe sailing, and what the voyage meant to him. Cliff Watson filmed several of these talks, though when I reviewed his tapes, I discovered that the sound tracks were too filled with the sound of rushing wind and water to understand all that was said. Nonetheless, watching the videos and catching parts of the talks gave me the impression that these sessions hit the mark. The crew enjoyed hearing from their fellows and finding out how they had become involved in the project and about their hopes and aspirations.

Take Archie Kalepa's tale. When he was twelve years old and wrapped up with paddling racing canoes, he heard that *Hōkūle'a* had just returned from Tahiti and would soon visit his island. So he asked his dad if he could take off from summer school and join his fellow paddlers to greet the canoe as she came in. His father flatly said no, pointing out that he had spent too much money paying for summer school to let him skip classes just to go see a canoe. Archie added with some glee that he cut school anyway to paddle out to *Hōkūle'a* as she was coming in, and that afterwards got "the worst lickin' of my life." But it was worth it, he told his amused comrades, because "seeing the canoe instilled a dream in me and made me proud to be a Hawaiian."

In discussing these talks with Cliff, Bruce summed up their impact:

> The really interesting thing about these talks is the way they affect the whole crew. It makes them come together a lot closer, in the sense you get a lot of aloha and good feeling that spreads through the whole crew, making them a lot stronger. What started as an impromptu event turned out to be a fabulous thing, and so we now are always looking forward to the next episode.

SINCE LEAVING NUKUHIVA, *Hawai'iloa*'s crew had been trolling for fish, catching one or two almost every day. Most were small tunas *(ahi)* or dorados *(mahimahi)* weighing from five to ten pounds. Bruce considered these to be an ideal size, just enough to feed the crew for a meal or two. He told Cliff that during previous voyages everyone liked to catch a lot of fish—the bigger the better—even if not all of them could be eaten or dried before they spoiled and had to be thrown overboard. Now Bruce said that he and his crewmates felt better about catching only one or two small fish at a time, just enough for everyone's needs without any wastage. To illustrate this new ethic, he pointed out that right after catching a small tuna on April 27th, they had hooked a big one that must have weighed 250–300 pounds. Rather than bring the fish on board and then have to throw most of it away, they released the giant creature and made do with the much smaller fish caught earlier.

AS APRIL GAVE WAY TO MAY, the northeast trades of the third segment were blowing steadily in the 20–25 knot range. Both *Te Au o Tonga* and *Hawai'iloa* were doing better than 7 knots, making daily runs of 170 miles or so. But *Te Au o Tonga* still maintained her lead. When she passed 17° north, *Hawai'iloa* was a half day behind and the other canoes were another day or so farther in the rear. Had any yachts happened across the canoes at this time, their sailors would have been thrilled to see these sleek vessels

Hōkūle'a *sails in 1976.*   Hōkūle'a *sails in 1995.*

sailing fast across the trades, gracefully riding over swell after swell. However, they might also have been puzzled by the strange collection of traditional and modern style sails powering these contemporary voyaging canoes.

On the first voyage to Tahiti, we had rigged *Hōkūle'a* with a pair of cotton sails modeled on petroglyphs and Western drawings of the Hawaiian "crab-claw" sail, which is the northern version of the basic triangular sail of Eastern Polynesia. To a yachtsmen used to the standard Bermuda rig, Hawaiian and other Eastern Polynesian sails appear to be rigged upside down, with the apex of the triangle pointing down instead of up. They are lashed onto two spars, with the thicker forward one serving as the mast and the slimmer aft one serving as the boom. In some of the archipelagos the boom and the trailing edge of the sail were straight, but they were curved in Hawai'i and Tahiti. (The way the upper part of the Hawaiian sail curves sharply back toward the mast is why it is likened to a crab claw.)

These tall, narrow, curved sails perform well, and *Hōkūle'a* had several daily runs of more than 160 miles while sailing back from Tahiti in 1976. However, in the 1980s, the *Hōkūle'a* sailors began modifying her sail rig. They made the booms heavier and more rigid, and finally, for ease of handling, took the curve out of the trailing edge of the sails and used straight booms. They also began mounting a jib forward of the two Hawaiian-style sails, and a staysail between them, to make the canoe sail faster, point higher into the wind and handle more easily. *Hawai'iloa,* and most of the other canoes of the fleet, followed this practice.

Although taking the curve out of the sails and booms was well within the bounds of Polynesian design, adding jibs and staysails was questionable. Although these sails have long been used on Western vessels, they do not appear in ancient Polynesian petroglyphs or in the early European drawings and descriptions of Polynesian canoes. Nonetheless, some of the sailors defended their use by saying that their ancestors must have developed them. On firmer ground were those who argued that since they had already demonstrated how well *Hōkūle'a* sailed with the old rig, they should be free to sail with whatever sails they now wished to use. The initially problematic but later synergistic alliance of experimental voyaging and cultural revival had served its purpose. Now the Hawaiians and other new Polynesian sailors were engaged in "identity voyaging"—sailing to celebrate their seafaring heritage and prove themselves by making their canoes sail as fast and as efficiently as possible.[5]

AFTER SEVERAL DAYS of fast sailing across the northeast trades, the *Hawai'iloa* sailors could almost taste land. The North Star was climbing higher and higher in the sky as the Southern Cross was sinking lower and lower. The wind and sea felt noticeably cooler. And they were now heading more directly toward the Big Island. Bruce had planned to turn more directly toward the island as they approached its latitude, but the wind did it for him by becoming more northerly, nudging the canoe onto a more northwesterly heading than that indicated by the reference course line.

While Bruce had no way of knowing it, by the morning of May 2, the thirteenth day at sea, the gap between his D.R. estimates and where the canoe was actually sailing had narrowed to around 25–30 miles. This provided another example of how misestimates do not necessarily add up in one direction to throw a navigator's reckoning increasingly off as a voyage progresses.

Hopes for a quick landfall were shattered later that day when tiny biting flies were reported on *Hawai'iloa*. The conclusion was that the canoe might be carrying the dreaded *nono*, a tiny sandfly (*Styloconops albiventris*) that infests the beaches of Te Henua 'Enana and sucks the blood from anyone so foolish as to linger on the sand or even walk slowly across it. Victims usually don't notice that they are providing a blood meal until twenty or thirty minutes later. By then the flies are engorged, and the victim begins to feel an intolerable itch. If vigorously scratched, the painful welts often become infected, adding to the misery.

Kimo Lyman radioed Nainoa that *Hawai'iloa* might be infested with *nono* flies, and asked him what to do. The real issue was not how to treat the bites, but how to prevent the flies from spreading to Hawai'i. If they were the noxious *nono*, it would be disastrous if they took hold in our islands, infesting the sandy shores. Beach life, so important to the local lifestyle as well as to tourism, would lose much of its appeal, and a consequent fall in visitor arrivals might send Hawai'i's economy, already weakened by overreliance on Japan's ailing yen, into a tailspin.

Nainoa was staggered by the news, but in a way he was conditioned to respond to it. While growing up, he had listened to his mother, Laura Thompson, a passionate environmentalist, talk about the dangers of introducing new plants, animals, and insects to Hawai'i. Later, as he began sailing around the islands, he saw for himself how sensitive they were to foreign invaders. During the search for *koa* trees, Nainoa had been struck hard by the realization that there were no big trees left to build double canoes. This led him to think about having the Polynesian Voyaging Society focus on protecting Hawai'i's vulnerable environment as well as on voyaging. After returning from the West Coast, he wanted to develop an environmental education program called *Mālama Hawai'i*, which literally means "Care for Hawai'i."

Although the original flora and fauna of the islands had been carried there by wind and sea, the arrival of humans, first in canoes, then ships and now aircraft, has brought many new plants, animals, and insects, as well as ways for radically reshaping the landscape. These introductions transformed a relatively isolated ecosystem, with a very high proportion of species native to the islands, into one under constant threat from the outside. The Hawaiian Islands now have the unwelcome distinction of leading the world in extinctions.

The original Polynesian settlers started this process by clearing the land, preying on flightless birds, and introducing new plants and animals. Even the little Polynesian rat that stowed away on the arriving canoes did major damage by eating ground-dwelling birds and their eggs, helping to drive several species to extinction. The islands were further transformed with the coming of ships, plantation agriculture and cattle ranches, and such unwanted pests as cockroaches, night-biting mosquitoes, and ground termites that had hitched rides on the ships. More recently, increased aircraft traffic has brought new diseases and insects, as well as snakes and other unwanted animals.

The prospect that *Hawai'iloa* might continue this cycle by introducing yet another pest spurred Nainoa to action. After hurriedly discussing the crisis aboard *Hōkūle'a*, he radioed Hawai'i to seek advice from government officials and scientists, and to consult with conservation specialists from the Sierra Club and the Nature Conservancy. Together they developed a plan to prevent the *nono*—or whatever bug was on the canoe—from reaching Hawai'i.

The canoes and their escorts would have to stop before they came within 100 miles of the Big Island. All fresh foods, plants, and other materials that might harbor insects were to be thrown overboard, after which the canoes and escort boats had to be thoroughly scrubbed, taking particular care to get rid of any sand or dirt that might have been brought aboard at Nukuhiva. After the vessels were sprayed inside and out using large insecticide canisters dropped from a Coast Guard plane, the fleet would have to wait 24 hours before setting sail for Hilo, the port on the Big Island's northeast coast. There, after tying up to a visiting pier, the canoes would be tented and fumigated with poison gas, the same treatment as that given to termite-infested houses in Hawai'i.

When Nainoa explained all this during an extended radio conference with the canoes and escort vessels, he pleaded for cooperation in order to avoid the awful possibility of introducing the *nono*. All captains readily agreed with the proposed measures but one, although after being assured that the order of the canoes would not be altered by the spraying, he finally accepted the arrangement. To have everyone in agreement was very important to Nainoa, for he was thinking ahead about how to implement *Mālama Hawai'i*. "I'd like to turn this *nono* thing around and make it into a long-term program on how to keep alien species out of Hawai'i," he told us over the radio. The *nono* crisis might be a bizarre way to end the voyage, but it could serve as a wake-up call for the people of Hawai'i to take better care of their islands.[6]

SINCE ALL THE CANOES hove to at the same time for cleaning, spraying, and the 24-hour pause that followed, upon getting underway again they sailed in the same order as before, with *Te Au o Tonga* in the lead. The big Rarotongan canoe had fairly steady winds all the way to the Big Island. After angling directly for the island rather than going all the way to 20° 30' north before turning, on May 5th she was off the port of Hilo, fifteen days after leaving Nukuhiva.

Hawai'iloa was not so fortunate. After turning downwind to head directly for Hilo, the canoe encountered a calm. To keep up the momentum, Bruce took a tow from *Kama Hele*, though he continued to navigate the canoe in an indirect way. After radioing the initial heading to the escort boat, he periodically called in course corrections. But just when Bruce was hoping to spy Mauna Kea off in the distance, a strange mist drifted over the canoe, preventing the anticipated landfall.

Although such mists are seldom seen in tropical Polynesia, one figures in the story of *Te Au o Tonga*. Papa Tom translates *Te Au o Tonga* as "The Mist of the South," or simply as "The Southern Mist." His choice of that historic name was unexpectedly validated on the day the completed hulls and other components were to be transported from the inland building site to the coast. That morning everyone was astonished to see that a thick mist, the likes of which no one could remember, had settled over the entire island. Visibility was reduced so much that an incoming airliner bearing the Prime Minister could not land and had to fly back to Tahiti. Taking this as a good omen for a canoe named after a legendary mist, the hundreds of people assembled enthusiastically carried the twin hulls and other components down to the sea.

FOR TUA PITTMAN AND PE'IA TAU'ATI, *Te Au o Tonga*'s co-navigators, making landfall on Mauna Kea capped their long years of study. Tua, a tall, well-spoken man whose full name is Teuatakiri Teri'itua Pittman, first saw *Hōkūle'a* in 1985 when the Hawaiians stopped at Rarotonga on their way to Aotearoa. He watched in silent awe as she entered the harbor, tied up to the pier, and Nainoa, Mau, and the others stepped ashore. He soon overcame his shyness and made himself so useful around the canoe that he was asked to watch over *Hōkūle'a* during the two months she was left at Rarotonga while waiting for seasonal winds suitable for sailing to Aotearoa. One thing led to another, and the following year Tua was chosen to join *Hōkūle'a*'s crew for the sail from Rarotonga to Tahiti.

At first he hesitated to accept, as several years earlier his father and grandfather had disappeared at sea during a fishing trip. This tragedy had given his whole family a fear of the deep ocean beyond the reef. He didn't dare tell his mother or grandmother about sailing on *Hōkūle'a*. However, when he finally decided to accept the invitation Tua explained to them that he had to go in order to overcome his fear of the sea and to find some closure with his father and grandfather. In Tua's words: "They were taken away from us by the ocean, and the only way I could get closer to them was actually getting out on the ocean, being there with them."

That voyage turned out to be one of *Hōkūle'a*'s roughest crossings, with frequent squalls forcing the crew to lower the entire sail rig scores of times. Tua recalls that:

> I went through hell on that trip. A lot of stages I was saying to myself, "what am I doing here?" But deep inside I knew that these two figureheads of my family, they went with me the whole way. So I battled it out and when the trip was over and I thought that I'd never do that again. And then I got the call for another trip.

Nainoa had trained both Tua and Pe'ia for the 1992 Pacific Arts Festival, and the two had acquitted themselves well in guiding their canoes to Rarotonga. Afterwards they continued studying navigation, travelling several times to Hawai'i to work under Nainoa's supervision. Between trips, they worked on their own at their respective islands of Rarotonga and Ma'uke, staying up far into the night going over star charts and studying the night sky. The two navigators were therefore very well prepared for the challenge of guiding *Te Au o Tonga* to Hawai'i.

The voyage went well for them, except for one incident. As they neared Hawai'i Island the captain insisted on turning *Te Au o Tonga* directly towards Hilo in order to save the time it would take to sail all the way up to 20° 30' north and then turn west. Nonetheless, after arriving in Hawai'i Tua recalled the positive aspects of navigating *Te Au o Tonga*:

> When we left Nukuhiva that was the start, really the start of the greatest challenge of our lives. First we were looking for the island of Eiao and we found it. And that was real for us, for me; I really felt good about it. And from then on whenever the stars came up, whenever the wind changed, we were on

126

top of it—we knew what was happening. We owe it all to Nainoa and Mau for teaching us and showing us the right way. And the system works, the navigation system really works. And that was a great feeling, especially when we saw Mauna Kea rise above the clouds. We knew the island was there somewhere, but we couldn't see it. And then the sun rose, the clouds cleared and Mauna Kea, the top of Mauna Kea, just sort of popped up.

ABOARD *HŌKŪLE'A*, Chad Baybayan also had the thrill of seeing the island suddenly appear out of the clouds:

> I knew where the island was and that all I had to do was to be patient and it would show itself to me. As I looked up toward the bow, and the clouds just opened up, you know, and it was like the island was there. . . . I saw the saddle [between Mauna Kea and Mauna Loa], and I saw the slopes coming down to Hilo. And [it was] really one of the few times in my life that I felt really proud about being strong and being Hawaiian.

FOR JACKO THATCHER, who was navigating *Te Aurere* with Piripi Evans, the peak experience came when they were crossing the equator. Until then Jacko had been very apprehensive about his navigating, particularly when the sun was too high in the sky to yield a bearing. In a post-voyage interview he talked about how difficult it was steering at midday by the ocean swells and how he never felt sure about where the canoe was heading until the sun neared the horizon and the stars started coming out. However, his confidence received a great boost when *Te Aurere* was approaching the equator:

> I was sitting on the platform and having a bit of a rest and Mariako wakes me up and he says have a look at this. I looked over the side, and there was a pod, must have been fifty to a hundred dolphins. Just everywhere they were, jumping and scooting under the hulls. And I looked up and said, "hey, hey, hey." And straightaway we knew what they were. They were *kaitiaki* or protectors who were leading us across the equator.

CLIFF INTERVIEWED BRUCE for the last time as *Hawai'iloa* neared Hilo, asking him about how he felt now that the voyage was finally coming to an end. Judging not only from the navigator's words, but also his tone of voice, Bruce was feeling somewhat down about recent events. He and the crew had really been looking forward to racing for the Big Island and making landfall on Mauna Kea. Instead, they had lost a day taking care of the *nono* problem, after which they had to take a tow when the wind died. Then the strange mist denied them the opportunity to sight Mauna Kea from afar.

Furthermore, when all fresh foods and plants had to be thrown overboard, a pair of popular experiments being conducted on *Hawai'iloa* were ruined. One tested ways for preserving the shoots of the taro plant (*kalo* in Hawaiian) on long voyages. The other involved selected crew members eating only native foods, including some fermented breadfruit paste and other foods that Tava Taupu had preserved by traditional 'Enanan methods. Their loss was greatly regretted, particularly as the taro experiment had been designed by schoolchildren from Moloka'i Island, and the diet experiment had been developed by dieticians at Kamehameha Schools who were interested in having Hawaiians give up "junk food" and go back to a healthful native diet.

Yet Bruce was too experienced, too even-minded, to dwell on what had gone wrong during the last days of the trip. The voyage had proceeded more or less as planned except for *Takitumu*'s brief disappearance and the *nono* problem. The winds had been fairly good most of the way. Even after spending an extra day at sea and another in Hilo for fumigation, it looked like *Hawai'iloa* and *Hōkūle'a* would easily reach O'ahu in time to be loaded aboard the Seattle-bound freighter.

Moreover, the navigator really felt good about how the crew and the canoe performed during the voyage, and he finished the interview by singing their praises. Without hesitation, he said that the passage from Nukuhiva to Hawai'i would go down as a great voyage, but not because of the navigation or anything else technical. Instead, Bruce stressed that it was:

> Great in the sense of any overall viewpoint of what in my mind a great voyage would entail, which would be good people, working together really respecting each other, and living aboard with each other as a functional, tight-knit group.

After elaborating on that theme, Bruce went on to pay special tribute to *Hawai'iloa*. He talked about how the canoe had a lot of *mana*, or spiritual power. This initially came from the Native Alaskan donors and their Hawaiian beneficiaries properly asking forgiveness from the gods and spirits for taking the lives of the two majestic spruce trees. Then by turning the logs into a handsome voyaging canoe, the Hawaiians had augmented that *mana*, further honoring the gods and spirits as well as their ancestors.

Bruce also talked about how well the canoe performed. Although *Hawai'iloa* had to be sailed stern-first because the forward sections of her hulls were too slim, to everyone's delight this reconfiguration transformed the canoe into a most seakindly vessel. Turning the broad, rounded sterns into the new twin bows gave *Hawai'iloa* a soft and comfortable ride. The reconfiguration also helped keep the canoe dry, for the

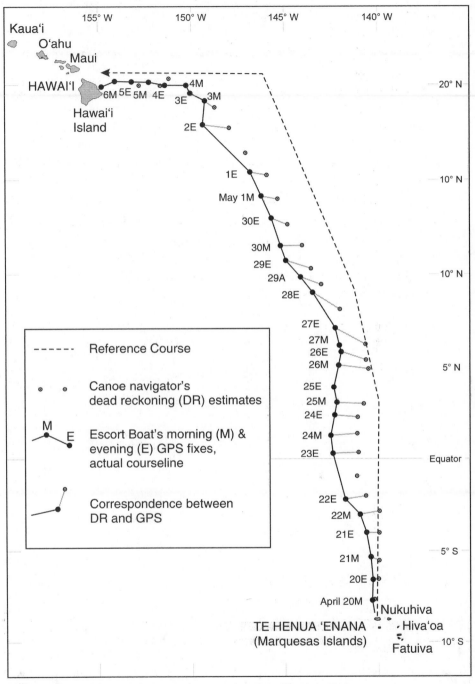

Route of Hawai'iloa *from Nukuhiva to Hawai'i, 19 April-6 May 1995.*

reversed hulls rode easily over the swells rather than plowing through them. This cut down the sea spray and kept all but the most insistent of swells from slopping over the gunnels onto the deck.[7] Bruce summed up his feelings about the canoe by saying:

> So this canoe has so much *mana* that it's hard to explain, but it keeps us safe. It rides the roughest oceans like a gem and it's so quiet and comforting to be on. It's like even in the roughest seas there is no hint of being worried that there is something that might not hold up. It's really a neat canoe. You know, I sailed down on this canoe, and I've sailed back, and it's really been memorable.

THE NAVIGATORS trained by Nainoa all passed the stern test of landfall. As a glance at the chart on the first page of the color insert shows, although there were variations, each had followed the same basic dogleg course through the four segments of the voyage to make landfall on Hawai'i Island. In fact, it would be difficult to pick out any significant differences between the tracks of the five canoes guided without instruments and that of *Takitumu*, whose navigator had relied on the precise position determinations of a GPS unit. Nainoa's navigational system really worked.

After years spent training his successors, then having to fight to keep the canoes separate so that each navigator could work on his own, Nainoa was immensely pleased. Upon reaching Hilo, he spoke of the drive and perseverance of the navigators, and that by guiding their canoes all the way to Hawai'i they had demonstrated that their ancestors "had the ability to explore and colonize the largest nation on earth," and had brought back to the islands "a sense of dignity as to who we are as a people."

Chapter Eight

Landed Ashore — The Work is Done

THE HAWAIIANS CHARACTERIZED the completion of the voyage with the saying, "*Ua Pae i kula*," which translates literally as "landed ashore" and figuratively as "the work is done."[1] Although the canoes stopped first in Hilo Harbor for fumigation, the sailors were not formally welcomed to Hawai'i until they reached O'ahu several days later. Actually, they landed ashore twice, first on May 11th at Kualoa on O'ahu's northeastern coast and two days later at Ke'ehi Lagoon on the southern coast. Whereas the landing at Ke'ehi was planned as a grand public event open to everyone, the one at Kualoa was meant primarily for *nā 'ohana holo moana*, "the voyaging families" of the canoes that had made the long journey.

The key word in that expression is *'ohana*, a metaphorical term for family based on the branching way the staple root crop *kalo* (taro) propagates. It includes a wide range of kin and now is often applied to groups whose members seek to embrace a family identity.[2] In the latter sense, each of the six canoes was considered to be the focus of an *'ohana* composed of those who had built, sailed, and navigated her, as well as their relatives and supporters. Many members of each of the six voyaging families, particularly those from Hawai'i, were expected to gather at Kualoa, and be joined there by Native Alaskans, 'Enanans, and others from around the Pacific who had been drawn into the endeavor. In addition, an *'ohana* from the adjacent valley of Hakipu'u would be there to represent lightly populated Kualoa and welcome the voyagers onto its sandy shores.

Kualoa is a small *'ahupua'a*, a land division at the northwestern end of Kāne'ohe Bay that extends from the sea to steeply rising uplands. It is said to be one of the most sacred places on O'ahu. Local historians talk about how when a high chief was in residence there, passing canoes had to lower their sails out of respect.[3] After building the hulls, crossbeams, and other components of *Hōkūle'a* in an old warehouse at Honolulu Harbor in 1975, we trucked them across the island to Kualoa, which had just become a beach park operated by the City and County of Honolulu. There on the sand and in the open air, we lashed the components together and launched the completed canoe into the welcoming waters of Kāneʻohe Bay. Now, twenty years later, *Hōkūleʻa* was coming home along with *Hawaiʻiloa* and the other canoes to complete the voyage from Te Henua ʻEnana.

After the fumigating tents were taken off the canoes at Hilo and the crews cleaned up their vessels, the fleet sailed for Oʻahu, though not directly. As there were a few days to spare, they stopped at Molokaʻi before making the short crossing to Oʻahu. Instead of staying with the fleet, I flew back to Honolulu to join our old skipper, Kāwika Kapahulehua, so that we could together watch the canoes sail into Kāneʻohe Bay. However, upon arriving at Kualoa on the appointed day, we received word that they had been slow to set sail and would not reach the park until late that afternoon.

That left plenty of time for those of us assembling there to exchange views about the voyage. Except for some joking about the *nono* crisis, I didn't hear anyone talk about the problems encountered in building *Hawaiʻiloa*, coordinating all the canoes, and actually making the voyage. Nor did I hear any discussion about how authentic *Hawaiʻiloa* and the other canoes were, whether Te Henua ʻEnana was really the Hawaiian homeland, or other issues that had once seemed so pressing. This was a relaxed and happy family reunion, and the people wanted to celebrate how six voyaging canoes from across Polynesia had sailed together to Hawaiʻi to commemorate the original discovery and settlement of the islands.

As the canoes began to arrive late that afternoon, the orators called them to land.[4] When each canoe neared the beach, the captain identified his canoe and asked permission to come ashore. Once permission was granted, the sailors landed and marched up the beach as chanters welcomed them to Kualoa. The cool and windy weather did not dampen the greetings, though the overcast cut the daylight short. By the time the last crew landed, it was almost dark. Everybody then moved back from the beach to an *ahu*, in this case a low stone cairn that had been erected for the *pōhaku* (stone) ceremony, the main event of the program. As the Hawaiians began sailing around Polynesia, they developed the practice of taking waterworn basalt stones from Hawaiʻi, and ceremonially presenting them to their hosts at their various destinations. This time stones brought by each of the crews were to be deposited on a cairn to stand as a monument to the voyage just completed and the cooperative efforts of all the voyaging families involved.[5]

MYRON THOMPSON, acting in his capacity of president of the Polynesian Voyaging Society, chose the *pōhaku* ceremony to give a brief and thoughtful speech. Instead of triumphantly reviewing the just-completed voyage, he focused on the vision, values, and social processes that had been crucial to ancient voyaging and were now driving its revival:

> As our ancestors did before us, we looked together over the horizon and envisioned new lands and new hopes for ourselves and the generations that will follow us. Like our ancestors, we set in our minds a clear vision of what that new hope can be. As of old, we sought out existing information and persevered in our quest for new knowledge to help that vision take shape. Following the example set by our ancestors, we defined each step needed to bring everyone to landfall safely. And, as of old, we have moved forward with courage and conviction to seek out and achieve our new hopes and dreams.

> And so today we come together to set our individual *pōhaku* on an *ahu* on these sacred grounds, forever memorializing the processes for success each of us has taken to assure a safe landfall for everyone. Ways established by our ancestors for successful achievement of their goals. Traditions which have been passed on to us, enabling us to achieve success in our collective endeavors. Processes which we can share with our children, grandchildren, and great-grandchildren.

> Our respective *pōhaku* are symbolic of these processes, these paths to success from our individual communities. We place our *pōhaku* in gratitude for being welcomed. We place these *pōhaku* as testament that the ways they represent can help Hawai'i and the lands from which each of us have come to be and remain healthy, productive and safe places in which to live and thrive—to become truly lands of aloha, our ultimate landfall!

These three paragraphs said a lot to me, though I realized that those who had not lived through the voyaging revival would need to know more about the elder Thompson in order to understand why he was connecting stones and canoes with ancestrally-inspired social processes and the overall welfare of the islands and their peoples. But as I was just then beginning to outline this book, I filed his speech away and promised myself that when it came time to writing the concluding chapter, I would feature it and the crucial role its author had played in the voyaging revival. That task was to be long delayed by teaching and research commitments. In fact, it was not until I retired from the University of Hawai'i in 2001 that I was able to work on this book in earnest.

By then Myron Thompson was in his late seventies and had retired or was in the process of retiring from the positions he held in a wide variety of community organizations. Later that year we learned that he was suffering from a serious illness, from which he was to die on Christmas day. During his last months, we had several long talks about the voyaging revival and how he had been working to make sure it benefited Hawaiians and others living in Hawai'i. When we had discussed voyaging in previous years, he always shied away from talking about himself, preferring to highlight the accomplishments of others. Now he was more willing to reflect about his life and the principles he had developed and applied during his long career as a social worker, administrator, and community organizer. In addition, Nainoa and other members of his family as well as his colleagues began to talk and write about the elder Thompson's life and contributions. All this enabled me to better understand how important this unique man had been to the voyaging revival.

MYRON BENNET THOMPSON was born in Honolulu in 1924. His mother had been so sure her child would be a girl that she decorated the baby's room all in pink. When Myron arrived, he naturally became known as "Pinky," a name that stuck to him throughout his life. As a child growing up in the 1920s and 1930s, Pinky was sensitized to the problems that many Hawaiian children and families were facing in what the United States then considered to be their "Territory of Hawai'i." His mother, a school-teacher, and his father, an accountant, also raised a dozen or so foster children from troubled homes who had been in and out of correctional institutions. Pinky became very close to them, feeling their pain as well as their happiness, an experience he later credited with orienting him toward social work.

As a teenager, Pinky was deeply affected by the attack on Pearl Harbor, and upon graduating from high school in 1943, he tried to enlist in the navy to become an aviator, only to be told by the recruiter that he was too dark to be selected. He tried the Army Air Corps and was accepted. But just before being sent to B-29 school, his unit was reassigned to the infantry for the impending invasion of occupied France. His officers knew he was from Hawai'i, though Pinky reckoned they must have thought he was like an American Indian, as they made him a scout.

After landing at Normandy and fighting his way across France as the chief scout of his unit, Pinky was shot through the head near the German border. The grievously wounded soldier was taken to a triage point, where he was judged beyond help and left to die. A pair of his buddies refused to accept the decision. They picked him up and were carrying him to a field hospital when one of them stepped on a land mine, killing him outright and wounding Pinky further. When Pinky finally reached the medical facility, the doctors managed to stabilize his condition, and he was evacuated to an Army hospital in Massachusetts that specialized in head wounds. Only after a painful and lonely two years did he finally recover his sight. While lying in bed, often with both eyes bandaged, the young soldier worked on his life's plan. Rather than sink into self-pity and depression, he instead began thinking about how he would go back to Hawai'i and dedicate himself to improving the well-being of his fellow Hawaiians.

Pinky went on to earn a B.A. in sociology at Maine's Colby College, then enrolled in the University of Hawai'i for an M.A. in social work. In post-war Hawai'i, he quickly became known as a highly effective social worker and administrator. He went on to direct a succession of government and private agencies, and to co-found such highly successful programs for Hawaiians as Alu Like for job training and Papa Ola Lōkahi for health services. Even after taking on the demanding full-time position as a trustee of the Kamehameha Schools/Bishop Estate, Pinky found time to serve a number of other community groups, and direct both the Polynesian Voyaging Society and Hui Nalu, one of the oldest and largest of the many outrigger canoe racing clubs in the islands. During his lifetime, he was widely honored for his leadership in social services, government, and Hawaiian causes, and his alma mater Colby College awarded him an honorary doctorate.

Into his seventies, Pinky, a compact, well-proportioned and active man, was still taking his turn steering Hui Nalu's senior men's team in canoe races. He could be intensely serious in meetings but was quiet and relaxed at home. He particularly enjoyed hosting the *pā'ina*, or feasts, that he and his wife Laura periodically held beneath the stars at the family compound in Niu Valley, where they, their son Nainoa, and daughter Lita and her husband, Bruce Blankenfeld, lived in modest wooden cottages.

When Nainoa signed up for the first voyage, Pinky supported his decision, even though it meant that his son would have to interrupt his education. As a teenager Pinky had been greatly inspired by Te Rangi Hiroa's portrayal of Polynesians as great seafarers. Now, after fully realizing the damage Hawaiians had sustained from the American takeover and the repression of their language and culture, he readily grasped the potential of *Hōkūle'a* as a means for Hawaiians to explore their past and demonstrate their worth. He and Laura were therefore proud that Nainoa would take part in the endeavor.

While growing up in pre-World War II, plantation-dominated Hawai'i, Pinky had felt that the Western system imposed upon Hawaiians carried the message that they were inferior. Although he refused to let that get him down, while doing social work he came to realize that many young Hawaiians succumbed to feelings of worthlessness and resentment generated by the colonial situation and then seemed to go out of their way to cause trouble at home, in school, and other places. To Pinky these disaffected youths were acting out frustrations that ultimately stemmed from Hawaiians being treated as second-class citizens in their own country.

Later, after collaborating with clinicians and researchers, Pinky came to accept that many of these youths were suffering from a specific form of depression now labeled as the "Kaumaha Syndrome." *Kaumaha* means "heavy," both literally and psychologically. In the latter sense, Hawaiian psychologist William Rezentes defines it as: "sad, depressed, dismal, dreary, downcast, troubled and wretched."[6] When Pinky told me about this syndrome, he added that when he saw the photographs taken of the crew when *Hōkūle'a* reached Tahiti in 1976, he could see from the faces of the disaffected sailors that they were *kaumaha*.

Nainoa has not been immune from reacting to how Hawaiians have been treated. During a talk presented in 1998 at the University of Hawai'i's Center for Hawaiian Studies, he told the students that while growing up, he spent much time with his paternal grandmother, a fluent Hawaiian speaker who had attended Kamehameha School in her youth. He recalled her telling him how she was beaten for speaking Hawaiian there— even though the school had been created for the education of Hawaiian children by the will of Bernice Pauahi Bishop, the last direct heir of Kamehameha. Not until much later, Nainoa said, did he realize how hearing about her suffering had subconsciously angered him. Only through sailing and navigating canoes, he told the students, was he able to get over that repressed rage by showing that his ancestors were not inferior.

Although Pinky supported the canoe project, he stayed in the background until the 1978 capsize. At that critical point, he challenged the leaders of the Polynesian Voyaging Society to get their act together, and some months thereafter became the society's new president. In addition to his considerable experience in administration and politics, Pinky brought to the shattered organization new ideas about applying native cultural values to troubled Hawaiian groups. During the 1960s, as the newly appointed executive-director of the Children's Center of the Queen Lili'uokalani Trust, Pinky surrounded himself with such knowledgeable advisers and staff members as Mary Kawena Pukui and noted psychiatrist Dr. E. W. Haertig. This group broke new ground in exploring how Hawaiian concepts, beliefs, and practices could be applied to problems besetting Hawaiian children and families.[7] One of the ideas that Pinky derived from this effort was that organizations as well as individuals could also benefit by focusing on such Hawaiian values as *lōkahi* (unity), *pono* (just, proper), and *aloha* (love, compassion) in order to develop a solid moral base from which to clarify their goals and work out ways of achieving them.

Pinky applied this approach to the Polynesian Voyaging Society, working closely with the board of directors and the crew to get the project back on track. He also made sure that the chauvinism that marred the preparations for the aborted 1978 attempt was not allowed to get in the way of bringing knowledgeable non-Hawaiians back into the project. The success of the 1980 return to Tahiti and subsequent voyages testifies as to how well he was able to turn the Society around and enable young Hawaiians to achieve the initially elusive goal of reviving voyaging.

Nonetheless, I have heard some skeptical comments about Pinky's explicitly cultural approach. For example, some critics said that he distorted reality by focusing solely on "positive" Hawaiian values and ignoring "negative" ones relating to aggression, warfare, and sorcery. Others argued that the values approach was really an American management fad clothed with nice-sounding Hawaiian words that resonate with New Age thinking. But surely Hawaiians, or any other group, have the right to be selective about what aspects of their cultural heritage they wish to emphasize. Furthermore, even if focusing on values, goals, and means of implementation might reflect some trends current in American organizations, consciously thinking these through in Hawaiian terms has been very effective.

In the late 1980s and early 1990s, Pinky and other leaders of the Society intensified this focus on Hawaiian ways of thinking, learning, and doing. Such Hawaiian terms as 'imi 'ike (seeking knowledge), a'o (learning, teaching), and mālama (caring for) began appearing in planning documents and discussions as the maturing organization sought new directions. Unexpectedly, this approach eventually led Pinky to realize that the values and concepts that had enabled the Polynesians to explore the world's greatest ocean and find new island homes were really universal in successful human endeavors. Sam Low, Nainoa's cousin and an accomplished anthropologist and filmmaker, recorded Pinky's thoughts about this:

> What struck me about voyaging was that before you set out to find a new island you had to have a vision of that island over the horizon. Then you had to figure out how you are going to get there; you had to make a plan for achieving the vision. You also had to experiment to try new things. Finally, you had to get out there and take a risk. And on the voyage you had to bind the crew to each other with aloha so they could work together to overcome the risk and achieve the vision. You find them throughout the world—seeking, planning, experimenting, taking risks and the importance of the team. That process is important to pass on to our young people. The same principles are the ones we use today and that we will use into the future. No matter what culture you are, or what race, this way of doing things works.[8]

A BIZARRE SITUATION developed just as the canoes were arriving at Taputapuātea for the ritual celebration of voyaging recounted in Chapter Three. A British catamaran designer dropped anchor in the lagoon after sailing all the way from the Canary Islands off Africa in a handsome catamaran of his own design that he advertised as a modern version of an ancient Polynesian double canoe. To everyone's consternation, he said that he had been invited to Ra'iātea by French Polynesia's Ministry of Culture to participate with the canoes in the ritual at Taputapuātea. It turned out that a Tahitian cultural official had indeed invited him, but that his would-be host was not coming to Ra'iātea and apparently had not coordinated the invitation with the organizers. The bewildered sailor was therefore getting nowhere in his plea to join the sail through the Sacred Pass and subsequent ceremonies on the *marae*. Neither he nor anyone else on his crew was Polynesian, and his catamaran looked far too modern to be considered a voyaging canoe.

Not surprisingly, the designer was angry about having been asked to sail almost halfway around the world to take part in celebrations that he now learned were off limits to him. After devoting much of his life to designing catamarans inspired by Polynesian designs and making construction kits that sold widely in Britain and continental Europe, he felt that he too had contributed to the voyaging revival. As his rage grew, he sought me out. I tried to explain that for contemporary Polynesians building and sailing voyaging canoes was an antidote to the depressing effects of Western colonialism and that they therefore wanted to celebrate their nautical accomplishments on their own. But the designer scoffed at my analysis as he had no real knowledge of the Pacific peoples and their colonization by Western powers, including his own country. He began accusing the Tahitians of being out-and-out racists, and even went so far as to say that he found all the talk he was hearing about native canoes, heroic voyagers, and Polynesian pride to be as bad as Hitler's ravings in *Mein Kampf*.

This unfortunate incident made me think about why I found it *pono* (just and proper) that the Polynesian Voyaging Society is now led by Hawaiians, and that the majority of those who sail *Hōkūle'a* and *Hawai'iloa* are Hawaiian. Was I too close to the situation not to see any problem with this? In searching my mind for an answer I recalled a discussion Pinky and I had about the society and other organizations devoted to traditional Hawaiian activities or to otherwise benefiting Hawaiians. Pinky firmly stressed that Hawaiians should lead such groups, but that their staff and membership should not be exclusively made up of Hawaiians. He recognized that Hawai'i had long been a multi-ethnic society, and believed that Hawaiians would inevitably suffer if they turned totally inward and worked exclusively among themselves. Although he headed the Polynesian Voyaging Society, and *Hawai'iloa* and *Hōkūle'a* were captained and navigated by Hawaiians, Pinky insisted that the organization's board as well as the canoe crews include non-Hawaiians. That might sound like tokenism, but it makes a great deal of sense in today's Hawai'i.

During the 1980s, some newly emergent Hawaiian nationalists began criticizing Pinky's insistence on reaching beyond the Hawaiian community, as well as his promotion of federally funded projects in Hawaiian health, education, and professional development. They thought that he should be trying to bring down the established order instead of working within it. In private, Pinky criticized them for "crying over spilt milk" by spending their energy protesting past injustices rather than doing something useful for the present. Pinky was a doer not a talker. Through his quiet but firm leadership, he worked effectively for the welfare of the Hawaiians, and indeed all the people of Hawai'i. Under his tutelage, the Polynesian Voyaging Society emerged as a stable and inspirational organization that has greatly helped Hawaiians gain a historical sense of their place in the greater Polynesian nation and a personal sense of being worthy heirs of a great seafaring tradition. So armed, they have not been shy about claiming their rightful place in their own islands.

ON THE EVENING OF SEPTEMBER 15, 2001, the Polynesian Voyaging Society held a special open-air event on the grounds of Lanikūhonua, an ocean resort on the southwestern coast of O'ahu. Although originally planned as a fundraiser, because of Pinky's illness, it had been transformed into a celebration of his life and works called "Ho'oilina Mau: Enduring Legacy." This turned out to be the last public chance to pay tribute to Pinky and his manifold contributions to making Hawai'i a better place to live.

Among the many accolades he received from family and friends, from his co-workers in the many organizations he had served, and from Senators Daniel Inouye and Daniel Akaka and other leaders was a *mele inoa,* or "name chant." Name chants were—and still are—composed for chiefs and other great persons to praise them in terms of their ancestral forebears as well as their own qualities and accomplishments. Professor Lilikalā Kame'eleihiwa—the director of the university's Center for Hawaiian Studies who says that her life was changed by sailing on *Hawai'iloa*—composed Pinky's name chant with great care and love. She has graciously given me permission to end this chapter with her tribute to the man whose vision and leadership was so crucial to realizing the dream of reviving ocean voyaging for the benefit of Hawaiians and all others who live in these islands.[9]

HE INOA NO MYRON BENNET PINKY THOMPSON,
HE KAMALEI-A-PAOA
Lilikalā Kameʻeleihiwa 15 Kepakemapa 2001

A NAME CHANT FOR MYRON BENNET PINKY THOMPSON
A BELOVED DESCENDANT OF THE CHIEF PAOA
Lilikalā Kameʻeleihiwa 15 September 2001

Hāwanawana ka leo a ke Aliʻi kūpono
Alakaʻi kūpono no ka lāhui ʻōiwi
Wiwoʻole i ka kaumaha mai ka ʻāina ʻē
Mahamaha lua ʻole i nā hoahānau, i nā malihini
Māliu mai i ka ʻuwalo a ka poʻe nele, ua lohe ʻia
I nā keiki makua ʻole
I hānai ʻia ai e Liliʻuokalani, ia lohe ʻia
I nā pua a Pauahi
I hiʻipoi ʻia ai e Kamehameha, ua lohe ʻia
I nā ʻilihune Hawaiʻi
I hoʻoikaika ʻia ai e Alu Like, ua lohe ʻia
I nā kānaka hoʻoluhi a nāwaliwali
I kākoʻo ʻia ai e Papa Ola Lōkahi, ua lohe ʻia
Koa kūpikiʻō a ke Kaua Nui ʻElua
Kaua ma ka ʻaoʻao o ka ʻōiwi Hawaiʻi
E loaʻa ka waiwai mai Wakinekona

Whispering like the sea is the voice of the righteous Chief
A righteous leader of the Native nation
Fearless in the face of foreign burdens
Gracious beyond compare to his people, and to guests
Compassionate to the cries of the people in need, he listened
To the orphans
Cared for by Liliʻuokalani, he listened
To the descendants of Pauahi
Cherished by Kamehameha, he listened
To destitute Hawaiians
Strengthened by Alu Like, he listened
To people burdened with sickness
Supported by Papa Ola Lōkahi, he listened

Fierce warrior in World War II
Prevailing on behalf of Native Hawaiians
To obtain support in Washington

O wai kēia Ali'i hanohano?
O wai lā?
'O Myron Bennet Pinky Thompson nō ia
'O Kamalei-a-Paoa
No hea mai 'o ia? No hea mai 'o ka 'ohana?
No hea mai lā?
Mai ka 'āina mamao o Hawai'inuiākea
Mai ka 'āina piko o Ra'iātea
Mai ka marae kapu o Taputapuātea
Mai ka maluhia kahiko o Teaouri me Teaotea
Mai Teaotearoa ā hiki i Rapa Nui
Mai Tahiti ā ke pae 'ana i Hawai'i
'O Paoa ka 'ohana kaulana i ho'olohe
I nā kāhuna o ka marae
Ua hele nō Paoauri me Paoatea
Mai kēia kihi ā kēlā kihi
Ma luna o nā wa'a kaulua kelekele nui
Kele aku ai i nā 'āina hūnā o Kānehunamoku

Who is this distinguished Chief?
Who indeed?
He is Myron Bennet Pinky Thompson
Beloved descendant of the Chief Paoa
Where is he from? Where is his family from?
From where indeed?
From the distant land of Hawai'inuiākea (Polynesia)
From the central homeland of Ra'iātea
From the sacred temple of Taputapuātea
From the ancient pan-Polynesian alliance of East and West
From Aotearoa to Rapa Nui
From Tahiti until the landing upon Hawai'i
Paoa is the family famous
In its service of temple priests
The Paoa chiefs of east and west traveled

From this corner to that corner
Upon the great double hulled voyaging canoes
Sailing to the hidden lands of Kānehunamoku (Floating Islands of Knowledge)

Hāhai aku i nā hōkū kilokilo o ka lani
Mai ka Moana nui a Kiwa
Ā hiki i ka piko o Wākea
'Imi aku iā Hōkūpa'a ā ka lani ākau
Ā pae i ka 'āina o Pele
Ma lalo pono o Hōkūle'a
Le'a nō 'o Paoa i ka pae 'āina o Hawai'i
E ho'okūkulu i ka lālani a Kanaloa, a Keawe

Following the navigational stars of the heavens
From the southern ocean of Kiwa
Until arriving at the navel of Wākea (Orion at the Equator)
Searching for Polaris in the northern heavens
Until landing in the land of Pele
Just under the zenith star of Hōkūle'a (Arcturus)
Joyous indeed was Paoa in the archipelago of Hawai'i
Establishing the lineage of the ocean god Kanaloa, and his offspring Keawe

A Keawenui-a-'Umi
Mai nā Mō'ī Kaikilani ā Keākealani
I wili 'ia me ka lālani a 'Ī
Ali'i 'Ī o Hilo me Māui
Nona ka mo'okū'auahau kapōhihi o Kumulipo
I ka pi'i aku ai i nā mamo o Manōkalanipō
'O Pi'ikoi nō ia, kahu a Kaumuali'i
Na Pi'ikoi lāua o Kamake'e
Nā pulapula hanohano he nui
'O David Pi'ikoi 'Ōku'u kekahi
'O David Pi'ikoi 'Ōku'u
Male aku iā Lu'ukia Keākealani Paoa
Ua hānau 'o Mary Kamaolipua Pi'ikoi 'Ōku'u
Male aku iā Isaac Haku'ole Harbottle
Keiki a Haku'ole me Naha Harbottle
Koho 'ia e Kalākaua e hele kula ma Iapana

Mo'opuna o Kapena Harbottle mai Pelekania mai
Kapena o ka moku kiakolu o Keōua
Hoaloha nui a Kamehameha
Na Mary Kamaolipua Pi'ikoi
Me Isaac Haku'ole Harbottle
Ka kaikamahine
'O Irmgard Kamu'ookalani Lu'ukia Harbottle
Wahine male a Henry Na'inoa Thompson
Keikikāne a David Thompson me Grace Kealoha Aona
Na Kamu'ookalani Lu'ukia me Na'inoa
Na keiki poina'ole 'o Myron Bennet Pinky Thompson
Pelekikena lua'ole o ka Hui Ho'okele o Polenekia
Kokua kūkulu no Hōkūle'a me Hawai'iloa
Wa'a ho'iho'i ka mana'olana a Hawai'i
Mau ana a ka hoe wa'a a Hui Nalu
Me ka lima pa'a i ho'okele ai
'O Myron Bennet Pinky Thompson
'O Kamalei-a-Paoa
E ō mai i kou inoa!
E ō mai ē!

Of the great Keawe, son of 'Umi
From the ruling chiefesses Kaikilani and Keākealani
Entwined with the lineage of 'Ī
Supreme chiefs of Hilo and Māui
For whom was chanted the sacred Kumulipo genealogy
Mingling with the descendants of Kaua'i chiefs
He was Pi'ikoi, guardian of Kaumuali'i, king of Kaua'i
From Pi'ikoi and Kamake'e, Hilo chiefess, came
Many famous offspring
David Pi'ikoi 'Ōku'u was one of these
David Pi'ikoi 'Ōku'u
Married Lu'ukia Keākealani Paoa
Born was Mary Kamaolipua Pi'ikoi 'Ōku'u
Who married Isaac Haku'ole Harbottle
Son of Haku'ole and Naha Harbottle
Chosen by King Kalākaua to study in Japan
Grandson of Captain Harbottle of England

Captain of the three-masted ship Keōua
Good friend of Kamehameha
From Mary Kamaolipua Piʻikoi
And Isaac Hakuʻole Harbottle
Came the daughter
Irmgard Kamuʻookalani Luʻukia Harbottle
Wife of Henry Naʻinoa Thompson
Son of David Thompson and Grace Kealoha Aona
From Kamuʻookalani Luʻukia and Naʻinoa
Was born the unforgettable son Myron Bennet Pinky Thompson
Unparalleled President of the Polynesian Voyaging Society
Whose support helped build *Hōkūleʻa* and *Hawaiʻiloa*
Canoes that returned hope to Hawaiʻi
Continued by the Hui Nalu paddler
Guided by the firm navigating hand of
Myron Bennet Pinky Thompson
Beloved descendant of the Chief Paoa
Answer your name chant!
Answer!

Epilogue

After being offloaded at Seattle, *Hawai'iloa* sailed north through the island-studded Inland Passage, stopping at villages and towns along the way so that the crew could thank the Native Alaskans for the spruce trees and show them the canoe that had resulted. Their hosts in turn honored them in gift-giving ceremonies, the likes of which the Hawaiians had never before experienced. The two groups also enjoyed swapping tales about their respective cultures, histories, and aspirations as the "First People" of their respective lands. An added bonus for the visitors was the chance to meet descendants of Hawaiians who over the last two centuries had settled in Alaska to work in fur trading, fishing, logging, and other industries.

While *Hawai'iloa* headed north, *Hōkūle'a* enjoyed a celebration with Hawaiian groups around Seattle, then stood out to sea and turned south to head down the West Coast. The canoe called at ports in Oregon, then reached San Francisco. There a flotilla of outrigger canoes from local Hawaiian racing teams greeted her as she sailed under the Golden Gate Bridge, where she was showered with blossoms from above. This visit, and the following ones at Santa Barbara, Long Beach, and San Diego, were organized by various Hawaiian Civic Clubs established by the many Hawaiians living in the Western states. The organizers also made sure that the Tongans, Samoans, and other Pacific Islanders, and above all Native Americans, were included in the celebrations. Well in advance, they had requested and gained permission from the native groups living around each port for *Hōkūle'a* to enter their tribal areas—something very few, if any, visitors think to do.

When the two canoes returned to Hawai'i late that summer, *Te Aurere, Te Au o Tonga,* and *Takitumu* were already home. The Cook Islanders headed straight for Rarotonga, as did the Māori, who after a stopover continued on to Aotearoa. Since then Hector Busby has been sailing *Te Aurere* around the North Island and has turned his home and grounds on Doubtless Bay into a center for teaching about canoe navigation and voyaging. Schoolchildren and youths travel there for day classes and residential courses taught by Hector, Jacko Thatcher, and other *Te Aurere* sailors. In 2000 Hector and his crew sailed *Te Aurere* west to New Caledonia to represent their nation at the Pacific Arts Festival being held there that year.

Takitumu arrived at Rarotonga much the worse for wear. Because her sail rig had not been properly fixed, and the plywood covering her hulls was beginning to separate, she was towed home. Soon after *Te Au o Tonga* reached Rarotonga (in much better shape than *Takitumu*), President Jacques Chirac announced that France was resuming nuclear testing at Moruroa Atoll in the Tuamotu chain. As the Cooks lie directly downwind from there, the government dispatched *Te Au o Tonga* to the testing zone to protest. However, a government ship ended up towing her there because there wasn't enough time to tack east against the southeast trades or to wait for seasonal westerlies. Nonetheless, as the only Polynesian canoe among the international flotilla of protesting yachts and motor vessels, *Te Au o Tonga* was the star media attraction. The following year Papa Tom caused another stir when he commandeered the canoe and sailed to the 1996 Arts Festival in Sāmoa, and then returned home via Aotearoa.

After the Hawaiian canoes returned from the West Coast, *Hawai'iloa* was hauled up to the great lawn at Bishop Museum for temporary exhibition there. Schoolchildren as well as regular museum visitors were able to climb aboard and get the feel of standing on the deck of a big voyaging canoe. While *Hawai'iloa* was on display, *Hōkūle'a* set out on a statewide educational sail, taking eight months to visit numerous ports and anchorages around the islands. At each stop, students learned about all the arts, crafts, and science that went into voyaging from the canoe sailors and volunteers. And the need to *mālama*, care for, Hawai'i was emphasized. In addition, the Polynesian Voyaging Society and teachers developed intensive courses and special programs at selected high schools, O'ahu's Windward Community College, and the main campus of the University of Hawai'i.

But it wasn't long before the Hawaiian sailors started talking about making more long voyages. After some discussion, the Big Island's Nā Kālaiwa'a Moku o Hawai'i chose to sail *Makali'i* to Micronesia, and the Polynesian Voyaging Society decided to sail *Hōkūle'a* to Rapa Nui.

By navigating *Hōkūle'a* to Tahiti and subsequently passing his knowledge on to Nainoa and others, Mau had become famous throughout Polynesia as a culture bearer from a remote region in the Pacific where traditional navigation had not died out. To honor him, the Big Island sailors wanted to take Mau on a tour through his native Micronesia, ending up at Satawal, his home atoll. In mid-1999 *Makali'i* set sail with Mau on board, stopping first at the atoll Republic of the Marshall Islands. There Mau's son Sesario joined the canoe and navigated her through the high islands and atolls of the Federated States of Micronesia to Satawal. *Makali'i* then turned north to complete the tour by visiting Saipan and Guam of the Marianas islands. The master navigator was welcomed everywhere as a hero. The fame Mau gained in helping Polynesians reclaim their maritime heritage had come full circle and was now stimulating hitherto indifferent Micronesian youths to go back to the sea.

Why sail *Hōkūle'a* all the way to Rapa Nui, which is much closer to South America than to Hawai'i? "Because we want to close the Polynesian Triangle," said the Hawaiians. Their islands stand in the North Pacific as the apex of this triangle, with Aotearoa in the southwest and Rapa Nui in the southeast as the base angles. *Hōkūle'a* had been born in Hawai'i, traveled as far away as Aotearoa and had touched upon the major islands and archipelagos in between. Now the Hawaiians wanted to sail to Rapa Nui to complete the canoe's Polynesian odyssey by symbolically closing the triangle.

Sailing so far to the southeast, and then finding this small and isolated island presented a major challenge. One way to sail there would have been to start out during mid-winter from Mangareva, located at the southeast end of the Tuamotu chain 1,400 miles from Rapa Nui, and sail east before the winter westerlies. However, Nainoa feared that the clouds and rain accompanying these winds would make it virtually impossible to navigate by the stars to such a small target. Instead, after working the canoe to Mangareva, he planned to set sail at the beginning of the trade wind season in order to have fair skies for navigating—even though he realized that the extra miles spent tacking back and forth into the trades could lengthen the voyage to six weeks or more.

However, in 1999 the trades were late. So when *Hōkūle'a* set off in the early spring, favorable northerly and northwesterly winds from a lingering low-pressure system enabled the Hawaiians to sail almost directly toward Rapa Nui. Although clouds plagued them for much of the way, sporadic star sights and some inspired dead reckoning enabled Nainoa and his assistant navigators to keep the canoe on course for Rapa Nui. Even though completely overcast skies and heavy rains forced the crew to steer by big southwest swells during the last two nights, at dawn on the 17th day at sea a dark line betraying the presence of Rapa Nui peeped out from under the overcast just as the canoe was about to sail past the island.

The people of Rapa Nui were delighted that *Hōkūle'a* had sailed all the way to their island, and also enjoyed the deluge of Hawaiian supporters, including three dance teams that flew in for the occasion. Yet when the Hawaiians explained to them that they had sailed to Rapa Nui to "close the triangle" the people were puzzled until an elderly lady wittily replied: "You have not closed the triangle, you have opened it for us!"

Endnotes

Prologue
1. Sharp (1956).
2. Finney (1967).
3. Finney (1977).
4. Finney (1979).
5. Finney, Kilonsky, Somsen, and Stroup (1986).
6. Heyerdahl (1953, 1978, 1981).
7. Finney, Frost, Rhodes, and Thompson (1989); Finney (1994a:125-162).
8. Bishop Museum (1998:3).

Chapter One
1. This scene was reconstructed from film footage taken by Gail Evenari for her 1999 film, *Wayfinders: A Pacific Odyssey.*
2. Pukui (1939:150-151).
3. Holmes (1981:17-24); Mueller-Dombois et al. (1981:309-311, 502-520); Spatz and Mueller-Dombois (1973).
4. Vancouver (1798:218-219).
5. Dr. Soboleff stressed to me that the Hawaiians had asked him to give the canoe a Kwakiutl name, as he would otherwise not have presumed to do so.
6. Tundra Times (1995:6).
7. This and subsequent sections on building the canoe are drawn from Kyselka et al. (1993) as well as from videotapes and interviews.
8. Davis (1979); Fornander 1878-1885; Chun (1993); Beckwith (1932).
9. Fornander (1919). Although Fornander wrote Hawai'i Loa as two words, this study follows the NHCAP and PVS practice of spelling it as one word.
10. Fornander (1919:278-279).
11. Fornander (1878:22-25, 132-138).
12. Howard (1967:55-60); Howe (1991; In Press); Sorrenson (1979).
13. Beckwith (1932:3-7); Cartwright (1929); Emory (1969); Kamakau (1991); Luomala (1951:38-41).
14. Buck (1938:246-249).
15. Burrows (1938:73-76); Kirch and Green (2001:96-97); Smith (1910:55-57); Taumoefolau (1996). One explanation for this distribution is that Polynesian culture jelled at Savai'i, the largest island of the Samoan chain, and that voyagers from there spread the name to Eastern Polynesia.
16. Barrère (1969:37).
17. Polynesian Voyaging Society (1994).
18. Pukui, Elbert, and Mo'okini (1974:43).
19. Holmes (1981:50-52).
20. Freycinet (1978:86).
21. Buck (1957:253-284); Clerke in Cook (1967, Part 1:129-130); Pâris (1843: vol. 2, plate 127); Pukui (1939).
22. Holmes (1981:115-117); Malo (1951:131); Townsend (1921).
23. Fornander (1916); Emerson (1893). See Silva (1989), one of the chanters at Pōka'ī, for his discussion of the then problematic vitality of Hawaiian chants.

Chapter Two
1. Jonassen (1994:308-311).

2. Although the Rarotongans also refer to themselves as *Māori* (native, indigenous), to avoid confusion I use that term only for the native Polynesians of Aotearoa.
3. Pukui and Elbert (1986:235).
4. Jonassen (1994:313-314).
5. Captain Cook (1968:151) named the six central islands of the leeward group the Society Isles because "they lay contiguous to one another." Later the entire chain came to be called the Society Islands. Tahitians now refer to it as *Te Mau Fenua Tōtaiete*, a translation of "The Society Islands" in which *taiete* is their way of rendering the English word "society" (Fare Vāna'a 1999:513).
6. Polynesian Voyaging Society (1993).
7. Pakoti (1895).
8. Low (1934). Buck (1938:97-100) gives a briefer, more colorful version.
9. Jonassen (1994:313-314).

Chapter Three

1. Te Ao Pēhi Kara graciously provided me with his Māori text and an equally poetic English translation, of which portions are quoted here.
2. The word *tapu* was introduced into late eighteenth century English through publication in the journals of Captain Cook. Although Cook wrote "taboo," the phonetically accurate spelling is *tapu*, except in post-missionary Hawai'i, where it is *kapu*.
3. Hobsbawm and Ranger (1983).
4. Keesing and Tonkinson (1982), Linnekin (1983), and Handler and Linnekin (1984) were early leaders in analyzing cultural revival in the Pacific, followed by Babadzan (1988), Hanson (1989), Chapman and Dupon (1989), Keesing (1989), Stevenson (1990, 1992), Linnekin (1991), Friedman (1992), Jolly (1992), Jolly and Thomas (1992), Sissons (1993), Norton (1993), White and Lindstrom (1993), Tobin (1994), Feinberg and Zimmer-Tamonoshi (1995), Lindstrom and White (1995), Turner (1997), and others. In an essay on the synergism generated by our dual experimental and cultural approach to voyaging, I used the term "re-invention" to characterize how oral traditions, early historical accounts, and similar ways of navigating in Micronesia were used to recreate Polynesian navigation (Finney 1991).
5. Linnekin (1983); Hanson (1989); Keesing (1989).
6. Grainger (1990); Nissen (1990); Noble (1990); Trask (1991).
7. Sahlins (1993:4); Turner (1997).
8. Lucas (1989); Kame'eleihiwa (1992:22).
9. MacAloon (1981).
10. Despite being geographically in the western half of Polynesia, since Aotearoa was settled from Eastern Polynesia it is part of that cultural province.
11. Henry (1928:119-128). John Orsmond arrived at Mo'orea in 1817 soon after most Tahitians had converted, nominally at least, to Christianity. He began learning Tahitian from Tahitian shipmates on the long voyage out from England, and soon became so fluent and developed such good rapport with Tahitian sages that King Pomare directed him to interview and record these keepers of oral tradition (Driessen 1982:5).
12. Smith (1898: 47).
13. As *roa* generally means "long," Henry initially translated Aotearoa as "Long-light-land." Yet noting that since *roa* can also mean "distant," she also suggested that Aotearoa might mean "Distant-light-land" in contrast to the islands nearer to Ra'iātea (Henry 1928:123). However, since *ao* can also mean "day," Biggs (1990:7) translates Aotearoa as "Long Daylight," explaining that the first voyagers to reach

this temperate land were struck by how much longer the summer days were there in comparison to those in the tropics.

14. Williams (1838:56, 104).
15. Finney (1979:278-286).
16. Professor Larry Kimura of the University of Hawai'i at Hilo kindly provided me with the text and translation, only a portion of which is quoted here.
17. Henry (1928: 123-126).
18. Clark (1993).
19. Kāne (1993).
20. Dening (1992:4-5, 203-205).
21. Buck (1938:81-82).
22. I would especially like to thank Hector Busby, Te Ao Pēhi Kara, Larry Kimura, and above all my host and longtime friend at Ra'iātea, Pierre Sham Koua for helping me to understand what was going on that day at Taputapuātea. See Finney (1999) for an earlier version of this chapter.

Chapter Four
1. Finney (1994a: 190-192, 196); Nelson (1991:70-71).
2. See Best (1976:23-62), Haddon and Hornell (1936:194-217), and Neyret (1977:73-84) for descriptions and drawings of Māori paddling and sailing canoes, including double-hull craft.
3. Davis (1992c); Haddon and Hornell (1936:265-273); Neyret (1977:113-115); Kernahan (1992); Clunie (1987, 1992). The *kalia* type was called *'alia* in Sāmoa and *ndrua* in Fiji.
4. Te Ariki Tara 'Are (1919:197, 2000:150); Hauete and Terei (1908); Cook Islands Voyaging Society (1995:12); Sissons (2002).
5. Walter (1998).
6. Nelson (1991:14-23).
7. Although *Makali'i* and its cognate forms of *matari'i, matariki,* etc. are often translated as the "tiny eyes" or stars that make up the Pleiades, the members of Nā Kālaiwa'a Moku o Hawai'i consider that *Makali'i* is a contraction of *Maka Ali'i,* meaning "Eye of the Chief."
8. I am indebted to Kiki Hugho for letting me read his vivid, first-hand account of this tragedy.
9. This and the following excerpts are quoted from recordings made for Gail Evenari's film, *Wayfinders: A Pacific Odyssey.*
10. Davis and Davis 1954; Davis 1992a.
11. Davis 1992b.

Chapter Five
1. Quiros (1904:20); Dening (1980:14).
2. Baert (1995); Le Cléac'h (1997:34, 45). See Kaiser and Elbert (1989:77) on the phonetic differences between the two dialects (or languages).
3. As with other Polynesian nouns, *fenua/henua* and *'enana/'enata* can be understood as either singular or plural depending upon context or the use of preceding quantifiers.
4. Emory (1959).
5. Ellis (1826:408).
6. Malo (1951:4-8).
7. See Pukui and Elbert (1986:112) for the various meanings of Kahiki.
8. Emory (1928:116-122; 1933; 1943; 1959:34-35; 1946).
9. Kirch (1985:15-16); Krause (1988:337-341); Emory, Bonk, and Sinoto (1968:ix).
10. Kirch (1985:16); Krause (1988:249-358); Emory, Bonk, and Sinoto (1968:3).

11. Krause (1988:370-378).
12. Krause (1988:378-390); Emory and Sinoto (1964).
13. Suggs (1960, 1961a, 1961b); Buck (1938:64-96; 1944:520-526); Emory (1962); Emory and Sinoto (1964).
14. Emory (1962; 1963); Emory and Sinoto (1965); Sinoto (1967).
15. Green (1966:20-26); Elbert (1982); Marck (1996:500-505, 1999). Green found that Hawaiian is closest to the Southern dialect of 'Enanan.
16. Green (1966:30; 1974); Bellwood (1970); Cordy (1974); Kirch (1986); Cachola-Abad (1993).
17. Kirch (1985:65-66).
18. Finney (1994a:276-277); Johnson et al. (1989:156-157); Bruner (1990).
19. "Abe" is the father of Gordon Pi'ianai'a, who has skippered *Hōkūle'a* on several long voyages, and his sister Ilima, who joined us on *Gershon* for the sail to Hawai'i
20. Kāne (1976:66); Pi'ianai'a (1990).
21. Porter (1815, 2:54-56).
22. Dening (1980:62-63).
23. Dening (1974:62-63, 266-267).
24. Porter (1822, 2:77).
25. Rolett (1998:250-262). Compare Walter (1998) on a similar decline in the Cook Islands.
26. Thomas (1990); Kirch (1991).
27. Melville (1846).
28. Candelot and Teikiehu'upoko (1995).
29. Teikiehu'upoko (1995). The salutations are, respectively, 'Enanan, Samoan, Māori, Tahitian, Hawaiian, and Māori again.
30. Spriggs and Anderson (1993); Anderson et al. (1994); Anderson (2001); Rolett and Conte (1994); Rolett (1998:55-57).
31. Quiros (1904:26); Beaglehole (1934:46-81).
32. Dening (1980).
33. Dening (1980:239-240, 265); Rallu (1992); Verneau (1929:xiii); ORSTOM (1993:72).

Chapter Six

1. See Kyselka (1987) and Finney et al. (1986) on how Nainoa learned navigation, and Lewis (1972) and Finney (1998) on Pacific canoe navigation.
2. A sealed transponder on the canoe continually transmitted a fixed signal that was received every several hours by passing satellites and relayed to an ARGOS ground station in France. There the position of the canoe was calculated and then sent to the University of Hawai'i for plotting.
3. Finney et al. (1986:85-86); Finney (1994a:90-93).
4. Although no firm evidence suggests that early Hawaiians reached North America, to explain the ancient presence in Polynesia of the sweet potato (*Ipomoea batatas*), a plant of South American origin, Yen (1974, 1991, 1998) and Green (2002) propose that Polynesians sailed to South America and brought this valuable tuber back to the islands. Seafarers from southeastern Polynesia could have reached South America by the same method as Hawaiians sailing to North America, except to reach the higher latitudes where westerlies blow they would have sailed south instead of north (Finney 1994b; 1994c).

Chapter Seven

1. The wind shadow also blocks canoes starting from O'ahu, Moloka'i, or Maui from sailing directly southeast past the Big Island's South Point (Ka Lae).

2. As the morning and evening D.R. and GPS positions were taken two hours apart, the lines connecting them can somewhat alter the gap between where the navigator estimated the canoe was and its actual position.
3. Krauss (1995).
4. Pukui and Elbert (1986:143).
5. See Linnekin (1990) for an analysis of cultural identity issues in the Pacific.
6. Miller (1995). The identification of the flies as *nono* was never confirmed.
7. By turning the hulls around, the Hawaiians had inadvertently followed a principle for making seakindly vessels that North Atlantic sailors characterize as "a cod's head and a mackerel tail" (Needham 1971:418). However, because of *Hawai'iloa*'s low freeboard, swells peaking directly underneath the canoe would sometimes smack the underside of the deck, once hard enough to break a deck plank.

Chapter Eight

1. Pukui (1983:311).
2. An example of the pitfalls of facilely charging cultural invention can be found in the pages of *Honolulu Magazine*. Scott Whitney (2001a) charged that *'ohana* is a neologism without ancient foundation, but was forced to recant when Hawaiian language authorities Cook, Hawkins, and McGregor (2001) pointed out that it was an old Hawaiian word with cognate forms in other Polynesian languages. Nonetheless, Whitney (2001b) stood by his contention that *'ohana* has been stretched far beyond its original meaning, and sharpened his point by charging that the term has "floated off into the murky pool of New Age mush."
3. Pukui, Elbert, and Mookini (1974:119); Finney (1979:3-6); Sterling and Summers (1978:177-184).
4. The voyaging canoes were joined by a pair of local double canoes, *Mo'olele* from Maui and *E'ala* from O'ahu.
5. This practice is somewhat reminiscent of an ancient custom of taking a stone from Taputapuātea to another island to serve as a foundation stone for a new *marae* of that name (Henry 1928:120, 122, 126-131; Emory 1933:61-62).
6. Rezentes (1996:37-38).
7. Oshiro (2002). One product of this was *Nānā i ke Kumu*, a work on Hawaiian beliefs, concepts, and practices by Pukui, Haertig, and Lee (1972).
8. I would like to thank Sam Low (who sailed from Te Henua 'Enana to Hawai'i on the escort boat *Rizalder*, captained by Randy Wichman) for allowing me to use this quote, as well as for his comments and suggestions on an earlier draft of this book.
9. Professor Kame'eleihiwa also kindly provided the translation, including the explanatory words in parentheses.

Glossary of Polynesian Terms Used

'Aha. (H, T) Cord braided from coconut fiber. Compare *kaha* (A, E), *ka'a* (C).

Aloha. (H) A greeting; love; compassion. Compare *ka'oha* (E), *arofa* (T), *aroha* (T, A), *aro'a* (C).

Alu Like. (H) "Work Together." Hawaiian organization for job training.

A'o. (H, T) Learning; instruction; teaching. Compare *'ako* (E), *ako* (A, C).

'Awa. (H) Plant *(Piper methysticum)*, the roots of which are pounded to make the drink also known as *'awa*. Compare *'ava* (T, E, C).

'Enana. (E) Person; native of Te Henua 'Enana. Compare *kanaka* (H), *ta'ata* (T), *tangata* (A, C).

Fa'Atau aroha. (T) The "Friendly Alliance" at Taputapuātea of islands belonging to Te-ao-uri (The Dark-land) and Te-ao-tea (The Light-land).

Haere mai. (T, A) Come hither. Compare *hele mai* (H), *he'e mai* (E), *'aere mai* (C).

Haka. (A) Fierce dance and chant. Compare *ha'a* (H), *pahaku* (E).

Haka'iki. (E) Hereditary chief. Compare *ali'i* (H), *ari'i* (T), *ariki* (R, A).

Hale. (H) House; compass point in Nainoa Thompson's conceptual compass. Compare *fare* (T), *whare* (A), *'are* (C), *ha'e* (E).

Haole. (H) White person; formerly any foreigner. Compare *hao'o, haore* (E).

Hau. (H, E) Tree *(Hibiscus tiliaceus)* providing light, strong wood for canoe components. Compare *fau* (T, E), *purau* (T), *'au* (C).

Haumea. (H) A female personification of "Earth Foundation," also known as Papa, who gave birth to islands and people.

Hawaiki. (A) The mythical Māori homeland; also used elsewhere in Polynesia for homeland or colony thereof in such forms as Savaiki, 'Avaiki, Havai'i, Hawai'i.

Hōkū Pa'a. (H) "Fixed Star." Polaris; North Star.

'Iako. (H) Crossbeam connecting two hulls of a double canoe, or the hull and a float of an outrigger canoe. Compare *kiato* (T, E, A, C).

'Imi 'ike. (H) To seek knowledge.

Kahiki. (H) Distant land(s), the South Pacific island of Tahiti.

Kahuna. (H) Expert, priest. Compare *tahu'a* (T), *tuhuka* (E), *tuhuna* (E), *tohunga* (A), *ta'unga* (C).

Kahuna kālai wa'a. (H) Master canoe carver.

Kahuna pule. (H) Prayer expert.

Ka'oha. (E) Greeting; expression of friendship and affection. Compare *aloha* (H), *arofa* (T), *aroha* (T, A), *aro'a* (C).

Kupuna. (H) Elder; ancestor. Compare *tupuna* (E, T, A, C).

Kaumaha. (H) "Heavy," both literally and psychologically. Compare *taumaha* (A), *tauma'a* (C), *teimaha* (T).

Kauri. (A) Aotearoa tree *(Agathis australis)* excellent for making big canoes.

Ki'i. (H) Statue; image. Compare *tiki* (E, A, C), *ti'i* (T).

Koa. (H) Hawaiian tree *(Acacia koa)* favored for making canoes.

Ko'i honua. (H) Genealogical chant.

Kōlea. (H) Pacific golden plover *(Puvialis fulda)*, a migratory bird. Compare *tōrea* (T, R), *to'ea* (E).

Lauhala. (H) Pandanus leaf, especially used in weaving. Compare *raufara* (T), *'auha'a* (E), *rau'ara* (C).

Lōkahi. (H) Unity; agreement.

Maika'i. (H) Good. Compare *meita'i* (E), *maita'i* (T), *meitaki* (C).

Mālama. (H) To take care of; preserve; protect. Compare *marama* (A).

Mālama Hawai'i. (H) "Care for Hawai'i." Environmental education movement.

Mamo. (H) Descendant; posterity; black Hawaiian honeycreeper.

Mana. (H, E, T, C, A) Power, spiritual power, authority.

Manu. (H) Ornamental extensions of canoe bow and stern pieces; entire bow piece *(manu ihu)* or stern piece *(manu hope)*; common word for "bird" throughout Polynesia.

Marae. (T, C, A) Temple, meeting ground. Compare *me'ae* (E).

Mele inoa. (H) Name chant.

Mo'o. (H) Side strakes (planks) added to raise freeboard of hulls; series; lizard. Compare *mo'o* (T), *moko* (C, A, E).

Nono. (T) Biting sandfly that infests the beaches of Te Henua 'Enana.

'Ohana. (H) Extended family; also applied to groups to protect a family identity.

'Ōhi'a lehua. (H) Hawaiian tree *(Metrosideros macropus)* noted for strong, dense wood, and bright red flowers.

Papa. (H, E, T, C, A) Female personification of "Earth Foundation," also known as Haumea, who gave birth to islands and people.

Papa Ola Lōkahi. (H) An organization for health care of Hawaiians.

Pōhaku. (H) Stone; rock. Compare *pōhatu* (A), *ko'atu* (C).

Pola. (H) Narrow platform between hulls of a double canoe.

Pono. (H) Just; proper. Compare *pono* (A, T, E).

Tapu. (E, T, R, A) Taboo; forbidden; restricted; sacred. Compare *kapu* (H).

Taputapuātea. (T) "Sacrifices from abroad;" temple at Ra'iātea.

Taro. (T, E, C, A) A staple root crop *(Colocasia esculenta)*. Compare *kalo* (H), *ta'o* (E).

Tau'a. (E) Prophet; shamanic priest. Compare *kaula* (H).

Te-ao-tea. (T) "The Light-land," composed of islands leeward of Ra'iātea.

Te-ao-uri. (T) "The Dark-land," composed of islands to windward of Ra'iātea.

Te Avamo'a. (T, C) The "Sacred Pass" through the reef to Taputapuātea.

Te Avarua. (T, C) The "Double Pass" through which aggrieved delegates from Te-ao-tea fled from Taputapuātea. Compare Te Awarua (A).

Te Henua 'Enana. (E) The Land of People; The Native Land; The Marquesas Islands. Te Fenua 'Enata in the southern dialect.

Tī. (T, C, A, E) Plant *(Cordyline terminalis)* with long green leaves. Compare *kī* (H).

Tipaerua. (T) A type of Tahitian double canoe.

Tōtora. (A) Aotearoa tree *(Podocarpus totora)* used for making canoe hulls.

'Ulu. (H) Breadfruit *(Autocarpus altilis)*. Compare *'uru* (T), *kuru* (C, A).

Wa'a. (H) Canoe. Compare *va'a* (T, E), *waka* (A), *vaka* (C, E).

Wākea. (H) Male personification of "Vast Space," who fertilized Papa (Haumea) to give birth to islands and people. Compare Ākea (E, T, C, A).

References Cited

Anderson, Atholl. 2001. The Chronology of Prehistoric Colonization in French Polynesia. In *Proceedings of the Fifth International Conference on Easter Island and the Pacific*, ed. Christopher M. Stevenson, Georgia Lee, and F. J. Morin, 247-265. Los Osos, California: Bearsville Press.

Anderson, Atholl, Helen Leach, I. Smith, and R. Walter. 1994. Reconsideration of the Marquesan Sequence in the Early Settlement of East Polynesia, with Particular Reference to Hane (MUH1). *Archaeology in Oceania* 29:29-52.

Babadzan, Alain. 1988. Kastom and Nation Building in the South Pacific. In *Ethnicities and Nations: Processes of Interethnic Relations in Latin America, Southeast Asia and the Pacific*, ed. R. Guidieri, F. Pellizzi, and S. J. Tambiah, 199-228. Houston: Rothko Chapel and University of Texas Press.

Baert, Annie. 1995. Îles Marquises, Fenua Enata, ou Henua Enana? Découvert ou Redécouvert? *Tahiti Pacifique* 5(48):47.

Barrère, Dorothy B. 1969. *The Kumuhonua Legends, A Study of Late 19th Century Hawaiian Stores of Creation and Origins*. Pacific Anthropological Records 3. Honolulu: Department of Anthropology, Bishop Museum.

Beaglehole, John C. 1934. *The Exploration of the Pacific*. London: A. & C. Black.

Beckwith, Martha. 1932. *Kepelino's Traditions of Hawaii*. Bishop Museum Bulletin 95. Honolulu: Bishop Museum.

Bellwood, Peter. 1970. Dispersal Centers in East Polynesia, With Special Reference to the Society and Marquesas Islands. In *Studies in Oceanic Culture History*, 2 vols., ed. Roger C. Green and Marion Kelly, 1:93-104. Honolulu: Department of Anthropology, Bishop Museum.

Best, Elsdon. 1976. *The Maori Canoe*. Dominion Museum Bulletin 7. Wellington: A. T. Shearer, Government Printer. Reprint of 1925 edition.

Biggs, Bruce. 1990. In the Beginning. In *The Oxford Illustrated History of New Zealand*, ed. Keith Sinclair, 1-20. Auckland: Oxford University Press.

Bishop Museum. 1998. *Bishop Museum's Native Hawaiian Culture and Arts Program 1987-1997, Accomplishments, Impact and Future*. Honolulu: Bishop Museum.

Blust, Robert. 1995. The Prehistory of the Austronesian Speaking Peoples: A View from Language. *Journal of World Prehistory* 9:453-510.

Bruner, Philip L. 1990. Personal communication, 14 November.

Buck, Peter H. (Te Rangi Hiroa). 1938. *Vikings of the Sunrise*. New York: Frederick A. Stokes; Philadelphia: J. B. Lippincott. (Reprinted in 1959 as *Vikings of the Pacific*, Chicago: University of Chicago Press.)

————. **1944.** *Arts and Crafts of the Cook Islands*. Bishop Museum Bulletin 179. Honolulu: Bishop Museum.

————. **1957.** *Arts and Crafts of Hawai'i*. Bishop Museum Special Publication 45. Honolulu: Bishop Museum.

Burrows, Edwin G. 1938. *Western Polynesia: A Study in Cultural Differentiation*. Erthnologiska Studier 7. Goteborg: Goteborg Ethnografiska Museum.

Cachola-Abad, C. Kēhaunani. 1993. Evaluation the Orthodox Dual Settlement Model for the Hawaiian Islands: An Analysis of Artefact Distribution and Hawaiian Oral Traditions. In *The Evolution and Organization of Prehistoric Society in Polynesia*, ed. Michael W. Graves and Roger C. Green, 13-32. New Zealand Archaeological Association Monograph 19. Auckland: New Zealand Archaeological Association.

Candelot, Jean-Louis, and Georges (Toti) Teikiehu'upoko. 1995. Discours Pour l'Arrivée des Pirogues Polynésiennes à Nukuhiva. *Bulletin de la Société des Études Océaniennes (Polynésie Orientale)* No. 267, 13(5): 78-85.

Cartwright, Bruce. 1929. The Legend of Hawaii-Loa. *Journal of the Polynesian Society* 38:105-121.

Chapman, Murray, and Jean-François Dupon. 1989. Renaissance du Pacifique. Special edition of *Ethnies, Droits de l'Homme et Peuples Autochtones* 4(8-10):1-124.

Chun, Malcolm Naea. 1993. *Na Kukui Pio Ole, The Inextinguishable Torches: The Biographies of Three Early Native Hawaiian Scholars, Davida Malo, S. N. Haleole and S. M. Kamakau.* Honolulu: First People's Productions.

Clark, Jeff. 1993. A Plant of Old Regains Prominence: Three Views on the Modern Hawaiian 'Awa Ceremony. *Ka Wai Ola O Oha* 10 (August):12, 23.

Clunie, Fergus. 1987. Ndrua and Kalia: The Great Tongan Voyaging Canoe. *Islands* (January-March):11-16.

————. **1992.** Letter to Herb Kāne, 29 March.

Cook Islands Voyaging Society. 1995. *Vaka.* Rarotonga, Cook Islands: Cook Islands Voyaging Society.

Cook, James. 1967. *The Voyage of the Resolution and Discovery 1776–1780*, 2 parts. Ed. J. C. Beaglehole. Cambridge: Hakluyt Society.

————. **1968.** *The Voyage of the Endeavour 1768–1771.* Ed. J. C. Beaglehole. Cambridge: Hakluyt Society.

Cook, Kenneth W., Emily Hawkins, and Davianna Pōmaiaka'i McGregor. 2001. 'Ohana Answers. *Honolulu* 36(5):12-14.

Cordy, Ross H. 1974. The Tahitian Migration to Hawaii ca 1100-1300 A.D.—An Argument Against its Occurrence. *New Zealand Archaeological Association Newsletter* 17:65-76.

Davis, Eleanor H. 1979. *Abraham Fornander, a Biography.* Honolulu: University of Hawai'i Press.

Davis, Thomas R. A. H. (Pa Tuterangi Ariki). 1992a. *Island Boy, An Autobiography.* Suva, Fiji: The Institute of Pacific Studies, University of the South Pacific; Canterbury, New Zealand: The Macmillan Brown Centre for Pacific Studies; Auckland: The Centre for Pacific Studies, University of Auckland.

————. **1992b.** *Vaka: Saga of a Polynesian Canoe.* Suva, Fiji: Institute of Pacific Studies, University of the South Pacific; Auckland, New Zealand: Polynesian Press, Samoa House.

————. **1992c.** The Drua and the Takitumu Canoe — Papa Tom's Column, *Cook Islands News*, 12 June.

Davis, Thomas R. A. H., and Lydia Davis. 1954. *Doctor to the Islands.* Boston, Massachusetts: Little, Brown.

Dening, Gregory M. 1974. *The Marquesan Journal of Edward Robarts 1797-1824.* Canberra: Australian National University Press.

————. **1980.** *Islands and Beaches.* Honolulu: University of Hawai'i Press.

————. **1992.** *Mr. Bligh's Bad Language.* Cambridge: Cambridge University Press.

Driessen, H. A. H. 1982. Outriggerless Canoes and Glorious Beings: Pre-contact Prophecies in the Society Islands. *Journal of Pacific History* 17:3-28.

Elbert, Samuel H. 1982. Lexical Diffusion in Polynesia and the Marquesan-Hawaiian Relationship. *Journal of the Polynesian Society* 91:499-518.

Ellis, William. 1826. *Narrative of a Tour through Hawaii, or Owhyhee; with Remarks on the History, Traditions, Manners, Customs, and Language of the Inhabitants of the Sandwich Islands.* London: H. Fisher, Son, and P. Jackson.

Emerson, Nathaniel B. 1893. *The Long Voyages of the Ancient Hawaiians.* Papers of the Hawaiian Historical Society No. 5. Honolulu: Hawaiian Historical Society.

Emory, Kenneth P. 1928. *Archaeology of Nihoa and Necker Islands*. Bishop Museum Bulletin 53. Honolulu: Bishop Museum.

———. 1933. *Stone Remains in the Society Islands*. Bishop Museum Bulletin 116. Honolulu: Bishop Museum.

———. 1943. Polynesian Stone Remains. In *Studies in the Anthropology of Oceania and Asia . . . in Memory of Roland Burrage Dixon*, ed. C. S. Coon and J. M. Andrews IV, 9-21. Peabody Museum of Archaeology and Ethnology Paper No. 20. Cambridge: Peabody Museum of Archaeology and Ethnology, Harvard University.

———. 1946. Eastern Polynesia: Its Cultural Relationships. Ph.D. Dissertation, Department of Anthropology, Yale University: New Haven.

———. 1959. Origin of the Hawaiians. *Journal of the Polynesian Society* 1959:29-35.

———. 1962. Changing Hidden Worlds of Polynesia. Unpublished paper presented at the Social Science Association. 3 December, Honolulu.

———. 1963. East Polynesia Relationships. *Journal of the Polynesian Society* 72:78-100.

———. 1969. *Preface* to *The Kumuhonua Legends, A Study of Late 19th Century Hawaiian Stores of Creation and Origins,* by Dorothy B. Barrère. Pacific Anthropological Records 3. Honolulu: Department of Anthropology, Bishop Museum.

Emory, Kenneth P., William J. Bonk, and Yoshihiko H. Sinoto. 1968. *Fishhooks*. Bishop Museum Special Publication 47. Honolulu: Bishop Museum.

Emory, Kenneth P., and Yoshihiko H. Sinoto. 1964. Eastern Polynesian Burials at Maupiti. *Journal of the Polynesian Society* 73:143-160.

———. 1965. Preliminary Report of the Archaeological Investigations in Polynesia: Field Work in the Society Islands, Tuamotu Islands, French Polynesia and American Samoa in 1962, 1963, 1964. Unpublished report. Honolulu: Department of Anthropology, Bishop Museum.

Fare Vana'a. n.d. *Grammaire de la Langue Tahitienne*. Pape'ete, Tahiti: Académie Tahitienne.

Feinberg, Richard, and Laura Zimmer-Tamakoshi. 1995. Politics of Culture in the Pacific Islands. Special issue of *Ethnology* 34:89-153.

Finney, Ben. 1967. New Perspectives on Polynesian Voyaging. In *Polynesian Culture History: Essays in Honor of Kenneth P. Emory*, ed. Genevieve Highland, Roland W. Force, Alan Howard, Marion Kelly, and Yoshihiko H. Sinoto, 141-166. Bishop Museum Special Publication 56. Honolulu: Bishop Museum.

———. 1977. Voyaging Canoes and the Settlement of Polynesia. *Science* 196:1277-1285.

———. 1979. *Hōkūle'a: The Way to Tahiti*. New York: Dodd, Mead.

———. 1991. Myth, Experiment and the Re-invention of Polynesian Voyaging. *American Anthropologist* 92:383-404.

———. 1994a. *Voyage of Rediscovery: A Cultural Odyssey through Polynesia*. With Marlene Among, Chad Baybayan, Tai Crouch, Paul Frost, Bernard Kilonsky, Richard Rhodes, Thomas Schroeder, Dixon Stroup, Nainoa Thompson, Robert Worthington, and Elisa Yadao. Berkeley: University of California Press.

———. 1994b. Polynesian Voyagers to the New World. *Man and Culture in Oceania* 10: 1-13.

———. 1994c. Polynesian-South American Round Trip Canoe Voyages. *Rapa Nui Journal* 8:33-35.

———. 1998. Traditional Navigation and Nautical Cartography in Oceania. In *The History of Cartography, Vol. 3, part 2: Cartography in Traditional African, American, Arctic, Australian, and Pacific Societies*, ed. G. Malcolm Lewis and David Woodward, 443-492. Chicago: University of Chicago Press.

———. 1999. The Sin at Awarua. *The Contemporary Pacific* 11:1-33.

Finney, Ben, Bernard Kilonsky, Steven Somsen, and Edward Stroup. 1986. Re-learning a Vanishing Art. *Journal of the Polynesian Society* 95:41-90.

Finney, Ben, Paul Frost, Richard Rhodes, and Nainoa Thompson. 1989. Wait for the West Wind. *Journal of the Polynesian Society* 98:261-302.

Fornander, Abraham. 1878-1885. *An account of the Polynesian race: its Origin and Migrations, and the Ancient History of the Hawaiian People to the Times of Kamehameha I.* London: Trubner & Co. (Reprinted in 1969 as one volume, Rutland, Vermont: Tuttle.)

———. **1916.** The History of Moikeha. Vol. 4, part 1:112-159 in *Fornander Collection of Hawaiian Antiquities and Folklore.* Memoirs of the Bernice P. Bishop Museum, Vols. 4-6. Honolulu: Bishop Museum.

———. **1919.** Legend of Hawaii-Loa, Compiled and Condensed in English from Kepelino and Kamakau. Vol. 6, part 2:266-281 in *Fornander Collection of Hawaiian Antiquities and Folklore.* Memoirs of the Bernice P. Bishop Museum, Vols. 4-6. Honolulu: Bishop Museum.

Freycinet, Louis. 1978. *Hawai'i in 1819, a Narrative Account by Louis Claude de Saulses de Freycinet,* trans. Ella L. Wiswell. Pacific Anthropological Records 26. Honolulu: Department of Anthropology, Bishop Museum.

Friedman, Jonathan. 1992. Myth, History and Political Identity. *Cultural Anthropology* 7:194-210.

Grainger, Matthew. 1990. Walker Rejects Analysis as Shallow. [Wellington] *The Dominion,* 24 February, 1.

Green, Roger C. 1966. Linguistic Subgrouping Within Polynesia: The Implications for Prehistoric Settlement. *Journal of the Polynesian Society* 75:6-33.

———. **1974.** Tahiti-Hawaii A.D. 1100–1300: Further comments. *New Zealand Archaeological Association Newsletter* 17: 206-210.

———. **2002.** The Introduction of the Sweet Potato and Other Plants from South America into Eastern Polynesia During 11th to 12th Centuries A.D. Unpublished paper presented at the Sweet Potato Session, Association of Social Anthropologists of Oceania (ASAO) Conference, 22 February, Auckland, New Zealand.

Haddon, A. C., and James Hornell. 1936. *Canoes of Oceania. Vol. 1: The Canoes of Polynesia, Fiji and Micronesia.* Bishop Museum Special Publication 27. Honolulu: Bishop Museum.

Handler, Richard, and Jocelyn Linnekin. 1984. Tradition, Genuine or Spurious. *Journal of American Folklore* 97:273-290.

Hanson, Allan. 1989. The Making of the Maori: Culture Invention and its Logic. *American Anthropologist* 91:890-902.

Hauete, Tivini (Stephen Savage), and Tamuera Terei. 1908. *E Tuatua Ai-Tupuna no Tangiia-nui* (The History of Tangiia-nui). Rarotonga, Cook Islands: S. Savage, Government Printer.

Henry, Teuira. 1928. *Ancient Tahiti.* Bishop Museum Bulletin 48. Honolulu: Bishop Museum.

Heyerdahl, Thor. 1953. *American Indians in the Pacific.* Chicago: Rand McNally.

———. **1978.** *Early Man and the Ocean.* London: Allen and Unwin.

———. **1981.** With Stars and Waves in the Pacific. *Archaeoastronomy* 4:32-38.

Hill, Adrian V. S., and Susan W. Serjeantson. 1989. *The Colonization of the Pacific: A Genetic Trail.* Oxford: Claendon Press.

Hobsbawm, Eric, and Terence Ranger. 1983. *The Invention of Tradition.* Cambridge: Cambridge University Press.

Holmes, Tommy. 1981. *The Hawaiian Canoe.* Hanalei, Kaua'i: Editions Limited.

Howard, Alan. 1967. Polynesian Origins and Migrations, A Review of Two Centuries and Speculation. In *Polynesian Culture History: Essays in Honor of Kenneth P. Emory*, ed. Genevieve A. Highland, Roland W. Force, Alan Howard, Marion Kelly, and Yosihiko Sinoto, 45-101. Honolulu: Bishop Museum.

Howe, Kerry R. 1991. *Singer in a Songless Land, A Life of Edward Tregear 1846–1831*. Auckland: Auckland University Press.

———. In Press. *The Quest for Origins*. Auckland, New Zealand: Penguin Books.

Johnson, Oscar W., Martin Morton, Philip I. Bruner, and Patricia M. Johnson. 1989. Fat Cyclicity, Predicted Migratory Flight Ranges, and Features of Wintering Behavior in Pacific Golden-Plovers. *The Condor* 91:156-177.

Jolly, Margaret. 1992. Specters of Inauthenticity. *The Contemporary Pacific* 4:49-72.

Jolly, Margaret, and Nicholas Thomas, 1992. The Politics of Tradition in the Pacific. Special issue of *Oceania* 62(4):24-362.

Jonassen, Jon. 1994. The Politics of Culture: The Case of the Voyaging Canoe. In *New Politics of the South Pacific*, ed. Werner von Busch, Marjorie Tuainekore Crocombe, Ron Crocombe, et al., 305-317. Rarotonga, Cook Island and Suva, Fiji: Institute of Pacific Studies, University of the South Pacific.

Kaiser, Michel, and Samuel H. Elbert. 1989. Ka'akai o te Henua 'Enana: History of the Land of Men. *Journal of the Polynesian Society* 98:77-83.

Kamakau, Samuel Mānaiakalani. 1991. *Tales and Traditions of the People of Old (Nā Mo'olelo a ka Po'e Kahiko)*. Honolulu: Bishop Museum.

Kame'eleihiwa, Lilikalā. 1992. *Native Land and Foreign Desires: How Shall We Live in Harmony?* Honolulu: Bishop Museum.

Kāne, Herb Kawainui. 1976. *Voyage, the Discovery of Hawai'i*. Honolulu: Island Heritage.

———. 1993. The Hawaiians did Have Traditional 'Awa Ceremony. *Ka Wai Ola O Oha* 10 (November):12.

Keesing, Roger. 1989. Creating the Past: Custom and Identity in the Contemporary Pacific. *The Contemporary Pacific* 1:19-42.

Keesing, Roger M., and Robert Tonkinson. 1982. Reinventing Traditional Culture: the Politics of Kustom in Island Melanesia. Special issue of *Mankind* 13(4):297-398.

Kernahan, Galal. 1992. Canoe Sketches Are of Drua Design Says Hawaiian Expert. *Cook Islands News*, 11 June.

Kirch, Patrick V. 1985. *Feathered Gods and Fishhooks: An Introduction to Hawaiian Archaeology and Prehistory*. Honolulu: University of Hawai'i Press.

———. 1986. Rethinking East Polynesian Prehistory. *Journal of the Polynesian Society* 95:9-40.

———. 1991. Chiefship and Competitive Involution: the Marquesas Islands of Eastern Polynesia. In *Chiefdoms, Power, Economy and Ideology*, ed. T. Earle, 119-145. Cambridge: Cambridge University Press.

———. 2000. *On the Road of the Winds*. Berkeley: University of California Press.

Kirch, Patrick V., and Roger C. Green. 2001. *Hawaiki, Ancestral Polynesia, An Essay in Historical Anthropology*. Berkeley: University of California Press.

Krauss, Bob. 1988. *Keneti: South Seas Adventures of Kenneth Emory*. Honolulu: University of Hawai'i Press.

———. 1995. Voyaging Canoes Sail into Hilo. *The Honolulu Advertiser*, 8 May, A1-2.

Kyselka, Will. 1987. *An Ocean in Mind*. Honolulu: University of Hawai'i Press.

Kyselka, Will, Elisa Yadao, Cliff Watson, and Monte Costa. 1993. Native Hawaiian Canoe Project. Unpublished report. Honolulu: Native Hawaiian Culture and Arts Program, Bishop Museum.

Le Cléac'h, Hervé. 1997. *Pona Tekao Tapapa 'Ia—Lexique Marquisien-Français*. Pape'ete, Tahiti: n.p.

Lewis, David. 1972. *We The Navigators*. Honolulu: University of Hawai'i Press.

Lindstrom, Lamont, and Geoffrey M. White. 1995. Anthropology's New Cargo: Future Horizons. *Ethnology* 34:201-209.

Linnekin, Jocelyn. 1983. Defining Traditions: Variations on the Hawaiian Identity. *American Ethnologist* 10:241-252.

———. 1990. The Politics of Culture in the Pacific. In *Cultural Identity and Ethnicity in the Pacific*, ed. Jocelyn Linnekin and Lin Poyer, 149-174. Honolulu: University of Hawai'i Press.

———. 1991. Cultural Invention and the Dilemma of Authenticity. *American Anthropologist* 93:446-449.

Low, Drury. 1934. The Story of Ru's Canoe and the Discovery and Settlement of Aitutaki. *Journal of the Polynesian Society* 69:17-24.

Lucas, Wilfrid. 1989. L'identité Culturelle du Peuple Polynésien et Sa Renaissance Contemporaine. In *Renaissance du Pacifique*, ed. Chapman, Murray, and Jean-François Dupon. Special edition of *Ethnies, Droits de l'Homme et Peuples Autochtones* 4(8-10):104-108.

Luomala, Katharine. 1951. *The Menehune of Polynesia and Other Mythical Little People of Oceania*. Bishop Museum Bulletin 203. Honolulu: Bishop Museum.

MacAloon, John J. 1981. *The Great Symbol: Pierre de Coubertin and the Origins of the Modern Olympic Games*. Chicago: University of Chicago Press.

Malo, David. 1951 (1903). *Hawaiian Antiquities (Mo'olelo Hawai'i)*. Trans. Nathaniel B. Emerson. Bishop Museum Special Publication 2. Honolulu: Bishop Museum.

Marck, Jeff. 1996. Eastern Polynesian Subgrouping Today. In *Oceanic Culture History: Essays in Honour of Roger Green*, ed. Janet Davidson, Geoffrey Irwin, Foss Leach, Andrew Pawley, and Dorothy Brown, 491-511. New Zealand Journal of Archaeology Special Publication. Otago, New Zealand: New Zealand Archaeological Association.

———. 1999. A Revision to the Standard Theory of Polynesian Linguistic Subgrouping and its Culture History Implications. In *Language and Archaeology, Vol. 4: Language change and cultural transformation*, ed. R. Blench and M. Spriggs, 95-122. Routledge: London and New York.

Melville, Herman. 1846. *Typee: A Peep at Polynesian Life During A Four Months' Residence in a Valley of the Marquesas*. New York: Wiley & Putnam.

Miller, Pi'ikea. 1995. Navigation with some "No-No"s. *The Nature Conservancy of Hawaii Newsletter* (Summer): 1.

Mueller-Dombois, Dieter, Kent W. Bridges, and Hampton L. Carson. 1981. *Island Ecosystems: Biological Organization in Selected Hawaiian Communities*. Stroudsburg, Pennsylvania: Hutchinson Ross.

Needham, Joseph. 1971. *Science and Civilization in China. Vol. 4: Physics and Physical Technology, Part 3: Civil Engineering and Nautics*. Cambridge: Cambridge University Press.

Nelson, Anne. 1991. *Nga Waka Maori, Maori Canoes*. Auckland: Macmillan-New Zealand.

Neyret, Jean. 1977. *Pirogues Océanniennes. Vol. 2: Polynésie, Micronésie, Indonésie, Inde, Austres Continents*. Paris: Association des Amis des Musée de la Marine.

Nissen, Wendy. 1990. Academics Stand up for Maoritanga Viewpoint. [Wellington] *Evening Post*, 1 March, 20.

Noble, John Wilford. 1990. Anthropology Seen as Father of Maori Lore. *New York Times*, 20 February, C-1, 12.

Norton, Robert. 1993. Culture and Identity in the South Pacific. *Man* 28:741-759.

ORSTOM (Office de la Recherche Scientifique et Technique d'Outre-Mer). 1993. *Atlas de la Polynésie Française*. Paris: Éditions de l'ORSTOM.

Oshiro, Masaru. 2002. Pinky Thompson's Life One of Accomplishment. *The Honolulu Advertiser*, 22 January, A-9.

Pakoti, John. 1895. Te Autara Ia Aitutaki: Tona Katiri Anga Ia. Ko Te Autara Ia Ru. *Journal of the Polynesian Society* 4:59-70.

Pâris, François Edmond. 1843. *Essai Sur La Construction Navale des Peuples Extra Européens, ou Collection Des Navires et Pirogues Construits Par Les Habitants de l'Asie, de la Malaisie, du Grand Océan et de l'Amerique Desinées et Measuré Par M. Pâris, Capitaine de Corvette, Pendant Les Voyages Autour du Monde de l'Astrolabe, la Favorite et l'Artémise*. 2 vols. Paris, France: Arthus Bertrand.

Pi'ianai'a, Abraham. 1990. Personal communication, 20 July.

Polynesian Voyaging Society. 1993. Highlights of the 1992 Voyage to Rarotonga: 1. The Voyage to Tahiti. *Polynesian Voyaging Society Newsletter* (Fall):4-5.

———. 1994. Hawai'iloa—The Discovery and Settlement of Hawai'i. *Polynesian Voyaging Society Newsletter*. Hilina Mā:2, 5.

Porter, David. 1822. *Journal of a Cruise made to the Pacific Ocean by Captain David Porter in the United States Frigate Essex*. 2 vols. New York: Wiley and Halsted.

Pukui, Mary Kawena. 1939. The Canoe Making Profession of Ancient Times. *Occasional Papers of the Bernice P. Bishop Museum* 15(13): 149-159.

———. 1983. *'Olelo No'eau: Hawaiian Proverbs & Poetical Sayings*. Bishop Museum Special Publication 71. Honolulu: Bishop Museum.

Pukui, Mary Kawena, and Samuel H. Elbert. 1986. *Hawaiian Dictionary*. Honolulu: University of Hawai'i Press.

Pukui, Mary Kawena, Samuel H. Elbert, and Esther T. Mo'okini. 1974. *Place Names of Hawai'i*. Rev. ed. Honolulu: University of Hawai'i Press.

Pukui, Mary Kawena, E. W. Haertig, and Catherine Lee. 1972. *Nānā i Ke Kumu (Look to the Source)*. 2 vols. Honolulu: Hui Hanai, Queen Lili'uokalani Children's Center.

Quiros, Pedro Fernández de. 1904. *The Voyages of Pedro Fernandez de Quiros, 1595-1606*. 2 vols. Trans. and ed. Clements Markham. London: Hakluyt Society.

Rallu, Jean Louis. 1992. From Decline to Recovery: the Marquesan Population 1886-1945. *Health Transition Review* 2:177-193.

Rezentes, William C. 1996. *Ka Lama Kukui, Hawaiian Psychology: An Introduction*. Honolulu: 'A'ali'i Books.

Rollett, Barry V. 1998. *Hanimiai: Prehistoric Colonization and Cultural Change in the Marquesas Islands (East Polynesia)*. Yale University Publications in Anthropology No. 81. New Haven: Department of Anthropology and Peabody Museum, Yale University.

Rollett, Barry V., and Eric Conte. 1995. Renewed Investigation of the Ha'atuatua Dune (Nuku Hiva, Marquesas Islands): A Key Site in Polynesian Prehistory. *Journal of the Polynesian Society* 104:195-228.

Sahlins, Marshall. 1993. Goodbye to Tristes Tropes: Ethnography in the Context of Modern World History. *Journal of Modern History* 65:1-25.

Sharp, Andrew. 1956. *Ancient Voyagers in the Pacific*. Memoir 32 of the Polynesian Society. Wellington, New Zealand: The Polynesian Society. (Reprinted in 1957, Harmondsworth, Middlesex, England: Penguin Books.)

Silva, Kalena. 1989. Hawaiian Chant: Dynamic Cultural Link or Atrophied Relic. *Journal of the Polynesian Society* 98:85-90.

Sinoto, Yoshihiko H. 1967. Artifacts from Excavated Sites in the Hawaiian, Marquesas, and Society Islands: a Comparative Study. In *Polynesian Culture History: Essays in Honor of Kenneth P. Emory*, ed. Genevieve A. Highland et al. Honolulu: Bishop Museum.

Sissons, Jeffrey. 1993. The Systematisation of Tradition: Maori Culture as a Strategic Resource. *Oceania* 64:97-115

Smith, S. Percy. 1898. *Hawaiki: The Whence of the Maori*. Wellington, New Zealand: Whitcombe and Tombs.

————. 1910. *Hawaiki: The Original Home of the Maori*. 3rd. ed. Christchurch, New Zealand: Whitcombe and Tombs.

Sorrenson, M. P. K. 1979. *Maori Origins and Migrations: The Genesis of Some Pakeha Myths and Legends*. Auckland: Auckland University Press.

Spatz, G., and Dieter Mueller-Dombois. 1973. The Influence of Feral Goats on Koa Tree Production in Hawaii Volcanoes National Park. *Ecology* 54:870-876.

Spriggs, Matthew, and Atholl Anderson. 1993. Late Colonization of East Polynesia. *Antiquity* 67:200-217.

Sterling, Elspeth P., and Catherine C. Summers. 1978. *Sites of O'ahu*. Rev. ed. Honolulu: Bishop Museum.

Stevenson, Karen. 1990. Heiva: Continuity and Change in a Tahitian Celebration. *The Contemporary Pacific* 2:255-278.

————. 1992. Politicization of La Culture Ma'ohi: The Creation of a Tahitian Cultural Identity. *Pacific Studies* 15:117-136.

Suggs, Robert C. 1960. *The Island Civilizations of Polynesia*. New York: New American Library.

————. 1961a. The Archaeology of Nuku Hiva, Marquesas Islands, French Polynesia. *American Museum of Natural History Papers* 14(1):1-205.

————. 1961b. The Derivation of Marquesan Culture. *Journal of the Royal Anthropological Institute of Great Britain and Ireland* 91:1-10.

Taumoefolau, Melenaite. 1996. From Sau 'Ariki to Hawaiki. *Journal of the Polynesian Society* 105:385-410.

Te Ariki-tara-are. 1919. History and Traditions of Rarotonga. Trans. S. Percy Smith. *Journal of the Polynesian Society* 28:183-207.

Te Ariki Tara 'Are. 2000. *History and Traditions of Rarotonga*. Trans. Richard Walter and Rangi Moeka'a. Polynesian Society Memoir No. 51. Auckland, New Zealand: The Polynesian Society.

Teikiehu'upoko, Georges (Toti). 1995. Speech for the Arrival of the Polynesian Canoes at Nukuhiva, 1995. Unpublished English translation by Tracey Smith and Debora Kimitete. Taiohai, Nukuhiva.

Thomas, Nicholas. 1990. *Marquesan Societies, Inequality and Political Transformations in Eastern Polynesia*. Oxford: Clarendon Press.

Tobin, Jeffrey. 1994. Cultural Construction and Native Nationalism: Report from the Hawaiian Front. *Boundary 2* 21:111-133.

Townsend, Ebenezer, Jr. 1921. *Extracts from the Diary of Ebenezer Townsend, Jr., Supercargo of the Sealing Ship "Neptune" on her Voyage to the South Pacific and Canton*. Hawaiian Historical Society Reprints No. 4. Honolulu: Hawaiian Historical Society.

Tundra Times. 1995. Gift of Spruce Comes Full Circle as Hawaiians Canoes Tours Southeast Villages, 19 July, 1, 6.

Trask, Haunani-Kay. 1991. Natives and Anthropologists: The Colonial Struggle. *The Contemporary Pacific* 3:159-167.

Turner, James West. 1997. Continuity and Restraint: Reconstructing the Concept of Tradition from a Pacific Perspective. *The Contemporary Pacific* 9:345-381.

Vancouver, George. 1798. *A Voyage of Discovery to the North Pacific Ocean, and Round the World . . . performed in the years 1790, 1791, 1792, 1793, 1794, and 1795*. 3 vols. London: G. G. and J. Robinson and J. Edwards.

Verneau, René. 1929. *Preface* to *Les Iles Marquises*, by Louis Rollin. Paris: Société d'Éditions Géographique, Maritimes et Coloniáles.

Walter, Richard. 1998. *Anai'o: The Archaeology of a Fourteenth Century Polynesian Community in the Cook Islands.* New Zealand Archaeological Association Monograph 22. Auckland: New Zealand Archaeological Association.

White, Geoffrey M., and Lamont Lindstrom. 1993. Custom in Oceania. Special issue of *Anthropological Forum* 6(4):459-654.

Whitney, Scott. 2001a. Inventing 'Ohana. *Honolulu* 36(3):42-45.

―――. **2001b.** 'Ohana Troubles. *Honolulu* 36(5):22.

Williams, John. 1838. *A Narrative of Missionary Enterprises in the South Sea Islands.* London: John Snow.

Yen, Douglas E. 1974. *The Sweet Potato and Oceania.* Bishop Museum Bulletin 236. Honolulu: Bishop Museum.

―――. **1991.** Polynesian Cultigens and Cultivars: the Questions of Origins. In *Islands, Plants and Polynesians*, ed. Paul A. Cox and Sandra A. Bannack, 67-95. Portland: Dioscorides Press.

―――. **1998.** Subsistence to Commerce in Pacific Agriculture: Some Four Thousand Years of Plant Exchange. In *Plants for Food and Medicine*, ed. N. L. Etkin, D. R. Harris, and P. J. Houghton, 161-183. Kew: Royal Botanic Gardens Press.

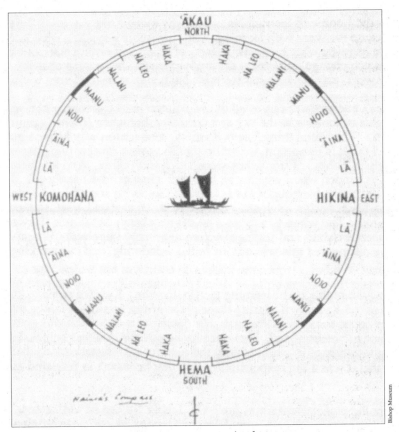

Nainoa Thompson's voyaging compass, committed to memory.

Index